Heart Smart® II Cookbook

By Henry Ford Health System
and The Detroit Free Press

ISBN 0-937247-72-3

Table of Contents

Acknowledgments

Henry Ford Health System and The Detroit Free Press would like to thank those who supported and assisted us in producing this book.

Editor: Steve Grimmer,
Detroit Free Press
Project Coordinator: Fay Fitzgerald,
Heart Smart® program
Copy Editor: Kathleen Knauss,
Detroit Free Press
Graphic Design: Hank Szerlag,
Detroit Free Press
Cover Illustration: Hank Szerlag,
Detroit Free Press
Illustrations: Bob Graham,
Detroit Free Press
Recipe Coordinator: Susan Selasky,
Detroit Free Press

Writers:
Steven Keteyian,
Director Cardiac Wellness Center,
Henry Ford Health System;
Bethany Ledford, registered dietitian,
Heart Smart® Program;
Steve Grimmer, Detroit Free Press

A special thank you to: Ann Baker, Meda Bower, Annette Habecker, Tracy Holmes, Corinna Johnson, Roxalana Karanec, Gwen Klein, Laura Ritter, Pat Siloac, Maria Stawarz, Jeanne Stevenson and the Henry Ford Hospital dietetic interns for their contributions to the Heart Smart® program and the Heart Smart® Cookbook.

Special support:
Douglas Weaver,
Division Head, Cardiovascular Medicine,
Henry Ford Hospital;
Sidney Goldstein,
Senior Cardiologist, Henry Ford Hospital;
Dwight Angell, Manager, Media Relations,
Henry Ford Health System;
Kelli Brady, Media Specialist,
Henry Ford Health System;
Dave Ellis, Director, Internal Communications,
Henry Ford Health System;
Mark McDowell, Market Communications
Consultant, Henry Ford Health System;
Dave Robinson, Deputy Managing Editor —
Sports and Operations, Detroit Free Press;
Thelma Oakes, Detroit Free Press

Foreword

One American dies every 34 seconds from cardiovascular disease, making it the nation's leading killer. Nearly 25 percent of adults have some form of cardiovascular disease, and one in five will die from it. Cardiovascular disease is the No. 1 cause of death of American women — nine times more common than breast cancer.

The medical outlook, however, is promising.

The incidence of heart disease has decreased by almost 30 percent in the past 15 years, and new medical treatments have provided hope for thousands of people. Unfortunately, many people put their faith into medical technology alone to cure their heart disease instead of actively trying to prevent it. Research clearly indicates that nearly half of all deaths from heart disease are preventable.

Seven of the 10 major risk factors for heart disease are related to lifestyle: high blood cholesterol, high blood pressure, obesity, diabetes, smoking, physical inactivity and a Type A (high achiever) behavior pattern. The first four can be modified by diet. By decreasing the intake of saturated fat from 12 percent to 9 percent, about 100,000 first-time heart attacks could be prevented by the year 2005.

We need to take action and accept responsibility for maintaining and promoting our own health. We can do this by learning about our health risks and how to reduce them.

It is our hope that these recipes, as in the first Heart Smart® cookbook, will help you to reduce your risk of heart disease by providing the information necessary to make healthier food and lifestyle choices.

Douglas Weaver, MD
Division Head
Cardiovascular Medicine
Co-Director, The Heart and Vascular Institute
Henry Ford Health System

Meal Planning

Chapter 1

The recipes in this book can be assembled for quick everyday meals, leisurely weekend dinners, special occasion feasts or casual snacking. You also can combine them with convenience foods from your supermarket and local deli to help you prepare quick, healthy meals.

Planning a meal that is as delicious and attractive as it is healthy is an acquired skill. Try some of our favorite menus and then experiment on your own using the following tips.

- Start with the main course. Add extra foods from the grain, vegetable and fruit groups. Be sure the flavors are compatible and do not compete. A strongly flavored main dish needs milder-flavored accompaniments for balance. A subtle main dish works well with boldly flavored side dishes.
- Choose foods with a variety of flavors, textures, colors, shapes and temperatures to add interest to your meal. And because vegetables of different colors contain different vitamins, they also increase the nutritional value of the meal.
- Use the Food Guide Pyramid in the appendix to help plan your meals for the day. Include at least the minimum recommended number of servings from each food group. To control fat, saturated fat and cholesterol, choose more foods from the bottom half of the pyramid and complement them with small servings from the meat and dairy groups.

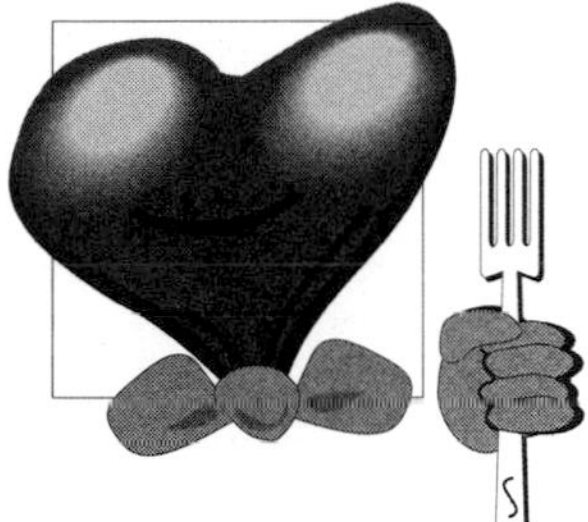

- The following meal plans include calorie counts for each meal and for the day. These calorie counts are based on single servings of recipes included in this book. If you are an active person and need to add extra calories, include more servings of fruits, vegetables or starches as part of a meal or as a snack.

Cook's note:

This symbol identifies useful information throughout this book.

15 30 45 60

This clock symbol indicates the approximate time required to prepare and cook each recipe. It does not account for time needed to marinate meats and poultry.

One Week's Meals

(* signifies a recipe in this book)

	Breakfast	calories	Lunch	calories	Dinner	calories
Day 1	Apple Pancakes with Cinnamon Sauce* Orange juice (1 cup) Skim milk (1 cup)	381	Pecan Chicken Salad* Melon slices (4) Bran-Raisin Muffins* Apple Spiced Tea*	481	Vegetable Shrimp Kabob* Brown Rice Pilaf* Green salad (2 cups) Tomato Parmesan Toasts* Pears Baked in Brandy*	591
Day 2	Bran cereal (1 oz.) Skim milk (1 cup) 1/2 grapefruit	310	Carrot & Potato Soup* Herbed Grilled Cheese* Fresh fruit (1 cup)	432	Spaghetti Verdura* Spinach salad (2 cups) Garlic bread (1 slice) Frozen fruit ice (1 cup) Almond Biscotti*	532
Day 3	Irish Soda Biscuits* 1/4 melon Skim milk (1 cup)	249	Tuna Crater* Pretzels (1 oz.) Fresh pear Crispy Marshmallow Bars*	432	Salisbury Steak with Vegetable Sauce* Garlicky Mashed Potatoes* Steamed green beans (1 cup) Frozen Peach Yogurt Pie*	739
Day 4	Sour Cream Cranberry Coffee Cake* Scrambled egg whites (2) Skim milk (1 cup)	327	Beef & Asparagus Salad* Sliced peaches (1/2 cup) Bread sticks (3) Applesauce Carrot Cake*	435	Parmesan Oven-Fried Chicken* Creamed New Potatoes with Peas & Onions* Waldorf Salad* Microwave Chocolate Pudding Cake*	689
Day 5	Whole wheat bagel with fat-free cream cheese Peach Yogurt Shake*	318	Garden Vegetable Pita* Black Bean Salad* Fresh fruit (1 cup)	334	Sloppy Joe* Oven fries (1 cup) Corn on the cob Deluxe Coleslaw* Nutty Apple Cake*	743
Day 6	Oatmeal Carrot Muffin* Nonfat fruit yogurt (1 cup) Fruit juice (6 oz.)	348	Skillet Pizza* Sweet Bunny Salad* Skim milk (1 cup)	338	Poached Salmon with Dill Sauce* Red-skinned potatoes (3 small) Asparagus (4 spears) Strawberry Shortcake*	578
Day 7	Spanish Omelet* English muffin Strawberries (1 cup) Skim milk (1 cup)	381	Seafood Vegetable Pasta Salad* Blueberry Lemon Bread*	419	Teriyaki Pork Chop* Baked potato Steamed Green Beans & Water Chestnuts* After-Dinner Cappuccino*	481

Special Meals

	calories	
Picnic in the Park	**586**	Heart Smart® Burger* Fresh Basil & Pepper Potato Salad* Mixed Green Salad with Honey Mustard Dressing* Chocolate Brownies*
Spring Brunch	**625**	Shrimp, Avocado & Spinach Salad* Fruit salad (1 cup) Pineapple Yogurt Muffin* Springtime English Trifle* Apple Spiced Tea*
Holiday Buffet	**597**	Roasted Garlic & Almond Dip* Low-fat crackers Herbed Flank Steak* Brown Rice Pilaf* Microwave Vegetable-Filled Squash* Sugar Cookies*
Super Bowl Party	**339**	Heart Smart® Party Mix* Quesadilla Appetizers* Sweet Pea Guacamole* Tex-Mex Bean Dip* Baked nacho chips Spicy Warm Cider*
Thanksgiving Dinner	**894**	Roast turkey (4 ounces) Garlicky Mashed Potatoes with Olive Oil* Turkey Gravy* Rum Raisin & Apple Stuffing* Whipped Sweet Potatoes * Brussels sprouts Gingerbread with Pear Sauce*
New Year's Eve	**753**	Vegetable Soup with Pesto* Orange Lamb Stuffed with Spinach & Mint* Baked potato Peas and onions (1/2 cup) Mixed green salad (2 cups) Strawberry Cheesecake*
Tailgate Party	**517**	Bulgur Chili* Corn Bread* Fresh vegetable sticks (1 cup) Spicy Warm Cider* Chocolate Chip Cereal Cookies*

Nutrition Through the Years

Cooking for a family is always a challenge. Not only do nutrient requirements vary as we move through our lives, but other factors affect how we eat. Let's look at the life stages and the key role that nutrition plays in each.

INFANTS (0-12 months):

From birth until about 6 months of age, dietary needs are met by breast milk or infant formula, and there is no need to introduce solid food.

In fact, early introduction of solid food may cause health problems. Until infants are about 3 months old, they are not able to digest starch and have limited ability to excrete waste from high levels of dietary protein and minerals. Early introduction of foods also may bring about allergies.

Many parents introduce solid foods early, believing that it helps the infant sleep through the night. But studies have shown that sleeping through the night has nothing to do with diet.

Iron-fortified rice cereal usually is the first solid food introduced. Add foods to the diet slowly. If any adverse effects such as a mild allergy or intolerance develop, avoid that food for a few months. Then reintroduce a small amount. Babies often outgrow allergies and food intolerances.

Do not feed an infant:

- *honey and corn syrup — in high doses, they may cause food poisoning.*
- *foods high in salt and sugar*
- *cow's milk*
- *foods that may cause choking — hot dogs, nuts, grapes, raw carrots and popcorn*
- *undiluted apple or pear juice — they can lead to diarrhea*

The goal of introducing solid foods during the first year is to let your infant become accustomed to a variety of foods. After one year of age, infants should switch from formula to whole milk and should start having most of their nutritional needs met through solid food.

TODDLERS (1-4 years):

Growth tapers off during these developmental years. As toddlers' appetites decrease, their activity level becomes greater. They also learn the power to say "no" to food. Mealtime can become a battleground. Don't panic.

Small servings and frequent meals and snacks are the answer. Provide finger foods that are easy to eat and colorful. Try cutting foods into interesting shapes and sizes. Introduce new foods at the start of the meal when your child is most hungry. If they refuse a particular food, try it again another day. Their food likes and dislikes change rapidly.

Food preferences are common with this age group. They may refuse to eat anything except one food at a meal. Such a situation is usually temporary. If a variety of nutritious foods are provided, toddlers usually will eat a well-balanced diet. Two-year-olds should start drinking skim milk in place of whole milk.

CHILDREN (5-12 years):

Obesity in childhood is related to obesity in adulthood, especially in females. It is very important to promote physical activity. Whether children compete in sports or walk with the family after dinner, they need to be active.

To encourage children to eat nutritious meals and snacks, involve them in the selection and preparation of the food. Remember you are competing with TV commercials and fast-food restaurants.

TEENS (13-19 years):

Teenagers make most of their own food choices. Because it is hard for teens to relate today's actions to tomorrow's health, their choices are not always the best.

Teenage girls are likely to fall prey to the latest diet fad in order to stay slim. These trendy diets often are inadequate in calcium, iron, vitamin A, vitamin B6, vitamin C and zinc. They need to develop an understanding of how low-fat choices from each food group will help keep them healthy.

Calcium is a must for teenage girls. A lack of milk may increase the risk of osteoporosis. If teenage girls are not drinking milk, they probably will need a calcium supplement. It is best, however, if they can get the nutrients they need from foods.

Active teenage boys often eat high-fat, high-cholesterol diets, setting the stage for coronary heart disease later in life.

For teen athletes, stress the importance of good nutrition for overall physical — especially muscle — development. And emphasize a well-balanced, low-fat dict to achieve weight goals for overweight teens.

ADULTS (20-55 years):

Adults can best promote health and prevent disease by eating a variety of foods and following the Food Guide Pyramid shown in the appendix.

SENIORS:

The current life span is 66 to 73 years for men and 74 to 79 years for women. Of those over 65, approximately 85 percent have some nutrition-related problems.

Nutritional deficiencies can be related to medications, depression, budget problems, and the inability to get and cook foods.

Some guidelines for promoting healthful eating in later years include:

- Eat regularly. Small frequent meals may be best.
- Keep easy-to-prepare foods on hand.
- Arrange things so food preparation and cleanup are easy.
- Eat when possible with friends, relatives or at a senior center.
- Share cooking responsibilities with a neighbor or use community resources.
- Stay physically active.
- Don't forget to drink plenty of fluids.

The following is a sample meal that is easy to prepare and appropriate for the whole family. Read the tips that follow to adjust this menu to meet the needs of your family.

Menu

Poached Salmon with Dill Sauce
Steamed Green Beans and Water Chestnuts
Broiled redskin potatoes
Rolls
Skim milk
Fresh fruit
Sugar cookies

Toddlers and Children
- Cut the salmon into bite-size pieces and serve without the sauce.
- Serve the green beans without the water chestnuts.
- Serve small portions (1 tablespoon to 1/2 cup, depending on your child's appetite).

Teenagers
- Weight-conscious teens should not add butter to rolls or vegetables.
- Active teens should have extra helpings of rolls, potatoes, green beans or fruit.

Adults
- Average adult servings are: one 4-ounce piece of salmon, 1/2 cup redskin potatoes, 1/2 cup green beans, 1 roll, 1 cup skim milk, 1/2 cup fruit and 1 cookie.
- Active adults may want to take extra helpings of rolls, potatoes, green beans or fruit.

Seniors
- Add extra sauce to moisten foods for seniors.
- Seniors need to drink something. If they can't tolerate milk, serve another beverage.

Health & Fitness

Take a good look around.

We're surrounded by labor-saving devices designed to make our life easier. Need the garage door opened? Push a button. Time to cut the lawn? Adjust the seat and turn the key. Want to change the channel on the television? Just aim and push.

Although some border on the frivolous, most of these technological advances are useful. These developments have come with a cost. In pursuit of increased comfort and safety, we have eliminated something essential to good health — daily physical activity.

How bad is it? Only about 25 percent of Americans engage in enough daily activity to help their health. Another 50 percent are somewhat active, but on an irregular schedule. That leaves the final 25 percent of our population leading inactive lives. This literally means no physical activity — at work or at leisure.

To compensate for our inactivity, we often join a fitness center or buy exercise equipment, only to quickly abandon our plans. We gravitate toward products claiming "inches off in days," "extra energy" and "fitness while sitting at your desk." Unfortunately no pill, potion, technique, elixir or quick fix exists.

So the question is: What can be done to move our families, friends, nation and ourselves toward a more active and healthy lifestyle?

Begin by deciding how much activity is needed to achieve the health benefits you seek. Goals could include increasing stamina, bone strength and good (HDL) cholesterol; lowering body weight, blood pressure, and risks for developing heart disease and certain cancers; or simply building self-esteem.

Research during the past decade shows that often simply making the inactive person more active is all that is needed to derive health benefits. Examples of being more active include cutting your lawn with a push mower; going for a 25-minute walk with the dog; parking farther away when going shopping or to work; occasionally shoveling the driveway by hand instead of using the snowblower; using the stairs instead of an elevator; raking leaves; or vacuuming the carpets. The secret is to regularly — preferably daily — include some of the above activities, or others like them, in your life.

For parents, leading an active life provides an additional benefit: It sets an excellent example for children. Common sense tells us that inactive children are likely to grow up to become inactive adults.

To motivate children — and yourself — begin taking weekly trips to the park with the family and play with the children instead of sitting on a bench. Or plot on a map how many miles your family should bike each week during summer vacation and reward yourselves when a goal is reached. You could also agree to play 15 minutes of video games with an inactive child in exchange for a

25-minute walk around the neighborhood with you.

Certainly, more vigorous exercise such as jogging, tennis, walking, swimming or cycling provides greater fitness gains and has been associated with even lower risks for lifestyle-related diseases. Remember, however, that many Americans do not engage in any regular activity. So adopting a plan of gradually increased activity is a logical and important first step. Significant improvements in health — in blood pressure, body weight and blood sugar — are achieved through moderate physical activity.

For those looking to start an exercise program, keep it simple. Activities such as swimming, walking, in-line skating and cycling are all satisfactory. Build up to a point where you are comfortably able to exercise continuously for 30-45 minutes four to five times per week. It may take you several months to accomplish this goal, but that's okay. And remember that more is not necessarily better — so keep the pace moderate.

Regularity of exercise is of greatest importance to a healthy lifestyle. This doesn't mean days or weeks of exercise, but refers to a commitment to years of activity. Try to see the big picture and plan to arrange your schedule for the long haul. Don't fret if you miss a day of exercise, and don't feel you are healthy after 12 weeks of regular walking.

To make an impact, you need to follow through with plans to modify your habits for the rest of your life. Helpful strategies include: exercising with a friend or spouse; charting your progress on a calendar or daily planner; and exercising in the morning, when your time is more available, versus the end of the day when other commitments often interfere.

The message is clear. Physical activity is one means to improve your health and the health of those around you.

Dining Out

Chapter IV

It's possible to watch your diet and still have a good time when eating out. Building your meal with low-fat items may be easier and tastier than you think. Here are some tips for healthy dining:

- Phone ahead to make special requests, such as having foods prepared without added salt, fat or monosodium glutamate (MSG).
- Examine the menu carefully. If foods that fit into your diet are not listed, don't be afraid to ask the wait staff if they are available.
- Choose raw fruits and vegetables as appetizers.
- Look for entrees that have been steamed, poached, baked, broiled or stir-fried.
- Order gravy, sauces and dressings on the side.
- For dessert choose fruit, fruit ice, sherbet or low-fat frozen yogurt.
- Drink water with a twist of lemon or lime instead of high-calorie alcoholic beverages.

Sampling dishes from various parts of the world can be fun and tasty. But if you're not careful, it also can be hazardous to your health. When eating at ethnic restaurants, it is sometimes difficult to determine if too much fat and salt are being used. Don't be afraid to ask questions. A 1988 National Restaurant Association survey found that nearly 90 percent of all table-service restaurants will alter food preparations on request.

Understanding the cuisine of different countries will help you make healthy selections. The following are examples of healthy choices in some ethnic cuisines.

ITALIAN

Italian cuisine offers wonderful dishes seasoned with basil, oregano, onions and garlic.

Northern Italy is dairy country, and butter, eggs and cream are used extensively. The pasta is usually flat and limp. Although wheat is the primary grain, polenta, or cornmeal, is also popular.

In Southern Italy, the pasta is stiff, brittle and usually made without eggs. The sauces are made with tomatoes rather than cream. Olive oil is used for cooking and for salads.

When dining in an Italian restaurant, avoid cheese dishes, fried calamari (squid), sausages, cream- and cheese-based sauces, antipasto and garlic bread.

A healthy selection could include:

Minestrone soup
Garden salad (limit cheese, olives, pine nuts and dressing)
Bread sticks (hard)
Pasta (spaghetti, angel hair, ziti, linguine) with marinara sauce or red clam sauce
Chicken, shrimp or veal with marinara sauce or red primavera sauce
Italian ice

CHINESE

This popular cuisine uses meat primarily for flavoring. Noodles, rice or vegetables supply the bulk of the dishes. That's the good news. The bad news is Chinese cuisine often includes soy sauce or monosodium glutamate, which are high in sodium. Request that your dish be served without MSG and with little or no soy sauce.

Some high-fat selections you may encounter in a Chinese restaurant are egg rolls, fried rice and deep-fried entrees.

A healthy selection could include:

Hot and sour soup
Chicken with black bean sauce
Vegetable, chicken, shrimp or lean beef stir-fry
Chow mein or chop suey
Yu-Shiang pork
Cantonese chicken and vegetables
White rice
Fortune cookie

MIDDLE EASTERN

Dishes characteristic of the Middle East are very popular today. With imaginative use of herbs, spices, grains and vegetables, small portions of meat go a long way. Even vegetarians can find many tasty dishes. Lamb is the meat of choice, and eggplant and tomatoes are favorite vegetables. The meal often includes a fine grain, such as couscous.

Ask that sour cream be eliminated or served on the side. Cheese, nuts, olives, hummus and tabbouleh are often served as appetizers. They are high in fat and should be eaten in limited amounts.

A healthy selection could include:

Vegetarian grape leaves
Lentil soup
Fattoush (served without fried pita bread)
Shish kabab (chicken, lean beef or lamb)
Rice pilaf
Pita bread
Fresh or dried fruits

MEXICAN

Mexican food is hot! So hot, in fact, that salsa has replaced ketchup as the top-selling condiment. Mexican food, however, also can be high in fat and calories.

But take heart. Mexican food doesn't necessarily taste Mexican because of the fat content, but rather because of the spices, chilies and cilantro found in nearly every dish.

Because sour cream and guacamole are high in fat and calories, salsa should be substituted. Ask that tacos and enchiladas not be deep-fried, and avoid refried beans unless lard is not used and they are low in fat.

A healthy selection could include:

Baked tortilla chips with salsa
Black bean soup
Chicken soft tacos or burritos
Chicken fajitas (prepared with a small amount of oil)
Chicken enchiladas (limit cheese)
Tropical fruit ice

Reading the Label

All nutrition information relates to this **serving size.**

A **calorie** is a measurement of the energy stored in foods. Excess calories are stored as fat.

To determine your calorie needs for normal daily activity (additional physical activity will require additional calories):

Men
Current weight
(in pounds) x 12*

Women
Current weight
(in pounds) x 11*

Eat less than 30 percent of your calories from **fat** to minimize the risk for obesity, heart disease and cancer.

Saturated fat does the most harm to your health so your intake should be as minimal as possible.

Nutrition Facts

Serving Size 1 Oz. (28.3g)
Servings per Container 14

Amount Per Serving

Calories 157 — Calories from Fat 94

	% Daily Value
Total Fat 10.4g	16%
Saturated Fat 3.8g	18.8%
Cholesterol 0mg	0%
Sodium 112 mg	4.7%
Total Carbohydrates 14.3g	4.8%
Dietary Fiber 0.9g	3.7%
Sugars <0.1g	
Protein 1.7g	

Vitamin A < 2.0%	Vitamin C 9%
Calcium < 2.0%	Iron < 2.5%

*Percent Daily Values are based on a 2,000 calorie diet. Your daily values may be higher or lower depending on your calorie needs.

	Calories	2,000	2,500
Total Fat	Less than	65g	80g
Sat Fat	Less than	20g	25g
Cholesterol	Less than	300mg	300mg
Sodium	Less than	2,400mg	2,400mg
Total Carbohydrate		300g	375g
Fiber		25g	30g

Calories per gram:
Fat 9 — Carbohydrate 4 — Protein 4

% **Daily Value** shows how a food fits into the 2,000-calorie daily diet.

Limit **cholesterol** intake to less than 300 mg per day to decrease the risk for heart disease.

It is prudent for everyone to limit their **sodium** intake.

To decrease the risk for heart disease and cancer, the average adult should consume 25 to 30 grams of **fiber** each day.

Daily **protein** needs vary from 50 grams to 65 grams for most adults.

Reference values are provided to help consumers learn good diet basics. They can be adjusted depending on a person's calorie needs.

The **conversion guide** helps consumers learn the calorie value of the energy-producing nutrients.

** To lose weight, subtract 500 to 1,000 calories from this total. Do not eat fewer than 1,200 calories per day.*

In the marketplace, you will find a wide array of healthy food choices — more than you did just a year ago.

Manufacturers are reformulating traditional products so fast that shopping for low-fat foods and fat-free foods has become much easier. Food labels also were changed to reflect nutritional concerns about total fat, saturated fat, percentage of calories from fat, cholesterol, sodium and fiber. The Nutrition Labeling and Education Act required that after 1994 almost all foods sold in supermarkets bear nutrition labels. This was the first extensive renovation of the food label since 1974.

The nutrition information is provided so consumers can make educated decisions on food choices.

In this chapter we hope to help you:

- Learn more about the label;
- Be able to zero in on the parts of the label that are important to you;
- Determine whether a food product will fit into your diet.

Before you can use the label to meet your needs, you need to know what your nutritional goals are. How many calories, how much fat, saturated fat, cholesterol, sodium and fiber should you be eating each day? Let's start with calorie needs. To estimate your calorie needs, use this formula:

Women: your current weight in pounds x 11 = estimated calorie needs

Men: your current weight in pounds x 12 = estimated calorie needs

This calculation gives you an idea of how many calories it takes to maintain your weight. If you would like to lose weight, you need to decrease this number.

Once you have determined your calorie goal, it will be easy to determine your fat goal. The American Heart Association recommends that most healthy adults consume less than 30 percent of their calories from fat (3 grams of fat per 100 calories). Remember, though, most research has shown that to prevent heart disease your fat intake should be less than 20 percent of your calorie intake (2 grams of fat per 100 calories).

To reverse existing heart disease, your fat intake should be 10 percent of your calorie intake (1 gram of fat per 100 calories).

The American Heart Association says less than 10 percent of your calories should come from saturated fat. The American Heart Association also recommends that adults eat less than 300 mg of cholesterol per day. Cholesterol is found only in food products from animals such as meat, milk and eggs.

To decrease your sodium intake, stop adding salt to foods during cooking and at the table. You should avoid fast foods, canned foods, frozen dinners and snack foods, which often are high in sodium. The general rule of thumb is: If it tastes salty, it contains too much sodium.

Even though fiber is good for your health, most Americans take in less than 15 grams of fiber per day. Try increasing your intake of fresh fruits and vegetables, whole grain breads and cereals, and beans and legumes.

Once you know your nutritional goals, you can use the labels to help determine what foods you should buy.

Serving size: The new label law includes a standardized, and we hope a more realistic, serving size. You may, however, eat more than one serving size. Because the nutritional numbers are based on the serving size, if you eat more, you must multiply the numbers accordingly. For instance, if the serving is 1 ounce, and you eat 2 ounces, all the nutritional numbers should be multiplied by 2.

Servings per container: If you eat the whole package, multiply all the nutritional numbers by the number of servings.

Calories: Now that you've calculated your goal, simply add up the calories from your

food labels to insure you stay within your calorie limit. Next to the calorie listing, the label tells you how many calories are from fat. From this you can estimate the percentage of calories from fat. For instance, the label in the example states 157 calories, with 94 calories coming from fat. 94 divided by 157 times 100 equals approximately 60 percent. So 60 percent of the calories in this product come from fat.

Total fat: In this nutrition label example, there are 10 grams of fat in a 1-ounce serving. If you are allowed only 50 grams for the day, this product is using up 20 percent of your allowance with just 1 ounce.

Listed underneath total fat is saturated fat, cholesterol and sodium. One way to determine if these numbers are too high for you is to take your daily allowance and divide by the number of meals you usually eat. For example, the American Heart Association recommends you consume less than 300 mg of cholesterol for the day. If you eat breakfast, lunch, and dinner, you can have 100 mg of cholesterol per meal.

Carbohydrate: Carbohydrates, whether in the form of sugar or starch, are a good source of energy. You need at least 100 grams per day. Dietary fiber makes up part of the total carbohydrates in your diet.

Americans tend to eat considerably less than the recommended 25 to 30 grams of fiber per day. When you look at food labels, ask yourself if the food helps you meet that goal. Fruits and vegetables are two good sources of fiber. By law, fruits and vegetables do not have to be labeled, although some grocery stores are posting nutrition labels in the produce section. If this information is not readily available, ask the grocery store manager for it. Most grocery stores keep notebooks that list the nutritional information.

The % Daily Values are listed on the right side of the label. These are based on a 2,000-calorie diet. For example, 20 percent next to the total fat on the label in the example does not mean that 20 percent of the calories are coming from fat, it means that the food provides 20 percent of the fat grams allowed on a 2,000-calorie diet.

On larger food containers there are reference values listed to help you remember some of your nutritional goals. But remember, fat and saturated fat will vary depending on your calorie level.

There also is a conversion guide at the bottom of all labels, which tells you how many calories there are per gram of fat, carbohydrate and protein.

The terms "light," "diet," and "low fat" are confusing.

Your best bet when grocery shopping is to not get caught up in the words on the package. Instead, look at the numbers. Once you know your nutritional goals, the numbers on the label can help you to determine if the food belongs in your diet. Reading labels will take some extra time — at first. But soon you'll have memorized the nutrition information about foods you frequently buy. Grocery shopping will become easier, more enjoyable and healthier.

Making Recipes Heart Smart®

Chapter VI

Trying new recipes is a fun way to make changes in your diet, but don't give up on your old favorites. By using new ingredients, techniques and equipment, traditional recipes can be transformed into Heart Smart® meals.

Soups
- For a creamy consistency, use evaporated skim milk.
- Use herbs and spices for flavoring in place of salt.
- Brown lean meat or poultry and drain the fat before adding to soup.
- To add richness, puree some broth with vegetables and return the mixture to the soup.
- To enhance flavor, reduce the stock by simmering it without a cover.
- Remove fat from the broth by refrigerating it and discarding the hardened fat that collects on the surface or use a fat skimmer.

Salads and sandwiches
- Use a variety of fruits and vegetables in salads.
- For main-dish salads or sandwiches, choose ultra-lean lunch meats and nonfat or low-fat cheese.
- Instead of butter, margarine or mayonnaise, use light or fat-free margarine or mayonnaise on sandwiches.
- Top salads with a nonfat or low-fat dressing, a flavored vinegar or lemon juice.
- Use seeds and nuts sparingly, all are high in fat.

Vegetables and sides
- Steam or microwave vegetables to retain vitamins.
- Season vegetables and other side dishes with herbs and spices instead of salt.
- In place of butter or margarine, use low-sodium, butter-flavored sprinkles.
- Add lean ham or smoked turkey in place of bacon or ham hocks.

Casseroles and pasta dishes
- Avoid egg noodles by using macaroni products or eggless noodles.
- Finely shredded or processed low-fat or nonfat cheese melts well in casseroles.
- For quick sauces in casseroles, use low-fat, low-sodium condensed soups.
- Fat-free sour cream or yogurt can be used in place of regular sour cream.
- For a creamy consistency, use nonfat ricotta cheese blended with skim milk.
- In place of butter or margarine, use reduced-fat margarine.
- For toppings, use plain bread crumbs or wheat germ.

Meat, chicken and seafood entrees
- Choose lean red meat and trim any extra fat.
- Use skinless chicken or turkey breast whenever possible.
- When browning meat or chicken, use a nonstick pan and vegetable oil cooking spray.
- Saute vegetables in broth, white wine, water or vegetable oil cooking spray.

• Bake, broil or stir-fry — avoid pan frying and deep-fat frying.

Baked goods

• Replace some or all of the fat with pureed fruits or fat-free yogurt.
• In place of baking chocolate, use 3 tablespoons of cocoa powder and 1 tablespoon of oil.
• Substitute two egg whites or 1/4 cup egg substitute for each whole egg called for in a recipe.
• Mix low-fat quick breads gently to prevent them from turning out tough and chewy.
• Keep fat-free products moist and fresh by not overbaking and by storing them in the refrigerator.

Appetizers

After-Dinner Cappuccino

15

Cappuccino and other specialty coffee drinks are delicious, but they are often prepared with cream. This After-Dinner Cappuccino made with skim milk cuts the calories to 101 per cup with just a trace of fat.

4 servings

4 cups skim milk
1/4 teaspoon vanilla extract
4 tablespoons instant decaffeinated coffee or instant decaffeinated espresso
1/4 teaspoon almond extract
1/2 teaspoon unsweetened cocoa, divided
4 sticks cinnamon (optional)

Nutrition Information Per Serving

			% of daily value
Calories	**101**		
Calories from fat	**5**	%	
Fat	**1**	g	2%
Saturated fat	**trace**	g	1%
Cholesterol	**4**	mg	1%
Sodium	**129**	mg	5%
Carbohydrate	**14**	g	5%
Fiber	**0**	g	
Sugar	**11**	g	
Protein	**9**	g	

■ Heat the milk in a medium-size saucepan over low heat until it's bubbly, but not boiling, about 6 to 8 minutes. Stir in the vanilla and coffee and remove from the heat. Stir in the almond extract.

Pour 1 cup of the milk mixture into the container of an electric blender; cover and process at the highest speed until frothy, about 30 seconds. Repeat three times with the remaining 3 cups of milk mixture. (You need room in the blender for the expansion of the hot mixture. If you put 2 cups or more in, the hot mixture could erupt from the blender.)

Divide the mixture equally into four mugs or large cups, and sprinkle each with 1/8 teaspoon of cocoa. Garnish each with a cinnamon stick, if desired.

1 milk

30

Apple Spiced Tea

Before you take the iced tea plunge, read the label. Although flavored iced teas have become popular, many contain more calories, sugar and caffeine than soda pop. Try preparing your own flavored teas such as Apple Spiced and Red Raspberry.

6 servings

1 cup apple juice
3 tablespoons brown sugar
1/2 teaspoon ground nutmeg
1/2 teaspoon ground cardamom
1/2 teaspoon whole cloves
1 tablespoon lemon juice
3 tea bags, decaffeinated
5 cups boiling water
6 cinnamon sticks

■ In a small saucepan, combine the apple juice, brown sugar, nutmeg, cardamom, cloves and lemon juice. Bring to a boil; reduce heat.

Cover and simmer for 20 minutes. Strain to remove the spices. Put the tea bags into a teapot. Pour the 5 cups boiling water over the tea bags; steep for 3 to 5 minutes.

Remove the tea bags.

Combine the apple juice and sugar mixture with the brewed tea. Chill. Pour over ice and garnish with a cinnamon stick.

Nutrition Information Per Serving

			% of daily value
Calories	**38**		
Calories from fat	**3**	%	
Fat	**trace**	g	1%
Saturated fat	**0**	g	0%
Cholesterol	**0**	mg	0%
Sodium	**7**	mg	1%
Carbohydrate	**10**	g	3%
Fiber	**0**	g	
Sugar	**8**	g	
Protein	**trace**	g	

Diabetic exchange

3/4 fruit

Red Raspberry Tea

Flavored teas may contain as much as 6 teaspoons of sugar per 6-ounce glass. This Heart Smart® Red Raspberry Tea uses only about 1 teaspoon of sugar, and artificial sweetner can be substituted to trim the calories even more. Fresh fruit provides the flavor and much of the sweetness.

8 servings

2 cups fresh or frozen raspberries
Juice and zest of one medium-size orange
3 tablespoons sugar
4 cups water
3 tea bags, decaffeinated
Lemon slices, for garnish

Nutrition Information Per Serving

			% of daily value
Calories	**41**		
Calories from fat	**0**	%	
Fat	**trace**	g	1%
Saturated fat	**0**	g	0%
Cholesterol	**0**	mg	0%
Sodium	**4**	mg	1%
Carbohydrate	**11**	g	4%
Fiber	**2**	g	
Sugar	**8**	g	
Protein	**trace**	g	

■ Puree the raspberries in a blender or food processor. Use a wooden spoon to further strain the puree through a fine sieve set over a bowl.

Put the orange juice, zest, sugar and water into a 2-quart saucepan. Bring to a boil and boil for 1 to 2 minutes until the sugar is dissolved. Remove the pan from the heat and add the tea bags. Let the tea steep for 3 to 5 minutes. Strain the tea into the puree, stir the mixture and chill.

Serve the raspberry tea over ice and garnish with lemon slices.

Diabetic exchange

3/4 fruit

15

Chocolate Banana Milk Shake

Children need the calcium from milk products for growth and development. If your children will not drink plain milk, try being a little creative. This chocolate milk shake is low in fat, packed with calcium, and delicious.

2 servings

3/4 cup skim milk
2 tablespoons chocolate-flavored syrup
1 cup vanilla ice milk
1 banana, peeled, cut into pieces

■ Combine the milk and chocolate syrup in a blender. Cover and blend on high speed for 2 seconds.

Add the vanilla ice milk and banana.

Cover and blend on low speed until smooth and creamy.

Nutrition Information Per Serving

			% of daily value
Calories	**238**		
Calories from fat	**10**	%	
Fat	**3**	g	5%
Saturated fat	**1.5**	g	8%
Cholesterol	**8**	mg	3%
Sodium	**139**	mg	6%
Carbohydrate	**48**	g	16%
Fiber	**1**	g	
Sugar	**39**	g	
Protein	**8**	g	

Diabetic exchange

1 milk, 1 fruit, 1 starch, 1/2 fat

Heart Smart® Party Mix

This recipe was designed to be served on those football Saturdays and Sundays. It's a super treat for the Super Bowl.

20 servings

3 cups toasted oat cereal
3 cups Rice Chex
2 cups Wheat Chex
1/4 cup peanuts
2 cups pretzel sticks
2 cups small pretzel twists
1/4 cup vegetable oil
1 tablespoon Worcestershire sauce
1 teaspoon garlic powder
1/2 teaspoon paprika
1/4 teaspoon ground red (cayenne) pepper

■ Preheat the oven to 250 degrees.

In a large baking dish, combine the toasted oat cereal, Rice Chex, Wheat Chex, peanuts, and pretzel sticks and twists. Set aside.

In a small bowl, whisk together the vegetable oil, Worcestershire sauce, garlic powder, paprika and ground red pepper. Pour over the cereal mixture. Stir to coat.

Bake for 1 hour, stirring every 15 minutes. Remove from the oven and let cool to room temperature. Store in an airtight container.

Nutrition Information Per Serving

			% of daily value
Calories	**123**		
Calories from fat	**29**	%	
Fat	**4**	g	6%
Saturated fat	**0.5**	g	3%
Cholesterol	**0**	mg	0%
Sodium	**259**	mg	11%
Carbohydrate	**19**	g	6%
Fiber	**0.5**	g	
Sugar	**1**	g	
Protein	**3**	g	

1 starch, 1 fat

15

Light Sangria

Will alcohol protect you from heart disease? Although some research shows that alcohol may increase your good cholesterol (HDL), it can contribute to other health problems. Moderation should be key. This sangria combines wine with sparkling water. The result is a refreshing beverage with less alcohol.

8 servings

1 bottle (750 ml) dry white wine
2 tablespoons superfine sugar
2 kiwifruits, peeled, inner stem removed and sliced
1 cup seedless green grapes, washed, dried
1 orange with rind, sliced thin
2 tablespoons Calvados or Armagnac or apple-flavored liqueur
3 tablespoons Cointreau or orange-flavored liqueur
3 cups bottled sparkling water
4 to 8 cups ice
Sprig of mint or edible flowers, optional

■ Place the wine in a large pitcher. Stir in the sugar until dissolved, then add the kiwifruit, grapes, orange, Calvados or Armagnac, and Cointreau to pitcher. Stir.

Cover and refrigerate for 4 or 5 hours.

To serve, stir in sparkling water. Pour over ice in tall glasses. Garnish with a sprig of mint or an edible flower.

Nutrition Information Per Serving

			% of daily value
Calories	**144**		
Calories from fat	**1**	%	
Fat	**trace**	g	1%
Saturated fat	**0**	g	0%
Cholesterol	**0**	mg	0%
Sodium	**10**	mg	1%
Carbohydrate	**12**	g	4%
Fiber	**1**	g	
Sugar	**7**	g	
Protein	**trace**	g	

Diabetic exchange

1 fruit, 1 1/2 fat

Quesadilla Appetizers

Mexican quesadillas made with avocado-based guacamole and topped with regular cheese can contain 800 calories per serving. These Quesadilla Appetizers are made with low-fat cheese, Salsa Cruda and Sweet Pea Guacamole. They have only 73 calories per appetizer serving with 30 percent of the calories from fat.

30 servings

1/2 small mango, peeled, seeded and cut into thin slices
1/4 pound shredded Monterey Jack cheese (low-fat, low-sodium, variety)
10 flour tortillas (8 inch)
Vegetable oil cooking spray
2 cups Salsa Cruda (page 28)
2 cups Sweet Pea Guacamole (page 29)

Nutrition Information Per Serving

			% of daily value
Calories	73		
Calories from fat	30	%	
Fat	3	g	5%
Saturated fat	0.5	g	3%
Cholesterol	3	mg	1%
Sodium	24	mg	1%
Carbohydrate	10	g	3%
Fiber	0.5	g	
Sugar	1	g	
Protein	3	g	

■ Divide the slices of mango and cheese into an even layer among five tortillas, leaving a 1/2-inch border. Top each tortilla with another tortilla and press lightly to compress. Spray a 10-inch skillet with the cooking spray and heat over medium heat. When hot, cook the quesadillas, one at a time, turning once, until very lightly browned on both sides, about 2 minutes per side.

Quesadillas are best served immediately, although they can be cooked several hours in advance and held at room temperature.

Reheat them before serving by placing them in a single layer on a baking sheet and baking at 400 degrees for 4 to 5 minutes.

To serve, cut each one into sixths, for a total of 30 slices, and arrange on a platter or in a large basket. Serve with guacamole and salsa on the side.

1 starch, 1/2 fat

15 (minutes)

Salsa Cruda

Cilantro is the seasoning that gives this salsa its unique taste. It is a type of parsley, but has a very strong, pungent flavor. It can be purchased year-round at most produce markets.

40 servings

1 large clove garlic, peeled
1 jalapeno or serrano pepper, seeded if desired
1/2 cup cilantro
1 small onion
2 medium tomatoes, seeded and diced
1 teaspoon red-wine vinegar
1 teaspoon light olive oil

■ Mince the garlic, pepper, cilantro and onion in a food processor or by hand, and place them in a bowl. Add the tomato to the bowl along with the vinegar and the oil, and mix well. Serve immediately or refrigerate for several days. Drain excess liquid and adjust seasonings before serving.

Nutrition Information Per Serving

			% of daily value
Calories	**5**		
Calories from fat	**34**	%	
Fat	**trace**	g	1%
Saturated fat	**0**	g	0%
Cholesterol	**0**	mg	0%
Sodium	**2**	mg	1%
Carbohydrate	**1**	g	1%
Fiber	**0**	g	
Sugar	**0**	g	
Protein	**trace**	g	

free food, up to 1/4 cup

Sweet Pea Guacamole

Traditional guacamole is made from avocados. But a tablespoon serving of the old "guac" contains 34 calories and 4 grams of fat. This low-fat variation still has the distinctive flavor of guacamole, but with less fat and fewer calories. It can be paired with baked tortilla chips for a delicious snack.

20 servings

10 ounces frozen peas
1 jalapeno pepper, seeds and stem removed
2 tablespoons olive oil
1 1/2 to 2 teaspoons fresh lemon juice
1/4 teaspoon ground cumin
1 medium onion, peeled, ends removed

■ Cook the peas according to the package directions. Drain well and pat with paper towels to remove as much moisture as possible. Mince the jalapeno pepper in a food processor or blender. Scrape down the sides of the container, add the oil and 1 1/2 teaspoons of lemon juice, and mix until the pepper is even more finely minced, about 30 seconds. Add the peas and cumin and puree, stopping once to scrape down the sides of the container. Cut the onion in half and add it to the container. Mix just enough to chop coarsely.

Chill well.

Adjust the seasonings and lemon juice before serving. This dish can be made up to two days in advance and refrigerated.

Nutrition Information Per Serving

		% of daily value
Calories	**24**	
Calories from fat	**51** %	
Fat	**1** g	2%
Saturated fat	**0** g	0%
Cholesterol	**0** mg	0%
Sodium	**3** mg	1%
Carbohydrate	**2** g	1%
Fiber	**0** g	
Sugar	**0** g	
Protein	**1** g	

Cook's note:

The percentage of calories from fat is high because the number of calories per serving are low.

free food, up to 1 tablespoon

15 minutes

Peach Yogurt Shake

Choose yogurt products wisely by comparing labels. Although yogurt sounds like a healthy choice, it can be very high in fat if it is made from whole milk. This Peach Yogurt Shake uses skim milk to provide a low-fat, high-energy treat.

4 servings

2 1/2 cups peaches, peeled, pitted, diced
1 medium-sized banana, peeled, strings removed
1 cup skim milk
8 ounces low-fat vanilla yogurt
4 teaspoons wheat germ, divided

■ In a blender combine the peaches, banana, skim milk and vanilla yogurt.

Process until smooth. Pour into 4 glasses, and sprinkle each glass with 1 teaspoon wheat germ.

Nutrition Information Per Serving

			% of daily value
Calories	138		
Calories from fat	8	%	
Fat	1	g	2%
Saturated fat	0.5	g	3%
Cholesterol	4	mg	1%
Sodium	72	mg	3%
Carbohydrate	27	g	9%
Fiber	2.5	g	
Sugar	19	g	
Protein	7	g	

1/2 milk, 1 fruit, 1/2 starch

YAK! Snack: Peanut Butter Crunchers

No food is forbidden in a healthy diet. Some foods, like milk, we need everyday and some are only once-in-a-while foods. It is not good to eat them everyday. Candy is a once-in-a-while food. These crunchers are better for you than most candy. Include them in your once-in-a-while foods.

24 servings

1/3 cup peanut butter, natural style
1/4 cup honey
1/2 cup instant nonfat dry milk (or a little more if needed to hold the shape)
1 1/2 cups rice cereal
Roll of waxed paper

Editor's note: This recipe for Peanut Butter Crunchers appeared in the Free Press' YAK! section for young readers. It's a quick, easy-to-assemble snack that your little ones will enjoy making.

Nutrition Information Per Serving

			% of daily value
Calories	44		
Calories from fat	35	%	
Fat	2	g	3%
Saturated fat	0.5	g	3%
Cholesterol	trace	mg	1%
Sodium	46	mg	2%
Carbohydrate	6	g	2%
Fiber	trace	g	
Sugar	4	g	
Protein	1	g	

■ First, make sure you have all the ingredients. You also will need measuring cups, spoons, a medium-size bowl, and a large spoon for stirring. You also will need a knife and an adult to help do the cutting.

To make it easy, measure your ingredients first and have them ready on the counter or table.

1. Put the peanut butter into the bowl.
2. Add the honey to the bowl.
3. Add the instant nonfat dry milk.
4. Stir all this together until it makes a moist dough that feels like clay. The dough should not be too dry or too sticky.
5. Roll the dough into a log shape. Put it on waxed paper.
6. Pour the cereal on the waxed paper and roll the dough log in the cereal until it is covered.
7. Have an adult cut the log into thin slices.
8. Keep in the refrigerator to chill. The crunchers can last up to two weeks in the refrigerator.

1/2 starch, 1/2 fat

60

Roasted Garlic & Almond Dip

If you are tired of snacking on cut vegetables or indulging yourself and then feeling guilty, this dip is for you. Serve it on fat-free or low-fat crackers or chips to trim even more fat and calories.

144 servings

1 cup blanched almonds (about 4 ounces)
3 heads garlic (about 36 cloves), peeled, ends removed
1 tablespoon vegetable oil
2 teaspoons Worcestershire sauce
1 1/2 teaspoons Dijon mustard
1 cup low-fat sour cream
1 cup low-fat mayonnaise
1/4 cup plus 2 tablespoons chopped fresh parsley
2 teaspoons dried rosemary
1/8 tablespoon freshly ground pepper

Nutrition Information Per Serving

			% of daily value
Calories	**15**		
Calories from fat	**79**	%	
Fat	**1**	g	2%
Saturated fat	**trace**	g	1%
Cholesterol	**trace**	mg	1%
Sodium	**4**	mg	1%
Carbohydrate	**trace**	g	1%
Fiber	**trace**	g	
Sugar	**0**	g	
Protein	**trace**	g	

■ Preheat the oven to 350 degrees. Spread the almonds out in a shallow baking dish, and toast in the oven 6 to 8 minutes or until golden. Remove from the oven and set aside.

Reduce the oven temperature to 300 degrees, and position the oven rack in the lowest third of the oven. Place the garlic in a small baking dish and toss with oil. Bake until the garlic is soft and golden, about 30 to 40 minutes. Remove from the oven, transfer to a blender and cool about 30 minutes.

Add the Worcestershire sauce and Dijon mustard to the garlic and blend until the garlic is finely chopped. Scrape the mixture into a large bowl. Stir in the almonds, sour cream, mayonnaise, parsley, rosemary and pepper. Cover and refrigerate at least two hours or overnight, to mellow the flavors. Let stand at room temperature for one hour before serving. Serve with assorted crackers, red pepper strips and snow peas if desired.

Nonfat sour cream and mayonnaise may be substituted.

Diabetic exchange

1/3 fat

Spicy Warm Cider

Many goodies served to children at festive times of the year aren't such a treat for their hearts. Chocolate is loaded with sugar and fat, particularly saturated fat, which contributes to atherosclerosis, or hardening of the arteries. But there are heart-healthy treats for children, including this Spicy Warm Cider.

30 servings

1 gallon apple cider
1 can (6 ounces) frozen concentrate orange juice
7 cinnamon sticks
1 1/2 teaspoons whole cloves
1 teaspoon whole allspice

■ Combine the cider and frozen orange juice in small soup pot. Place the cinnamon sticks, cloves and allspice in a double layer of cheesecloth, tied with kitchen string. Lower the bag into the juice. Simmer the mixture, covered, for one hour over low heat. Strain if not using a cheesecloth bag.

Serve the cider warm (it can be reheated).

Nutrition Information Per Serving

			% of daily value
Calories	**56**		
Calories from fat	**0**	%	
Fat	**0**	g	0%
Saturated fat	**0**	g	0%
Cholesterol	**0**	mg	0%
Sodium	**0**	mg	0%
Carbohydrate	**14**	g	5%
Fiber	**0**	g	
Sugar	**0**	g	
Protein	**trace**	g	

1 fruit

15 minutes

Tex-Mex Black Bean Dip

With many fat-free products available, you can easily adjust your recipes without losing flavor. A typical spread has 3 grams of fat per tablespoon, with 80 percent of its calories from fat. By substituting fat-free cream cheese, fat-free sour cream and fat-free mayonnaise in your dips and spreads, you eliminate most of the fat. This Tex-Mex Black Bean Dip eliminates cheese to reduce the percentage of calories from fat to 4 percent.

24 servings

1 can (15 ounces) black beans, rinsed and drained
Vegetable oil cooking spray
1/2 cup chopped onion
2 garlic cloves, peeled, ends removed, minced
1/2 cup diced tomatoes
1/3 cup mild picante sauce
1/2 teaspoon ground cumin
1/2 teaspoon chili powder
1/4 cup chopped fresh cilantro
1 tablespoon fresh lime juice
Fat-free corn or flour tortilla chips

■ Place the black beans in a small bowl. Partially mash the beans until they are chunky; set aside.

Spray a medium-size nonstick skillet with the cooking spray. Place it over medium heat, add the onion and garlic; saute 4 minutes or until tender.

Add the beans, tomatoes, picante sauce, cumin and chili powder; cook 5 minutes or until thickened, stirring constantly. Remove from the heat. Add the cilantro and lime juice.

Serve warm or at room temperature.

Nutrition Information Per Serving

			% of daily value
Calories	23		
Calories from fat	4	%	
Fat	trace	g	1%
Saturated fat	0	g	0%
Cholesterol	0	mg	0%
Sodium	25	mg	1%
Carbohydrate	4	g	1%
Fiber	1	g	
Sugar	0	g	
Protein	1	g	

Diabetic exchange

1/3 starch

Breads & Breakfast

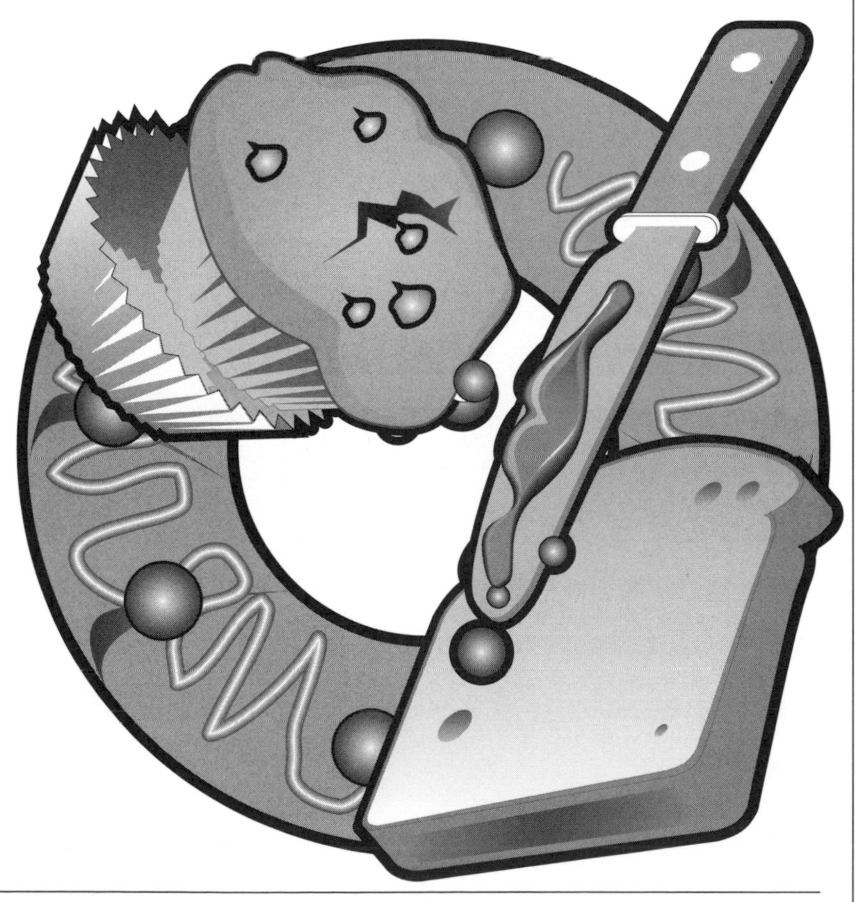

Apple De-Light Muffins

By choosing an Apple De-Light Muffin for breakfast instead of stopping at a fast-food restaurant for a danish, you trim 400 calories and 36 grams of fat.

18 servings

Vegetable oil cooking spray
2 cups all-purpose flour
3/4 cup granulated sugar
2 teaspoons baking soda
1 1/2 teaspoons ground cinnamon
1/2 teaspoon salt
3/4 cup nonfat liquid egg substitute or 6 egg whites
1/2 cup sweetened applesauce
1/2 cup skim milk
1 1/2 teaspoons vanilla extract
2 cups coarsely chopped apples (about 3 small apples peeled, cored, seeded)
2 cups grated carrots

■ Preheat the oven to 375 degrees. Spray a muffin pan with the cooking spray.

In a large bowl, combine the flour, sugar, baking soda, cinnamon and salt. In another bowl, combine the egg substitute or egg whites, applesauce, skim milk and vanilla extract. Mix well. Stir the egg mixture into the flour mixture just until moistened. Fold in the apples and carrots.

Fill the prepared muffin cups with batter. Bake for 20 to 25 minutes, or until a wooden pick inserted into the center comes out clean. Remove the muffins from the oven and serve.

Nutrition Information Per Serving

			% of daily value
Calories	**103**		
Calories from fat	**2**	%	
Fat	**trace**	g	1%
Saturated fat	**0**	g	0%
Cholesterol	**trace**	mg	1%
Sodium	**172**	mg	7%
Carbohydrate	**23**	g	8%
Fiber	**1**	g	
Sugar	**12**	g	
Protein	**3**	g	

Diabetic exchange

1 starch, 1/2 fruit

45 (time)

Apple Pancakes with Cinnamon Sauce

Pancakes are a favorite among people of all ages. This variation replaces the sugary syrup with a tasty yogurt sauce. This recipe will also help children learn good breakfast habits.

4 servings

Vegetable oil cooking spray
2 Granny Smith apples, washed, peeled, cored, seeded, coarsely chopped
1/2 cup flour
1 cup skim milk
1 tablespoon sugar
4 egg whites
1 tablespoon vegetable oil

Sauce:
1 cup nonfat vanilla yogurt
1 teaspoon cinnamon
2 tablespoons apple juice
1 tablespoon sugar

Nutrition Information Per Serving

			% of daily value
Calories	**232**		
Calories from fat	**16**	%	
Fat	**4**	g	6%
Saturated fat	**0.5**	g	3%
Cholesterol	**2**	mg	1%
Sodium	**122**	mg	5%
Carbohydrate	**41**	g	14%
Fiber	**1.5**	g	
Sugar	**18**	g	
Protein	**10**	g	

■ Spray a large skillet with the cooking spray.

Over medium heat, gently saute the apples until almost soft, about 6 to 10 minutes. Set aside to cool.

In a medium-size bowl, mix the flour, milk, sugar and egg whites. Stir in the vegetable oil, cover the batter and set aside for at least 20 minutes.

In a small bowl, mix together the yogurt with the cinnamon, apple juice and sugar until creamy. Refrigerate until ready to serve.

Preheat the nonstick griddle to 375 degrees or heat a large skillet sprayed with the cooking spray. Mix the cooled apples into the batter.

Pour 1/2 cup of the batter on the griddle or skillet. Cook each pancake for 2 to 3 minutes, or until lightly browned. Turn with a spatula and cook the second side until lightly browned.

Serve 1/4 cup of the sauce on the side with each pancake. Refrigerate any extra sauce for another use.

Diabetic exchange

2 starch, 1/2 milk, 1/2 fat

Bran-Raisin Muffins

Skipping meals often leads to bingeing on high-calorie foods when hunger takes over and resistance is low. Plan ahead for a busy day and carry these tasty muffins with you. They are high in fiber and carbohydrates, so they will give you a full feeling as well as an energy boost — a perfect pick-me-up.

12 servings

Floured baking spray
1 cup All-Bran cereal
2/3 cup raisins
1 1/4 cups skim milk
3 tablespoons vegetable oil
2 egg whites
1 cup all-purpose flour
2 teaspoons baking powder

Nutrition Information Per Serving

			% of daily value
Calories	**129**		
Calories from fat	**29**	%	
Fat	**4**	g	6%
Saturated fat	**0.5**	g	3%
Cholesterol	**trace**	mg	1%
Sodium	**158**	mg	7%
Carbohydrate	**20**	g	7%
Fiber	**2.5**	g	
Sugar	**5**	g	
Protein	**4**	g	

■ Preheat the oven to 400 degrees. Spray a 12-cup muffin pan with the floured baking spray.

In a large bowl, mix the cereal and raisins. Add the milk, stir and let stand several minutes. Add the vegetable oil and egg whites. Beat well.

In a small bowl whisk together the flour and baking powder. Add to the bran mixture. Stir until the flour is just blended or moistened.

Evenly spoon the mixture into the prepared muffin pan. Bake for 15 minutes. Remove from the oven, and remove the muffins from the pan immediately and place on a cooling rack.

Diabetic exchange

1 starch, 1/2 fat, 1/3 fruit

30

Corn Bread

This corn bread prepared with pimiento and green chilies is so flavorful it needs no added fat. It tastes great served with chili or stew or a crisp summertime salad.

6 servings

Vegetable oil cooking spray
1 cup skim buttermilk
2 egg whites
1 tablespoon vegetable oil
1 tablespoon sugar
1 tablespoon pimiento, drained, finely chopped
1 can (4 ounces) chopped green chilies, drained
1 cup all-purpose flour
3/4 cup yellow cornmeal
2 teaspoons baking powder
1/2 teaspoon baking soda

■ Preheat the oven to 450 degrees. Spray an 8-by-8-inch square baking pan with the cooking spray.

In a small bowl, whisk together the buttermilk, egg whites, oil and sugar. Stir in the pimiento and green chilies.

In a large bowl, combine the flour, cornmeal, baking powder and baking soda. Pour in the buttermilk mixture and stir just until the dry ingredients are moistened; do not overmix. Pour the batter evenly into the prepared pan.

Bake 25 minutes, or until golden and a wooden pick inserted in the center comes out clean. Remove from the oven and cool on a wire rack for 5 minutes.

Nutrition Information Per Serving

			% of daily value
Calories	**196**		
Calories from fat	**15**	%	
Fat	**3**	g	5%
Saturated fat	**0.5**	g	3%
Cholesterol	**trace**	mg	1%
Sodium	**293**	mg	12%
Carbohydrate	**35**	g	12%
Fiber	**1.5**	g	
Sugar	**4**	g	
Protein	**6**	g	

2 starch, 1/2 fat

Dill-Onion Bread

A well-balanced diet includes at least six servings of breads and cereals every day, which may seem like a lot to people who are watching their weight. To keep from overloading on calories, choose low-fat breads such as this tasty Dill-Onion Bread.

16 servings

1/4 ounce active dry yeast
1/2 cup warm water (110 to 115 degrees)
2 egg whites, beaten
1/2 cup 1-percent low-fat cottage cheese
1/3 cup onion, peeled, ends removed, finely chopped
1 tablespoon tub margarine, melted
2 1/4 cups all-purpose flour, divided
1/2 cup wheat germ
1/3 cup whole bran cereal
1 tablespoon sugar
1 tablespoon dill seed
1/2 teaspoon salt
1/4 teaspoon baking soda
Vegetable oil cooking spray

■ In a small bowl or measuring cup, soften the yeast in the warm water. In a medium bowl, combine the egg whites, cottage cheese, onion and margarine. Mix well.

In a large bowl, stir together 2 cups of the flour, wheat germ, bran cereal, sugar, dill seed, salt and baking soda. Add the yeast mixture and cottage cheese mixture to the flour mixture, stirring well. Cover with a clean tea towel; let rise in a warm place until the dough doubles, about 1 hour. Spray a 9-by-1 1/2-inch round baking pan with the cooking spray. Stir the dough down.

Using the remaining 1/4 cup of flour, lightly flour the work surface and knead the dough for 1 minute. Pat the dough into a prepared pan. Cover with a clean tea towel and let rise until it nearly doubles, about 1 hour.

Before baking, preheat the oven to 350 degrees. With a knife, gently score the top of the bread in a diamond pattern. Bake in the oven for 40 minutes or until golden. Remove from the pan. Cool on a wire rack. Serve warm.

Makes 1 loaf.

Nutrition Information Per Serving

			% of daily value
Calories	94		
Calories from fat	14	%	
Fat	1	g	2%
Saturated fat	trace	g	1%
Cholesterol	trace	mg	1%
Sodium	136	mg	6%
Carbohydrate	16	g	5%
Fiber	1	g	
Sugar	2	g	
Protein	4	g	

Diabetic exchange

1 starch

30

Irish Soda Biscuits

Irish Soda Biscuits can be prepared in advance and warmed in the microwave for a quick breakfast. For a complete meal, simply add fruit or juice and a glass of milk.

32 servings

Vegetable oil cooking spray
4 1/4 cups flour, sifted, divided
1/3 cup sugar
1 teaspoon baking powder
1 teaspoon baking soda
2 tablespoons tub margarine, frozen
1 1/2 cups raisins
1 1/2 cups buttermilk
1 egg
2 egg whites

■ Cover a baking sheet with foil and spray with the cooking spray. Preheat the oven to 350 degrees.

In a large bowl, blend together 4 cups of the flour, sugar, baking powder and baking soda. Cut in the frozen margarine using a pastry blender or 2 knives. Add the raisins.

In a small bowl, whisk together the buttermilk, egg and egg whites. Add to the flour-raisin mixture.

Sprinkle the remaining 1/4 cup flour on the work surface. Knead the dough for 1 to 2 minutes on the floured surface.

Roll or pat the dough so that it is about 3/4-inch thick. Cut out rounds with a 2-inch biscuit cutter or the rim of a small glass, and place the biscuits on the prepared baking sheet. Gather up the scraps of dough, form them into a ball and repeat the process.

Bake until the biscuits are golden brown, about 15 minutes. Remove from the oven.

Nutrition Information Per Serving

			% of daily value
Calories	**99**		
Calories from fat	**10**	%	
Fat	**1**	g	2%
Saturated fat	**trace**	g	1%
Cholesterol	**7**	mg	2%
Sodium	**64**	mg	3%
Carbohydrate	**20**	g	7%
Fiber	**1**	g	
Sugar	**7**	g	
Protein	**3**	g	

1 starch, 1/3 fruit

15

Old-Fashioned Bread Stuffing

We used a small amount of oil and chicken broth in place of butter to keep the flavor in this family favorite with less fat. Use this tip to adjust your favorite stuffing recipe.

8 servings

1 tablespoon vegetable oil
1 cup finely chopped celery
1/2 cup chopped onion
1 teaspoon poultry seasoning
1/4 teaspoon black pepper
16 slices dry bread, cubed
3/4 to 1 cup chicken broth

Nutrition Information Per Serving

			% of daily value
Calories	**161**		
Calories from fat	**22**	%	
Fat	**4**	g	6%
Saturated fat	**0.5**	g	3%
Cholesterol	**0**	mg	0%
Sodium	**368**	mg	15%
Carbohydrate	**26**	g	9%
Fiber	**1.5**	g	
Sugar	**2**	g	
Protein	**5**	g	

■ Heat the vegetable oil in a small saucepan over medium heat. Add the celery and onion and cook until tender, but not brown. Remove from the heat. Stir in the poultry seasoning and add the black pepper.

Place the dry bread cubes in a large bowl. Add the onion mixture and drizzle with enough broth or water to moisten. Toss lightly to evenly coat.

Use the stuffing to stuff a 8- to 10-pound turkey.

Diabetic exchange

2 starch, 1/2 fat

45 minutes

Oatmeal Carrot Muffins

In half of all American families, at least one person regularly skips breakfast. The most common reason is a lack of time. These muffins are easy to make ahead and freeze, and it takes only minutes to heat them in a microwave. Grab a glass of skim milk and an orange, and you have a healthy start to your day.

12 servings

1 cup skim milk
1 cup regular oatmeal, uncooked
1/2 cup raisins
Vegetable oil cooking spray or paper muffin liners
1/2 cup carrots, peeled, ends removed, grated
1/4 cup packed brown sugar
1/4 cup granulated sugar
1/4 cup vegetable oil
2 egg whites
1 teaspoon orange rind
1/2 cup all-purpose flour
1/2 cup whole-wheat flour
1 tablespoon baking powder
1/2 teaspoon baking soda

■ In a large bowl, pour the skim milk over the oats and raisins; stir to mix. Cover and let stand for two hours, or refrigerate overnight.

Preheat the oven to 400 degrees. Spray the muffin tins with the cooking spray or line with paper liners.

In a medium-size bowl, mix together the carrots, brown sugar, granulated sugar, oil, egg whites and orange rind. Stir into the oat mixture. In a medium-size bowl, sift together the flours, baking powder and baking soda. Stir into the batter just until moistened.

Spoon the batter into the prepared muffin cups, filling them almost to the top. Bake in the oven for 20 to 25 minutes or until firm to the touch. Remove from the oven and let stand for 2 minutes before removing the muffins from the pan.

Nutrition Information Per Serving

			% of daily value
Calories	**138**		
Calories from fat	**32**	%	
Fat	**5**	g	8%
Saturated fat	**0.5**	g	3%
Cholesterol	**trace**	mg	1%
Sodium	**142**	mg	6%
Carbohydrate	**22**	g	7%
Fiber	**1.5**	g	
Sugar	**13**	g	
Protein	**3**	g	

Diabetic exchange

1 starch, 1 fat, 1/2 fruit

Pineapple Yogurt Muffins

The healthy combination of pineapples and yogurt lends a unique taste to these quick breakfast muffins.

12 servings

Vegetable oil cooking spray or paper muffin liners
1/4 cup sugar
2 egg whites
1/4 cup vegetable oil
1 cup nonfat plain yogurt
1 1/2 cups all-purpose flour
1 teaspoon baking powder
1/2 teaspoon baking soda
1 cup crushed pineapple, well drained

Nutrition Information Per Serving

			% of daily value
Calories	**122**		
Calories from fat	**22**	%	
Fat	**3**	g	5%
Saturated fat	**trace**	g	1%
Cholesterol	**trace**	mg	1%
Sodium	**86**	mg	4%
Carbohydrate	**19**	g	6%
Fiber	**0.5**	g	
Sugar	**7**	g	
Protein	**3**	g	

■ Preheat the oven to 375 degrees. Spray the muffin pan with the cooking spray or line with paper liners that are sprayed on the inside.

In a medium-size bowl, combine the sugar, egg whites, oil and yogurt. Beat until well combined.

In another medium bowl, sift together the flour, baking powder and baking soda. Add the yogurt mixture to the flour mixture and stir until moistened. Stir in the pineapple.

Evenly divide the batter among the 12 muffin cups. Bake for 15 to 20 minutes, or until a wooden pick inserted into the center comes out clean and muffins are golden. Remove from the oven and let cool on a wire rack.

Cook's note:

Low-fat muffins tend to stick to paper liners. Spraying the paper liners with vegetable oil cooking spray alleviates this problem.

Diabetic exchange

1 starch, 1/2 fat, 1/4 fruit

30

Rum Raisin & Apple Stuffing

Every family seems to have a favorite stuffing for holiday meals. Trim some of the fat from yours by sauteing vegetables in a small amount of oil or vegetable oil cooking spray. Moisten bread with low-fat chicken broth instead of butter, or start a new tradition by serving Rum Raisin & Apple Stuffing.

12 servings

1/2 cup raisins
1/3 cup rum, or 1/2 teaspoon rum extract mixed with 1/3 cup hot tap water
1 loaf (1 1/2 pounds) whole-wheat, pumpernickel or bran bread, or any combination, dried (see directions)
1 1/2 cups (one 12-ounce can) low-sodium chicken broth, chilled and defatted (see directions)
Fresh ground pepper, to taste
1 teaspoon thyme
1 1/2 teaspoon sage
1/2 teaspoon savory
1/4 cup chopped parsley
3 medium apples, unpeeled, cored, chopped
2 large onions, chopped (about 2 cups)
4 stalks celery, diced (about 1 1/2 cups)
3 tablespoons margarine, melted
3 egg whites, lightly beaten

■ Place the raisins in a small bowl and cover with rum or rum extract and water; marinate at least 1 hour, allowing the raisins to absorb the liquid.

If the bread needs to be dried, spread the slices on a rack for half a day or place in a 300-degree oven until dried, about 15 minutes. Cut the bread into cubes or break into crumb size with a spoon or food processor.

Chill the low-sodium chicken broth overnight in the refrigerator or 1 hour in the freezer, then skim off the fat. Set aside.

Combine the bread crumbs with the pepper, thyme, sage, savory and parsley; mix well. Add the apples, onion, celery and margarine, and mix well. Add the defatted broth and beaten egg whites; mix well. This recipe makes enough to stuff a 10- to 14-pound turkey. Spoon the stuffing into a cleaned turkey. Don't pack too tightly; allow some space for expansion upon heating.

After cooking, remove the stuffing and place in a separate bowl before carving the turkey. Keep the stuffing warm in a 200-degree oven until ready to serve.

Nutrition Information Per Serving

			% of daily value
Calories	**232**		
Calories from fat	**20**	%	
Fat	**6**	g	9%
Saturated fat	**0.5**	g	3%
Cholesterol	**0**	mg	0%
Sodium	**423**	mg	18%
Carbohydrate	**38**	g	13%
Fiber	**8**	g	
Sugar	**12**	g	
Protein	**7**	g	

Cook's note:

If you aren't cooking a whole turkey, place the stuffing in a 5-quart oven-proof baking dish sprayed with vegetable oil cooking spray. Bake the stuffing, alone or topped with turkey cut into 1/4-inch slices, in a preheated 350-degree oven for 20 minutes, uncovered, and 35 to 40 minutes more, covered.

1 1/2 starch, 1 fruit, 1 fat

Sour Cream Cranberry Coffee Cake

A special brunch can be elegant, delicious and healthy, too. Simply serve fresh fruit and an assortment of low-fat quick breads. This coffee cake, with only 2 grams of fat per serving, is such a treat you may decide to serve it on other special occasions.

9 servings

Vegetable oil cooking spray
1 1/2 cups all-purpose flour
3/4 cup sugar
1 teaspoon baking soda
1/2 teaspoon ground cinnamon
1/2 cup apple juice concentrate
1/4 cup nonfat sour cream
1 egg white, lightly beaten
2 1/2 cups cranberries, rinsed, coarsely chopped
3 tablespoons walnuts, coarsely chopped
1/2 cup confectioners' sugar
1 to 2 tablespoons hot water

■ Preheat the oven to 350 degrees. Spray a 9-by-9-inch baking dish with the cooking spray.

In a medium bowl, combine the flour, sugar, baking soda and cinnamon. Stir to mix well. Stir in the apple juice concentrate, sour cream and egg white. Fold in the cranberries and walnuts.

Spread the batter evenly into the prepared baking dish. Bake for 30 to 35 minutes, or until a wooden pick inserted into the center comes out clean. Remove from the oven and cool 10 minutes. Invert onto a wire rack and cool completely.

To prepare the glaze: In a small bowl, mix together the confectioners' sugar and enough hot water to form the desired consistency of glaze. Drizzle the glaze over the cooled cake.

Nutrition Information Per Serving

			% of daily value
Calories	**203**		
Calories from fat	**9**	%	
Fat	**2**	g	3%
Saturated fat	**trace**	g	1%
Cholesterol	**trace**	mg	1%
Sodium	**108**	mg	5%
Carbohydrate	**43**	g	14%
Fiber	**0.5**	g	
Sugar	**16**	g	
Protein	**4**	g	

Diabetic exchange

2 starch, 1 fruit

30

Spanish Omelet for Four

Next time you are tempted to eat an egg and cheese sandwich at a fast-food restaurant, consider that it contains 400 to 525 calories. Then consider that 55 to 60 percent of those calories come from fat. That's like eating 5 to 7 teaspoons of butter.

4 servings

2 eggs
6 egg whites
1/4 cup skim milk
1/4 teaspoon salt (omit to reduce sodium)
1/8 teaspoon pepper
1 cup thinly sliced potatoes (about 2 medium)
1 teaspoon vegetable oil
1/2 cup thinly sliced onions
1/2 cup julienned green pepper strips
1 clove garlic, minced, or garlic powder to taste
1/3 cup thin tomato wedges

■ Combine the eggs and egg whites, milk, salt and pepper in a medium bowl; beat well. Set aside.

Put the potatoes in a microwave dish, cover and microwave on high power about 5 minutes, until they are firm but cooked; or put the potatoes in a saucepan, cover with water and cook, covered, about 10 to 15 minutes; drain well.

Heat the vegetable oil in a 10-inch nonstick skillet over medium heat. Saute the cooked potato, onion and green pepper until tender and browned; add the garlic and tomatoes and cook for 2 more minutes. Cover and set aside.

Preheat the oven to 350 degrees. Heat a 6-inch nonstick skillet over medium heat on top of the stove until a drop of water sizzles on contact.

Pour half the egg mixture into the hot pan. Allow a thin layer of the mixture to cook for approximately 30 seconds. Using a spatula, gently lift the edges while tilting the pan, allowing the uncooked portion to flow underneath. When cooked, loosen and place on a heated plate. Spoon half the vegetable mixture onto half of the omelet; gently fold the other half of the omelet over the mixture. Cut into two portions and put on an ovenproof plate in the oven to keep warm. Repeat the procedure with the remaining portions.

Serve at once.

Nutrition Information Per Serving

			% of daily value
Calories	151		
Calories from fat	23	%	
Fat	4	g	6%
Saturated fat	1	g	5%
Cholesterol	107	mg	36%
Sodium	261	mg	11%
Carbohydrate	18	g	6%
Fiber	1.5	g	
Sugar	3	g	
Protein	11	g	

1 starch, 1 meat

Spinach-Potato Pancakes

These pancakes make a tasty side dish for any meal.

12 servings

1 1/4 cups skim milk
1/8 teaspoon ground nutmeg
1 cup plus 1 tablespoon flour
2 tablespoons vegetable oil
1/2 pound potatoes, peeled, eyes removed, finely grated
1 egg
4 egg whites
1/2 teaspoon sugar
1 package (10 ounces) frozen chopped spinach, thawed and squeezed dry
1/2 onion, peeled, ends removed, finely grated
Vegetable oil cooking spray

Nutrition Information Per Serving

			% of daily value
Calories	**101**		
Calories from fat	**25**	%	
Fat	**3**	g	5%
Saturated fat	**0.5**	g	3%
Cholesterol	**18**	mg	6%
Sodium	**63**	mg	3%
Carbohydrate	**15**	g	5%
Fiber	**1**	g	
Sugar	**2**	g	
Protein	**5**	g	

■ In a blender or food processor, mix the milk, nutmeg, flour and oil.

In a medium bowl, combine the potatoes, egg, egg whites, sugar, spinach and onion. Pour the milk mixture over the potato mixture and toss to combine.

Spray an electric skillet or griddle with the cooking spray. When hot, spoon on 1/4 cup of the pancake batter.

Cook several minutes on each side, or until the pancakes are nicely browned. Spray the skillet as it becomes necessary while cooking the remaining pancakes.

Makes 12 pancakes.

Diabetic exchange

1 starch, 1/2 fat

90

Strawberry Almond Bread

Nuts add taste and a great crunchy texture to quick breads. Remember they are high in fat so use them sparingly. The almonds in this recipe add less than 1 gram of fat per serving.

16 servings

Vegetable oil cooking spray
1 1/4 cups all-purpose flour
1/2 cup sugar
1 1/2 teaspoons baking powder
1/4 teaspoon baking soda
1/4 teaspoon ground cloves
2 egg whites
1/2 cup plain nonfat yogurt
1/4 cup vegetable oil
1 teaspoon almond extract
1 1/2 cups strawberries, washed, stems and leaves removed, diced
2 tablespoons almonds, finely chopped
1 tablespoon sugar

■ Preheat the oven to 350 degrees. Spray an 8 1/2-by-4 1/2-by-3-inch loaf pan with the cooking spray. In a large bowl, combine the flour, sugar, baking powder, baking soda and cloves; stir well.

In a medium bowl, combine the egg whites, yogurt, oil and almond extract. Add to the dry ingredients, stirring well. Fold in the strawberries. Spoon the batter into the prepared loaf pan. Sprinkle with almonds and sugar.

Bake for 55 minutes, or until a wooden pick inserted near the center comes out clean. Remove from the oven and let cool in the pan for 10 minutes. Remove from the pan, invert onto a wire cooling rack, and let cool for 1 hour. Cover and chill for 8 hours.

Nutrition Information Per Serving

			% of daily value
Calories	**127**		
Calories from fat	**28**	%	
Fat	**4**	g	6%
Saturated fat	**0.5**	g	3%
Cholesterol	**trace**	mg	1%
Sodium	**57**	mg	2%
Carbohydrate	**21**	g	7%
Fiber	**2**	g	
Sugar	**12**	g	
Protein	**2**	g	

Diabetic exchange

1 starch, 1/2 fruit, 1 fat

15

Tiny Corncakes

This is a great way to get kids to eat their vegetables. These Tiny Corncakes are easy to make and taste delicious. Serve them with a vegetarian chili for a meatless meal with complete protein.

15 servings

3/4 cup all-purpose flour
1/2 cup cornmeal
1 teaspoon baking powder
1/4 teaspoon salt, optional
1/2 teaspoon sugar
1 can (14 3/4 ounces) cream-style corn
1/2 cup skim milk
2 egg whites, slightly beaten
Vegetable oil cooking spray

Nutrition Information Per Serving

			% of daily value
Calories	66		
Calories from fat	5	%	
Fat	trace	g	1%
Saturated fat	0	g	0%
Cholesterol	0	mg	0%
Sodium	166	mg	7%
Carbohydrate	14	g	5%
Fiber	1	g	
Sugar	1	g	
Protein	2	g	

■ In a large bowl, combine the flour, cornmeal, baking powder, salt and sugar. Stir well. Make a well in the center of the mixture.

In a medium bowl, combine the cream-style corn, skim milk and egg whites. Add the milk mixture to the well in the flour mixture. Stir to combine, just until moistened.

Preheat a griddle or large skillet and spray with the cooking spray. For each corncake, pour 3 tablespoons of the batter onto the hot griddle or skillet. Turn the corncakes when the tops are covered with bubbles and the edges look cooked, and cook on the other side until done.

Diabetic exchange

1 starch

15 minutes

Tomato Parmesan Toasts

The combination of tomato and Parmesan cheese usually is reserved for an evening pasta meal. In this Heart Smart® recipe for toasts, the cheese is melted over a mixture of tomatoes, olives and cilantro. Delicious!

8 servings

Vegetable oil cooking spray
16 slices from a baguette, each cut 1/2-inch thick
2 tomatoes, washed, cored, seeded, cut into 1/4-inch dice
2 tablespoons black olives, pitted, cut into 1/4-inch slices
4 tablespoons fresh cilantro, washed, dried, stems removed, minced
1/8 teaspoon freshly ground black pepper
1 1/2 tablespoons freshly grated Parmesan cheese

■ Preheat the oven to 400 degrees. Cover a baking sheet with foil. Spray the foil with the cooking spray. Arrange the baguette slices on the sheet, and bake for 3 to 4 minutes or until lightly browned. Remove from the oven and set aside.

In a medium-size bowl, combine the tomatoes, olives, cilantro and pepper. Divide and spoon the mixture evenly on top of each piece of toast. Sprinkle with Parmesan cheese. Return to the oven for 5 minutes, or until heated through. Remove from the oven and serve warm.

Nutrition Information Per Serving

			% of daily value
Calories	**117**		
Calories from fat	**19**	%	
Fat	**3**	g	5%
Saturated fat	**0.5**	g	3%
Cholesterol	**1**	mg	1%
Sodium	**266**	mg	11%
Carbohydrate	**20**	g	7%
Fiber	**1.5**	g	
Sugar	**3**	g	
Protein	**4**	g	

Diabetic exchange

1 starch, 1/2 fat

Wild Mushroom Stuffing

Wild mushrooms are available in most supermarkets. If you have not tried them, you are missing out on a treat. They have a strong, woodsy taste, and in this stuffing they provide a unique flavor.

12 servings

1 pound loaf white bread, cut into 1/2-inch cubes
1/2 pound loaf whole-wheat bread, cut into 1/2-inch cubes
1 tablespoon vegetable oil
3 medium onions, peeled, ends removed, chopped
4 ounces shiitake mushrooms, stems removed, or porcini mushrooms, cleaned, sliced
12 ounces fresh button mushrooms, cleaned, sliced
2 cups celery, washed, ends removed, chopped
1 cup fresh parsley, washed, dried, chopped
3 tablespoons fresh rosemary, washed, dried, minced; or 2 teaspoons dried, crumbled
3 tablespoons fresh tarragon, washed, dried, minced; or 2 teaspoons dried, crumbled
1/4 teaspoon black pepper
1/4 cup walnuts, shelled, chopped
1 1/2 cups low-sodium defatted chicken broth
Vegetable oil cooking spray

■ Preheat the oven to 250 degrees. Place the bread cubes on two baking sheets and bake until dry but not hard, stirring occasionally, about 40 minutes. Remove from the oven and let cool.

Increase the oven temperature to 350 degrees. Place the cubes in large bowl. Heat the oil in a heavy large skillet over medium heat. Add the onion and cook until tender, about 8 minutes. Add all the mushrooms and celery and saute until tender, about 8 minutes. Add the mushroom mixture to the bread cubes. Mix in the parsley, rosemary, tarragon, black pepper and walnuts. Drizzle the chicken broth over the mixture, gently tossing until absorbed.

Spray a 4-quart baking dish with the cooking spray. Transfer the mixture to the baking dish and cover with foil. (Can be prepared one day ahead. Cover and refrigerate. Bring to room temperature before baking.) Bake the stuffing until heated through, about 1 hour.

Remove from the oven and serve.

Nutrition Information Per Serving

			% of daily value
Calories	198		
Calories from fat	23	%	
Fat	5	g	8%
Saturated fat	0.5	g	3%
Cholesterol	0	mg	0%
Sodium	326	mg	14%
Carbohydrate	32	g	11%
Fiber	4	g	
Sugar	3	g	
Protein	7	g	

Diabetic exchange

2 starch, 1 fat

90

Blueberry Lemon Bread

Blueberries are excellent raw or cooked. They can be eaten by the handful or added to cereal, muffins, pancakes, fruit salads or yogurt. You can buy them in season and freeze them for later use. Don't wash berries before freezing. Simply spread them out in a single layer on a cookie sheet, then place them in the freezer until they are frozen solid, and then transfer the berries to a heavy plastic bag. They will keep for 10 to 12 months. Before using frozen berries, quickly rinse them under cold water.

16 servings

Vegetable oil cooking spray
2 cups all-purpose flour
2 teaspoons baking powder
1/4 teaspoon salt
1/3 cup canola oil
1 1/3 cups sugar, divided
4 egg whites
1/2 cup skim milk
1 teaspoon lemon extract
1 1/2 cups blueberries, any stems removed, rinsed
1/4 cup fresh lemon juice

■ Preheat the oven to 350 degrees. Spray a 9-by-5-inch loaf pan with the cooking spray; set aside.

In a medium bowl, combine the flour, baking powder and salt. Set aside. In a large mixing bowl, beat the canola oil and 1 cup of the sugar on low speed until blended. Increase the speed to medium; beat until thoroughly combined, about 5 minutes. Reduce the mixer speed to low. Add the egg whites one at a time, beating after each addition until well blended. Scrape the sides of the bowl occasionally.

Alternately add the flour mixture and the skim milk to the batter, mixing just until blended. Add the lemon extract. Gently fold in the blueberries. Spoon the batter into the prepared loaf pan.

Bake for 1 hour and 5 minutes, or until a wooden pick inserted into the center comes out clean. Remove from the oven and cool 10 minutes.

Meanwhile, to prepare the glaze, combine the remaining 1/3 cup of sugar and the lemon juice in a small bowl.

Remove the loaf from the pan and transfer to a wire rack. Place a plate underneath the rack. Using a metal or wooden skewer, prick the top and sides of the warm cake in several places. Using a pastry brush, coat the top and sides of the warm cake with the lemon glaze. Continue to cool or serve immediately.

Nutrition Information Per Serving

			% of daily value
Calories	**172**		
Calories from fat	**24**	%	
Fat	**5**	g	7%
Saturated fat	**0.5**	g	3%
Cholesterol	**trace**	mg	1%
Sodium	**93**	mg	4%
Carbohydrate	**31**	g	10%
Fiber	**1**	g	
Sugar	**17**	g	
Protein	**3**	g	

Cook's note:

Fresh blueberries will keep in the refrigerator for up to 10 days. Look for plump, dry, firm, even-colored berries. If they are in a box that is cellophane-wrapped, examine the berries you can see, then check the box for dampness and stains, which indicate the fruit below may be decaying.

2 starch, 1 fat

Soups & Sandwiches

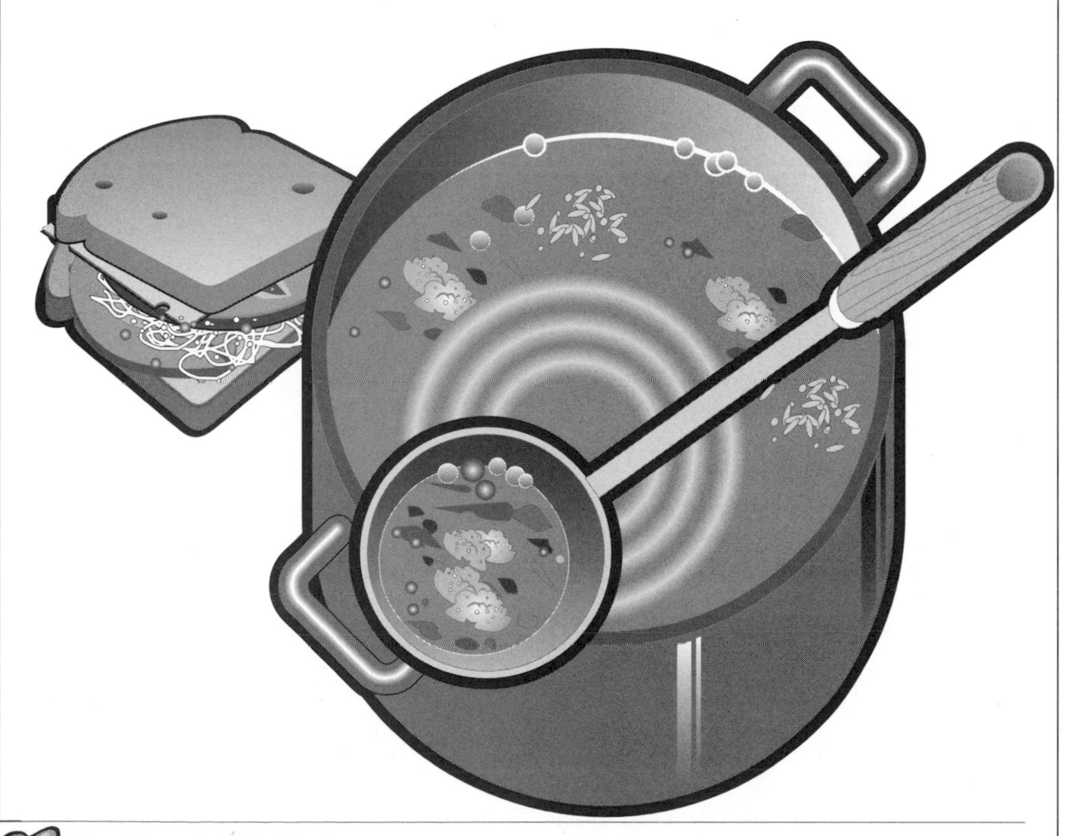

Asparagus Soup

Many researchers believe that having enough potassium in your diet may be as important in blood pressure control as reducing your sodium. This Asparagus Soup is delicious served hot or cold and contains more than 700 mg of potassium, more than one-third of the daily requirement. Choose low-sodium chicken broth to reduce the amount of sodium in your soup.

6 servings

Boiling water
2 pounds asparagus, washed, trimmed, cut into 1-inch pieces
Ice water
Vegetable oil cooking spray
1 small onion, peeled, ends removed, chopped (about 1/2 cup)
1/2 cup uncooked rice
5 cups low-fat chicken broth
1/2 teaspoon white pepper
1/4 cup evaporated skim milk

■ In a medium-size saucepan with boiling water, blanch 12 asparagus tips for 2 minutes. Remove and plunge them into the ice water. Reserve these tips for a garnish.

Spray a large nonstick saucepan with the cooking spray.

Add the onion and saute over medium heat for 3 minutes, or until the onion is translucent.

Add the rice, the remaining asparagus pieces and the chicken broth. Bring the soup to a boil, reduce the heat and simmer, covered, for 25 minutes or until the rice is tender.

Remove the soup from the heat and cool it slightly. Working in batches, puree the soup in a food processor fitted with a metal blade or in a blender. Strain the soup through a sieve over a large bowl.

Add the white pepper and evaporated skim milk. Return the soup to a medium saucepan and heat until warmed through.

Ladle the soup into bowls and garnish with the reserved asparagus tips. Or refrigerate the soup to serve cold.

Nutrition Information Per Serving

			% of daily value
Calories	145		
Calories from fat	14	%	
Fat	2	g	3%
Saturated fat	0.5	g	3%
Cholesterol	1	mg	1%
Sodium	666	mg	27%
Carbohydrate	22	g	7%
Fiber	1.5	g	
Sugar	1	g	
Protein	10	g	

(Using low-sodium broth will reduce sodium to 19 mg - 8% daily value.)

Cook's note:

Potassium is found in most fruits and vegetables. As you use fewer processed foods and more fresh fruits and vegetables, your sodium intake will go down and your potassium levels will increase naturally. Limit your sodium to 2,400 mg per day and try to include five servings of fruits and vegetables to provide the 2,000 mg of potassium you need daily.

Diabetic exchange

1 vegetable, 1 starch, 1 lean meat

45

Cabbage & White Bean Soup

Researchers have found some vegetables decrease the risk of cancer by increasing the body's ability to protect our cells. Cabbage and other vegetables in the cabbage family offer the best protection.

4 servings

1 tablespoon olive oil
1 large onion, peeled, ends removed, finely chopped (1 cup)
2 carrots, peeled, ends removed, halved lengthwise, sliced crosswise
1 large stalk celery, washed, ends removed, halved lengthwise, sliced crosswise
1 teaspoon caraway seeds
2 cups chopped green cabbage
3 cups chicken broth
1 tablespoon light brown sugar
1 can (16 ounces) crushed tomatoes in juice
1 can (15 ounces) white beans, drained and rinsed
1 tablespoon cider vinegar
1/4 teaspoon ground white pepper
1/4 cup fresh parsley or chives, washed, dried, chopped, optional

■ In a medium soup pot, heat the olive oil and saute the onion for 3 minutes. Add the carrots and celery; saute 3 minutes. Add the caraway seeds; cook, stirring for 1 minute.

Stir in the cabbage, chicken broth and brown sugar. Simmer, covered, for 5 minutes. Stir in the tomatoes with juice. Simmer, covered, for 20 minutes. Add the white beans, vinegar and white pepper.

Simmer, uncovered, for 5 minutes until heated through. Stir in the parsley or chives if desired. Serve hot.

Nutrition Information Per Serving

			% of daily value
Calories	**173**		
Calories from fat	**18**	%	
Fat	**4**	g	6%
Saturated fat	**0.5**	g	3%
Cholesterol	**1**	mg	1%
Sodium	**429**	mg	18%
Carbohydrate	**27**	g	9%
Fiber	**2.5**	g	
Sugar	**8**	g	
Protein	**10**	g	

1 starch, 2 vegetable, 1/2 meat

Carrot & Potato Soup

A single cup of soup can contain 600 to 2000 mg of sodium. There are, however, new lower-sodium varieties of soups. Choose a soup with less than 500 mg per cup to stay within the American Heart Association's recommendation of 2400 mg of sodium or less per day.

8 servings

1 tablespoon oil
2 medium onions, peeled, ends removed, diced (about 2 cups)
1 clove garlic, peeled, ends removed, crushed
8 cups low-fat, low-sodium chicken broth
1 1/2 pounds potatoes, peeled, eyes removed, diced into 1-inch cubes (about 4 cups)
1 pound carrots, peeled, ends removed, cut into 1/2-inch slices (about 2 cups)
1 teaspoon ground white pepper
Parsley or chives, optional

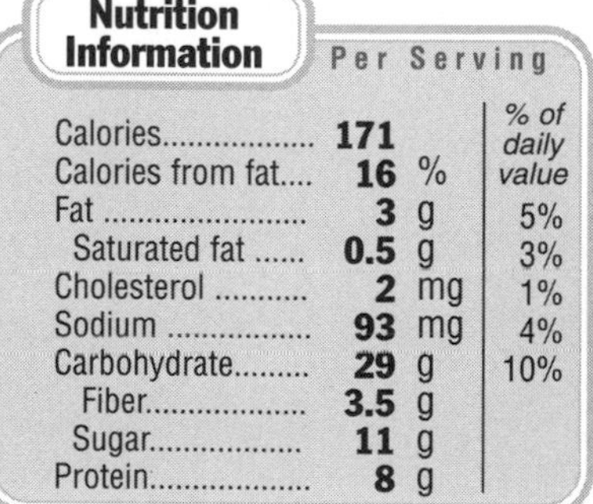

Nutrition Information Per Serving

			% of daily value
Calories	**171**		
Calories from fat	**16**	%	
Fat	**3**	g	5%
Saturated fat	**0.5**	g	3%
Cholesterol	**2**	mg	1%
Sodium	**93**	mg	4%
Carbohydrate	**29**	g	10%
Fiber	**3.5**	g	
Sugar	**11**	g	
Protein	**8**	g	

■ In a stockpot, heat the oil over medium heat and saute the onion and garlic until translucent, about 3 to 4 minutes. Add the broth, potatoes and carrots. Bring to a boil. Reduce heat and simmer over medium heat for 1 1/2 hours. Cool, strain and reserve the broth.

Puree the potatoes and carrots in a food processor or a vegetable mill, and add back to the broth.

Reheat the soup. Season it with white pepper. Serve very hot, garnished with parsley or chives.

Diabetic exchange

1 vegetable, 1 1/2 starch, 1/2 meat

60

Corn Chowder

Corn has a reputation as a fattening food. Actually, it is low in fat and high in complex carbohydrates and fiber. But an ear of corn that has only 70 calories can easily jump to 170 calories when it is dripping with butter. Try a new way of serving corn without the fat by preparing this New England-style corn chowder.

10 servings

4 cups fresh or frozen corn, cut from the cob (about 8 large ears), divided
1/2 tablespoon oil
2 cups onion, peeled, ends removed, chopped
1 cup celery, washed, ends removed, diced
4 ounces lean ham (5 percent fat), trimmed, diced
2 cloves garlic, peeled, ends removed, minced
2 cans (10 1/2 ounces each) low-sodium chicken broth
2 cups raw potato, peeled, eyes removed, diced
1/4 cup all-purpose flour
1/2 teaspoon black pepper
1/8 teaspoon ground red (cayenne) pepper
2 cups skim milk
1 teaspoon Worcestershire sauce

■ Process 2 1/2 cups of the corn in a food processor or blender until smooth; set aside.

Heat the oil in a large Dutch oven over medium heat. Add the onion, celery, ham and garlic, and saute 10 minutes or until the vegetables are tender, stirring occasionally. Add the broth and diced potato; bring to a boil. Reduce heat and simmer, uncovered, for 20 minutes, stirring frequently. Add the corn puree and remaining 1 1/2 cups of corn; cook 10 minutes.

Place the flour and black and red pepper in a small bowl. Gradually add the milk and the Worcestershire sauce, blending with a wire whisk. Gradually add the mixture to the chowder. Cook over medium heat for 10 minutes or until thickened, stirring constantly.

Nutrition Information Per Serving

			% of daily value
Calories	167		
Calories from fat	8	%	
Fat	2	g	3%
Saturated fat	0.5	g	3%
Cholesterol	7	mg	2%
Sodium	184	mg	8%
Carbohydrate	33	g	11%
Fiber	3	g	
Sugar	5	g	
Protein	8	g	

Diabetic exchange

2 starch

Curried Pumpkin Soup

The value of pumpkin, one of the orange vegetables that are high in beta carotene, is often overlooked in cooking. This pumpkin soup is a fall favorite, but you can make it year-round using canned pumpkin.

8 servings

1 tablespoon vegetable oil
1/2 cup chopped onion
1 clove garlic, peeled, ends removed, mashed and diced
2 cups pumpkin puree, freshly made, or 1 pound canned
4 cups chicken stock, defatted
1 bay leaf
Pinch of sugar
1/3 teaspoon curry powder, or to taste
Pinch of nutmeg
1/4 teaspoon freshly ground black pepper
2 cups plain low-fat yogurt
Fresh chives to garnish, chopped, optional

■ In a small soup pot, heat the vegetable oil. Add the onion and saute 2 minutes. Add the garlic and continue to saute 3 more minutes.

Add the pumpkin puree and chicken stock; stir well to mix. Add the bay leaf, sugar, curry powder, nutmeg and pepper. Bring to a boil, lower to simmer and cook for 30 minutes, covered.

Remove from the heat and whisk in the yogurt. Return to the heat only to bring the temperature of the soup back to hot. Do not boil.

Remove and discard the bay leaf. Serve in hot soup bowls. Garnish with chives if desired.

Nutrition Information Per Serving

			% of daily value
Calories	91		
Calories from fat	30	%	
Fat	3	g	5%
Saturated fat	1	g	5%
Cholesterol	4	mg	1%
Sodium	436	mg	18%
Carbohydrate	10	g	3%
Fiber	1.5	g	
Sugar	3	g	
Protein	7	g	

1/2 starch, 1/2 vegetable, 1/2 meat

30

Fish Chowder

There is nothing more comforting than a warm bowl of creamy soup. But most creamed soups contain between 15 and 20 grams of fat per serving. To prepare a soup with a creamy taste without all the fat, try using skim milk, cornstarch and light cream cheese.

4 servings

1 package (16 ounces) frozen mixed broccoli, carrots, cauliflower (cut up any large pieces)
1 3/4 cup low-sodium chicken broth, divided
3 green onions, washed, ends removed, sliced
1 1/2 cups skim milk
1 tablespoon cornstarch
3 ounces light cream cheese, cubed
8 ounces halibut or cod, rinsed, patted dry, cooked, flaked, bones removed

■ In a large saucepan, combine the vegetables, 1 cup of the broth and onion. Bring to a boil. Reduce heat. Cover and simmer over low heat for 5 to 7 minutes or until the vegetables are crisp-tender. Stir in the skim milk.

In a small bowl, stir the remaining 3/4 cup of the broth into the cornstarch. Stir until the cornstarch is dissolved, then add it to the vegetable mixture. Cook and stir until thick and bubbly. Add the cream cheese. Bring to a boil, stirring, to melt the cheese. Add the fish. Heat through.

Nutrition Information Per Serving

			% of daily value
Calories	192		
Calories from fat	31	%	
Fat	7	g	11%
Saturated fat	3.5	g	18%
Cholesterol	36	mg	12%
Sodium	189	mg	8%
Carbohydrate	14	g	5%
Fiber	3.5	g	
Sugar	8	g	
Protein	19	g	

Diabetic exchange

2 lean meat, 2 vegetable, 1 fat, 1/2 starch, 1/4 milk

Lentil Soup

If you think bean soup takes forever to make, think again. Lentils are small beans that cook quickly and do not need soaking to soften.

10 servings

1 tablespoon vegetable oil
1 large onion, peeled, ends removed, chopped
1 cup chopped celery
1 cup chopped carrots
1 clove garlic, peeled, ends removed, chopped
2 cups lentils, rinsed and sorted
9 cups boiling water
1 cup chopped lean ham
1 bay leaf
1/4 teaspoon thyme
Black pepper to taste

■ In a large soup pot, heat the vegetable oil. Add the onion, celery, carrots and garlic. Saute until tender, about 10 minutes. Stir in the lentils.

Add the boiling water, ham, bay leaf, thyme and black pepper. Bring back to a boil.

Reduce the heat and simmer, covered, for about 45 minutes to 1 hour, or until the lentils are tender.

Remove the bay leaf and serve.

Nutrition Information Per Serving

			% of daily value
Calories	**140**		
Calories from fat	**19**	%	
Fat	**3**	g	5%
Saturated fat	**0.5**	g	3%
Cholesterol	**8**	mg	3%
Sodium	**211**	mg	9%
Carbohydrate	**19**	g	6%
Fiber	**5**	g	
Sugar	**3**	g	
Protein	**11**	g	

1 starch, 1 lean meat, 1 vegetable

90

Ratatouille Soup

Orzo is a pasta made from wheat, and it's shaped like long-grain rice. Try it. It gives this soup a delicious and unique flavor.

8 servings

Vegetable oil cooking spray
1 cup chopped onion
1 cup chopped green pepper
2 cloves garlic, peeled, ends removed, chopped
3 cups eggplant, peeled, cut into 1/4-inch cubes
1 can (32 ounces) tomatoes, undrained, crushed or chopped
2 cups zucchini, washed, unpeeled, cut in half lengthwise, then sliced 1/4-inch thick
4 cups water
1 bay leaf
1 1/4 teaspoons dried basil
1 1/4 teaspoons dried oregano
1/8 teaspoon pepper
1/2 cup (3 ounces) orzo or favorite small pasta

■ Spray a large soup pot with the cooking spray and warm over medium heat. Add the onion, green pepper and garlic. Cook until tender, about 5 minutes.

Add the eggplant. Cook 5 minutes, stirring frequently and adding small amounts of water, if necessary, to prevent sticking.

Add the tomatoes, zucchini, 4 cups of water, bay leaf, basil, oregano and pepper. Bring the mixture to a boil, then reduce the heat to low, cover and cook 45 minutes.

Add the orzo and cook, uncovered, for 10 minutes. Remove and discard the bay leaf before serving.

Nutrition Information Per Serving

			% of daily value
Calories	**96**		
Calories from fat	**5**	%	
Fat	**trace**	g	1%
Saturated fat	**0**	g	0%
Cholesterol	**0**	mg	0%
Sodium	**292**	mg	12%
Carbohydrate	**22**	g	7%
Fiber	**3**	g	
Sugar	**5**	g	
Protein	**3**	g	

Diabetic exchange

4 vegetable

60

Red Snapper Soup

Fish helps protect against heart disease. The American Heart Association recommends you include at least three fish meals a week in your diet. If you are looking for a different way to serve fish, try this Red Snapper Soup. Red snapper is such a mild fish that even those who don't usually enjoy fish will love it.

8 servings

1 tablespoon oil
1 large onion, peeled, ends removed, chopped
1 rib celery with leaves, washed, ends removed, chopped
1 large clove garlic, peeled, ends removed, minced
1 can (32 ounces) tomatoes, chopped with juices
1/2 cup clam juice
2 tablespoons snipped parsley
1/4 teaspoon marjoram
1/4 teaspoon thyme
1/8 teaspoon black pepper
1 pound red snapper, washed, patted dry, any visible bones removed, cut into bite-size pieces

■ In a large sauce pot, heat the oil over medium heat. Add the onion, celery and garlic, and saute until tender, about 5 minutes.

Stir in the tomatoes with juices, clam juice, parsley, marjoram, thyme and pepper. Cover and simmer gently about 30 minutes, stirring occasionally. You can refrigerate or freeze the soup at this point.

To finish the soup, bring the base to a boil. Add the fish and reduce the heat. Simmer gently for 7 to 10 minutes or until the fish flakes and is opaque. Do not overcook.

Nutrition Information Per Serving

			% of daily value
Calories	**111**		
Calories from fat	**21**	%	
Fat	**3**	g	5%
Saturated fat	**0.5**	g	3%
Cholesterol	**21**	mg	7%
Sodium	**362**	mg	15%
Carbohydrate	**10**	g	3%
Fiber	**1.5**	g	
Sugar	**3**	g	
Protein	**13**	g	

1 lean meat, 2 vegetable

60

Vegetable Soup with Pesto

This soup uses basil pesto to provide a hearty flavor. Prepare pesto when fresh basil is available at your local market. Freeze extra in ice-cube trays and transfer to plastic bags. You will have homemade pesto on hand to use all winter long.

8 servings

4 cups chicken broth
3/4 pound potatoes, peeled, cut into 1-inch pieces (about 1 3/4 cups)
1/4 pound carrots, (3/4 cup) peeled, ends removed, sliced
1 celery stalk, washed, ends removed, sliced
1/2 cup sliced green onion (white part only)
2 medium tomatoes, washed, cored, cut into 1-inch cubes
1/4 pound zucchini, (1 small) washed, ends removed, cut into 1-inch cubes
1/4 pound green beans, washed, trimmed (about 3/4 cup)
1/2 cup lima beans
1/2 cup corn
1 clove garlic, peeled, ends removed, crushed
1 tablespoon chopped fresh parsley
3 tablespoons Pesto Sauce

(Pesto recipe is listed under the Sauces section.)

■ In a large saucepan, combine the chicken broth, potatoes, carrots, celery, green onion, tomatoes, zucchini, green beans, lima beans, corn, garlic and parsley. Bring to a boil.

Reduce heat; cover and simmer until the vegetables are tender. Stir in the Pesto Sauce. Serve.

Nutrition Information Per Serving

			% of daily value
Calories	**123**		
Calories from fat	**18**	%	
Fat	**2**	g	3%
Saturated fat	**1**	g	5%
Cholesterol	**1**	mg	1%
Sodium	**476**	mg	20%
Carbohydrate	**20**	g	7%
Fiber	**3.5**	g	
Sugar	**4**	g	
Protein	**7**	g	

(Using low-sodium broth will reduce sodium to 51 mg — 2% daily value).

Diabetic exchange

1 starch, 1 vegetable, 1/2 fat

Garden Vegetable Pita

Germinated beans and seeds bring us tender, crisp sprouts. When eaten raw, sprouts add a bit of crunch and moisture to salads and sandwiches. Choose fresh-looking sprouts with buds attached, and be sure to keep them refrigerated if they're not used right away. In this Garden Veggie Pita, the alfalfa sprouts bring volume and texture to a vegetable-laden meal.

4 servings

1/2 cup cauliflower, washed, dried, chopped
1/2 cup broccoli, washed, dried, chopped
1/2 cup yellow summer squash, washed, ends removed, chopped
1/2 cup zucchini, washed, dried, ends removed, chopped
1/4 cup carrots, peeled, ends removed, chopped
1/4 cup mushrooms, cleaned, sliced
1/3 cup nonfat plain yogurt
2 tablespoons nonfat mayonnaise
2 teaspoons red onion, peeled, ends removed, finely chopped
1 teaspoon lemon juice
1 teaspoon Worcestershire sauce
1/4 teaspoon dried basil
2 whole-wheat 6-inch pitas, halved, divided
4 lettuce leaves, washed, dried, divided
1/4 cup alfalfa sprouts, divided

■ In a medium bowl, mix together the cauliflower, broccoli, squash, zucchini, carrots and mushrooms. Set aside.

In a small bowl, mix together the yogurt, mayonnaise, red onion, lemon juice, Worcestershire sauce and basil. Pour over the vegetable mixture and toss to coat.

Line each pita half with a lettuce leaf. Spoon the vegetable mixture into each pita half and add 1 tablespoon of alfalfa sprouts. Serve immediately.

Nutrition Information Per Serving

			% of daily value
Calories	**91**		
Calories from fat	**5**	%	
Fat	**1**	g	2%
Saturated fat	**trace**	g	1%
Cholesterol	**trace**	mg	1%
Sodium	**240**	mg	10%
Carbohydrate	**18**	g	6%
Fiber	**2**	g	
Sugar	**3**	g	
Protein	**5**	g	

1 starch, 1 vegetable

15 minutes

Tuna Craters

Here is a quick-to-fix sandwich that children will love. Even better, these Tuna Craters can be stored for up to one month in the freezer for a Heart Smart® take-to-school lunch.

4 servings

1/4 cup plain nonfat yogurt
2 tablespoons nonfat mayonnaise or salad dressing
1 teaspoon prepared mustard
1/4 teaspoon dried dill weed
Dash pepper
1 can (6 1/2 ounces) water-packed tuna, drained and flaked
1/4 cup chopped onion
1/3 cup chopped celery
2 hot dog buns, split
1/2 cup low-fat shredded cheddar cheese (2 ounces)

■ In a medium-size mixing bowl, stir together the yogurt, mayonnaise or salad dressing, mustard, dill weed and pepper.

Stir the tuna, onion and celery into the yogurt mixture. Use a fork to hollow out the tops and bottoms of buns, leaving 1/4 shells.

Sprinkle the shredded cheese into the hollowed-out hot dog buns. Then spoon the tuna mixture over the cheese. The cheese prevents the bread from getting soggy.

Nutrition Information Per Serving

			% of daily value
Calories	**182**		
Calories from fat	**24**	%	
Fat	**5**	g	8%
Saturated fat	**0.5**	g	3%
Cholesterol	**27**	mg	9%
Sodium	**496**	mg	21%
Carbohydrate	**14**	g	5%
Fiber	**1**	g	
Sugar	**3**	g	
Protein	**20**	g	

Diabetic exchange

1 starch, 2 lean meat

Veggie Sandwich

Using seven-grain bread to make a sandwich sounds like a healthy choice, but don't be fooled. It may be mostly white bread with a little crushed wheat, a sprinkling of six other grains and food coloring. A whole grain should be listed as the first ingredient. If enriched wheat flour is listed first — instead of whole-wheat flour — many of the vitamins and minerals and much of the fiber were lost in processing. After you have found a bread that contains whole grains, look at the nutrition facts and be sure that two slices contain no more than 4 grams of fat and 300 milligrams of sodium.

2 servings

4 slices seven-grain or whole-wheat bread
1/3 avocado, sliced
4 thin slices of red onion
1/2 medium tomato, thinly sliced
1/2 cup shredded lettuce
2 tablespoons grated carrot, optional
2 slices low-fat Swiss cheese (1/2 ounce each)
1/4 cup alfalfa sprouts
2 tablespoons nonfat ranch dressing

■ Layer the ingredients in the slices of bread to make two sandwiches. Add the ranch dressing. Serve immediately.

Nutrition Information Per Serving

			% of daily value
Calories	263		
Calories from fat	35	%	
Fat	11	g	16%
Saturated fat	1	g	5%
Cholesterol	9	mg	3%
Sodium	427	mg	18%
Carbohydrate	34	g	11%
Fiber	4	g	
Sugar	4	g	
Protein	11	g	

2 starch, 1 vegetable, 1/2 meat, 1 1/2 fat

15 minutes

Herbed Grilled Cheese Sandwich

Everyone loves grilled cheese sandwiches, but considering all the fat they contain, most of us have shied away from them. Now with the new low-fat and nonfat cheeses available, we can enjoy them without guilt.

4 servings

4 slices crusty French or rye bread
1/2 to 1 ounce dry white wine
Dijon mustard
4 ounces sliced low-fat Swiss cheese
1 medium tomato, sliced
Freshly ground pepper to taste
Fresh basil leaves, optional

■ Toast the bread lightly on a grill or under a broiler.

Moisten one side of the bread lightly with wine. Spread on a thin layer of mustard, then add the cheese and tomato. Season generously with pepper and basil.

Return the sandwiches to the grill or broiler until the cheese is melted. Serve immediately.

Nutrition Information Per Serving

			% of daily value
Calories	**201**		
Calories from fat	**30**	%	
Fat	**7**	g	11%
Saturated fat	**3**	g	15%
Cholesterol	**17**	mg	6%
Sodium	**277**	mg	12%
Carbohydrate	**19**	g	6%
Fiber	**1**	g	
Sugar	**2**	g	
Protein	**14**	g	

Diabetic exchange

1 starch, 1 1/2 meat

Salads

Pecan Chicken Salad

Salads, often thought of as diet food, are an excellent source of vitamins and minerals and contain few calories. If you're not careful, however, your salad can become more fattening than a meat-and-potato meal. The biggest culprit is the dressing. Regular salad dressing contains 65 to 100 calories per tablespoon and 6 to 11 grams of fat. Fortunately, there are many low-fat and fat-free dressings that are quite tasty. They range from 2 to 20 calories and from 0 to 2 grams of fat per tablespoon. This recipe for Pecan Chicken Salad uses a mixture of fat-free yogurt and fat-free mayonnaise for the dressing.

6 servings

1 1/2 pounds boneless, skinless chicken breasts, washed, patted dry
3 cups water
1 low-sodium chicken bouillon cube
1/2 pound seedless green grapes, rinsed
1/2 cup pecan halves
1/2 cup diced celery
1/2 cup fresh chopped dill
3/4 cup nonfat yogurt
3/4 cup nonfat mayonnaise
Freshly ground black pepper, to taste
1 bunch watercress, washed, dried, optional
Dill sprigs, washed, dried, optional

Cook's note:

Nuts and seeds, at about 85 calories and 7 grams of fat per tablespoon, are a fatty addition to salads. Use them sparingly.

■ Preheat the oven to 350 degrees. Arrange the chicken breasts in a single layer in a shallow pan.

Bring 3 cups of water to a boil and add the bouillon cube. Stir to dissolve. Pour enough bouillon into the baking pan to just cover the chicken breasts.

Lay a sheet of cooking parchment or aluminum foil over the chicken and bake until cooked through, about 30 minutes. Allow the chicken to cool in the liquid, then discard the liquid.

Cut the chicken into bite-size pieces and place in a large bowl. Add the grapes, pecans, celery and chopped dill; toss well.

In a separate small bowl, mix together the nonfat yogurt and nonfat mayonnaise. Toss this mixture into the chicken salad. Season with pepper. Cover and refrigerate for 2 hours.

At mealtime, serve on a bed of watercress or other salad green and garnish with dill sprigs if desired.

Nutrition Information Per Serving

			% of daily value
Calories	254		
Calories from fat	23	%	
Fat	7	g	11%
Saturated fat	1.5	g	8%
Cholesterol	81	mg	27%
Sodium	486	mg	20%
Carbohydrate	16	g	5%
Fiber	1.5	g	
Sugar	7	g	
Protein	33	g	

Diabetic exchange

1/2 fruit, 4 1/2 lean meat, 1/2 starch

15

Black Bean Salad

This Black Bean Salad is a delicious way to add fiber to your diet. Although apples are the most common fruit source of pectin, a soluble fiber that lowers blood cholesterol, dry beans such as kidney, pinto and black beans also provide healthy amounts of soluble fiber.

4 servings

1 pound can black beans, rinsed, drained
1 cup frozen corn, thawed, drained
1/4 cup celery, washed, ends removed, chopped
1/4 cup purple onions, peeled, ends removed, chopped
1/4 cup carrots, peeled, ends removed, chopped
2 tablespoons lemon juice
1 tablespoon olive oil
1 teaspoon honey
1/2 clove garlic, peeled, ends removed, minced
1/4 teaspoon cumin, or to taste

■ In a medium-size bowl, combine the beans with the corn, celery, purple onion and carrots. Set aside.

In a small bowl, mix together the lemon juice, olive oil, honey, garlic and cumin. Pour the dressing over the bean mixture. Chill at least 4 hours before serving.

Nutrition Information Per Serving

			% of daily value
Calories	**183**		
Calories from fat	**18**	%	
Fat	**4**	g	6%
Saturated fat	**0.5**	g	3%
Cholesterol	**0**	mg	0%
Sodium	**447**	mg	19%
Carbohydrate	**31**	g	10%
Fiber	**1.5**	g	
Sugar	**3**	g	
Protein	**8**	g	

Diabetic exchange

2 starch, 1/2 vegetable, 1/2 fat

Broccoli Salad

Because all nuts are loaded with fat and calories — 90 grams of fat and 900 calories per cup — be careful not to go overboard using them in your recipes. But small amounts of walnuts added to casseroles and salads provide crunch, flavor and essential fatty acids to your diet.

8 servings

3 cups broccoli florets and tender stalks, cut into bite-size pieces
1 cup red seedless grapes, rinsed
4 green onions, washed, ends removed, finely chopped
3 tablespoons coarsely chopped walnuts
1/2 cup fat-free coleslaw dressing

Nutrition Information Per Serving

			% of daily value
Calories	51		
Calories from fat	31	%	
Fat	2	g	3%
Saturated fat	trace	g	1%
Cholesterol	0	mg	0%
Sodium	159	mg	7%
Carbohydrate	7	g	2%
Fiber	1.5	g	
Sugar	2	g	
Protein	2	g	

■ Place all the ingredients in a medium-size bowl. Add the coleslaw dressing, and gently toss the mixture until all the ingredients are evenly coated.

Cover and refrigerate overnight, then serve.

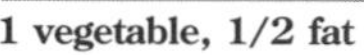

Diabetic exchange

1 vegetable, 1/2 fat

15

Deluxe Coleslaw

There are hundreds of variations of coleslaw — each with its own cook's secret. This recipe uses fat-free mayonnaise and nonfat yogurt to give the slaw its creamy texture. Try using a coleslaw blend that uses red cabbage as well as green for variety.

12 servings

1 package (16 ounces) shredded coleslaw vegetables
1 to 2 tablespoons lemon juice
1 tablespoon fresh chopped chives
1/2 cup nonfat plain yogurt
1/2 cup fat-free mayonnaise
1/2 teaspoon celery seed
1/2 teaspoon sugar
1/4 teaspoon freshly ground white pepper
1/4 cup raisins
2 tablespoons chopped walnuts, optional

■ Place the coleslaw vegetables in a large bowl. Add the lemon juice and chives and toss gently.

In a small bowl, mix together the yogurt, mayonnaise, celery seed, sugar and pepper.

Pour the yogurt mixture over the coleslaw. Add raisins and, if desired, walnuts. Mix well.

Serve immediately or cover and chill.

Nutrition Information Per Serving

			% of daily value
Calories	**43**		
Calories from fat	**21**	%	
Fat	**1**	g	2%
Saturated fat	**trace**	g	1%
Cholesterol	**0**	mg	0%
Sodium	**144**	mg	6%
Carbohydrate	**8**	g	3%
Fiber	**1**	g	
Sugar	**4**	g	
Protein	**1**	g	

Diabetic exchange

1 1/2 vegetable

East Indian Spinach Salad

This East Indian Spinach Salad is made special by the addition of 1/4 cup of mango chutney. Made famous in Jamaica, this chutney uses mangoes, garlic, habanero peppers, ginger and sugar. It can be found in supermarkets and stores specializing in ingredients for Caribbean cuisine.

6 servings

2 teaspoons white wine vinegar
1 tablespoon oil
1/4 cup chicken broth
1/4 cup mango chutney
1 teaspoon curry powder
1 teaspoon dry mustard
8 cups (about 10 ounces) fresh spinach, washed, dried, torn into bite-size pieces
2 cups unpeeled apples, chopped
1/2 cup raisins
2 tablespoons peanuts
2 tablespoons sliced green onion

■ In a jar with a tight-fitting lid, combine the white wine vinegar, oil, chicken broth, mango chutney, curry powder and dry mustard. Cover and chill at least two hours so the flavors blend.

Just before serving, place the spinach in a large salad bowl and top with the apples, raisins, peanuts and green onion. Remove the dressing from refrigerator and shake well. Pour the dressing over the salad and toss to coat.

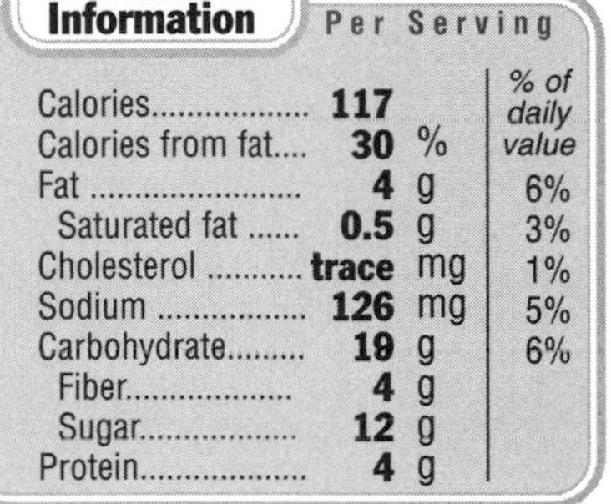

Nutrition Information Per Serving

			% of daily value
Calories	**117**		
Calories from fat	**30**	%	
Fat	**4**	g	6%
Saturated fat	**0.5**	g	3%
Cholesterol	**trace**	mg	1%
Sodium	**126**	mg	5%
Carbohydrate	**19**	g	6%
Fiber	**4**	g	
Sugar	**12**	g	
Protein	**4**	g	

Diabetic exchange

2 vegetable, 1/2 fruit, 1 fat

45

Fresh Basil & Pepper Potato Salad

Try adding fresh herbs instead of salt to your summer dishes. It's a great way to reduce the sodium in your diet and still enjoy flavorful food. This fine Fresh Basil and Pepper Potato Salad uses only 1/4 teaspoon of salt but doesn't lack for the subtle flavors that seasonings provide.

6 servings

1 quart boiling water
3 medium potatoes (about 1 pound)
1 cup nonfat mayonnaise
2 tablespoons fresh parsley washed, dried, snipped
1 tablespoon fresh basil, washed, dried, snipped
1 tablespoon sliced green onion
1/4 teaspoon salt
1/8 teaspoon white pepper
1/2 cup frozen peas
1/2 cup chopped sweet red pepper
2 medium tomatoes, washed, cored, cut into wedges

■ In a large saucepan, cook the potatoes in the boiling water for 25 to 30 minutes or until tender.

Drain and cool. When the potatoes are cool, peel and cube.

In a large mixing bowl, combine the mayonnaise, parsley, basil, green onion, salt and white pepper. Add the cubed potatoes, frozen peas and red pepper. Stir lightly to coat.

Cover and chill several hours before serving. Garnish with tomato wedges and serve.

Nutrition Information Per Serving

			% of daily value
Calories	**107**		
Calories from fat	**0**	%	
Fat	**0**	g	0%
Saturated fat	**0**	g	0%
Cholesterol	**0**	mg	0%
Sodium	**244**	mg	10%
Carbohydrate	**24**	g	8%
Fiber	**2**	g	
Sugar	**13**	g	
Protein	**2**	g	

Diabetic exchange

1 1/2 starch

Ginger Fruit Salad

This Ginger Fruit Salad, with only 1 gram of fat and 38 mg of sodium per serving, is packed with vitamins and minerals — and tastes delicious.

4 servings

1 cup low-fat lemon yogurt
2 teaspoons brown sugar
1/2 teaspoon ground ginger
1 teaspoon lemon juice
1 cup strawberries, washed, hulled, halved
1 orange, peeled, membrane removed, sectioned
1/2 cup fresh pineapple chunks
1 banana, sliced
1 apple, washed
8 bib lettuce leaves, washed

■ In a large bowl, combine the yogurt, brown sugar, ginger and lemon juice. Cover and refrigerate for 1 hour.

Remove the dressing from the refrigerator and add the strawberries, orange sections and pineapple chunks. Peel and remove the strings from the banana and slice. Core, seed and coarsely chop the apple. Add the banana and apple quickly to the dressing mixture.

Stir gently until the fruit is covered.

Arrange the lettuce on 4 plates and top with the fruit mixture.

Nutrition Information Per Serving

			% of daily value
Calories	145		
Calories from fat	8	%	
Fat	1	g	2%
Saturated fat	trace	g	1%
Cholesterol	0	mg	0%
Sodium	38	mg	2%
Carbohydrate	32	g	11%
Fiber	3.5	g	
Sugar	18	g	
Protein	3	g	

Diabetic exchange

2 fruit, 1/4 milk

45 minutes

Heart Smart® Pasta Salad

This Pasta Salad was first published in The Free Press in August 1988. It has been a favorite with readers ever since. Both simple to prepare and nutritious, it is a good choice for an outdoor buffet because it will not easily spoil.

12 servings

1 package (1 pound) rotini pasta (try the multicolored kind)
1 package (8 ounces) fresh mushrooms
1/4 cup boiling water for cooking broccoli (if not using microwave)
1 cup broccoli florets
3 cups ice water for cooling broccoli
1 sweet green pepper, seeded, diced
1 sweet red bell pepper, seeded, diced
2 green onions, including green tops, diced; or 1/2 small Bermuda onion, peeled, chopped fine
1/4 cup olive oil
1/4 cup red wine vinegar
3/4 teaspoon salt
1/4 teaspoon pepper
1/4 cup chopped fresh parsley
1 teaspoon dried tarragon or dried oregano; or 1 tablespoon of either herb, fresh
16 cherry tomatoes, halved

■ Cook the pasta al dente according to package directions, omitting salt. While the pasta is cooking, clean and slice the mushrooms. Place in a nonstick skillet over medium heat and saute until the mushrooms are tender and give up their liquid, about 5 minutes. Drain well and set aside.

Place the broccoli in microwave-safe dish and cook on full power, covered with plastic wrap, for 3 minutes. Remove and plunge into ice water to stop cooking. Or, if not cooking in the microwave, place the broccoli on a rack in a small saucepan with 1/4 cup boiling water and steam, covered, over medium heat for 4 minutes. Remove from heat and cool as above, in ice water. Do not overcook — the broccoli should remain firm and bright green.

Drain the broccoli and set aside.

Drain the pasta and let cool about 5 minutes. Mix the pasta, mushrooms, broccoli, green and red peppers, and onion in a large serving bowl. Set aside in the refrigerator.

In a covered jar, combine the oil, vinegar, salt, pepper, parsley, tarragon or oregano, and shake well. Pour the dressing over the pasta-vegetable mixture and toss well. Chill about 3 hours before serving. Just before serving, add the tomatoes.

Nutrition Information — Per Serving

			% of daily value
Calories	198		
Calories from fat	24	%	
Fat	5	g	8%
Saturated fat	0.5	g	3%
Cholesterol	0	mg	0%
Sodium	143	mg	6%
Carbohydrate	32	g	11%
Fiber	1	g	
Sugar	2	g	
Protein	6	g	

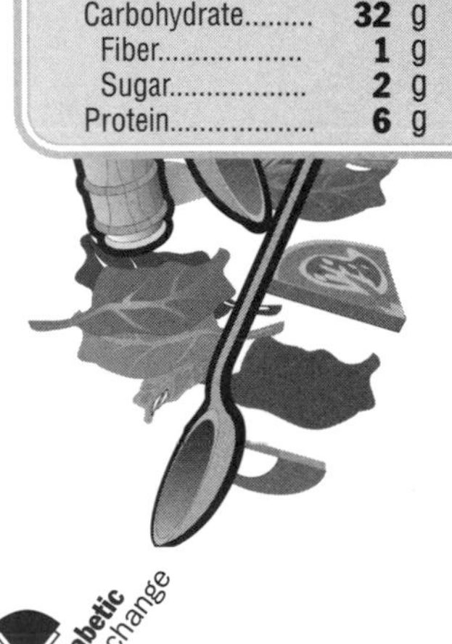

Diabetic exchange

2 starch, 1 fat

Mixed Green Salad with Honey Mustard Dressing

The low-fat sweet and sour Honey Mustard Dressing makes this Mixed Green Salad hum with flavor. Add to that the toasted poppy seeds and a splash of grapefruit juice and you have a unique salad full of complex flavors.

8 servings

2 teaspoons poppy seeds
6 cloves garlic, peeled, ends removed
1/3 cup water
2 tablespoons white wine vinegar
2 tablespoons olive oil
1 tablespoon coarse-grained prepared mustard
1/2 teaspoon honey
1/3 cup grapefruit juice
Freshly ground black pepper, to taste
1 pound (16 cups) lettuce greens, washed, trimmed and torn
1/2 red onion, peeled, ends removed, thinly sliced

Nutrition Information Per Serving

			% of daily value
Calories	62		
Calories from fat	51	%	
Fat	4	g	6%
Saturated fat	0.5	g	3%
Cholesterol	0	mg	0%
Sodium	31	mg	1%
Carbohydrate	7	g	2%
Fiber	1	g	
Sugar	2	g	
Protein	1	g	

■ Heat a small skillet over medium heat. Add the poppy seeds and toast, stirring constantly, until aromatic, 1 to 2 minutes.

Place the garlic cloves in a small saucepan and add water to cover. Bring to a boil, then reduce to a simmer over medium heat; cook until tender, about 3 minutes. Remove from the heat and drain.

In a blender or a food processor fitted with a metal blade, combine the white wine vinegar, olive oil, mustard, honey, cooked garlic and grapefruit juice. Blend until creamy. Season with pepper and poppy seeds.

In a large salad bowl, combine the lettuce greens with the onion. Drizzle with the dressing and toss to coat. Arrange on salad plates and garnish with the toasted poppy seeds.

Cook's note:

"Salad in a bag" is wonderful for people who have little time to chop ingredients. Avoid packaged salads with croutons and dressing because they contain as much as 16 grams (4 teaspoons) of fat per serving.

Diabetic exchange

1 vegetable, 1 fat

45

New Potato & Turkey Salad

Boiled new potatoes, served cold, are a wonderful addition to a Heart Smart® diet. Filling and delicious, new potatoes are any variety of potato harvested before the sugars in the flesh can convert completely to starch. The height of the new-potato season is late spring to early summer, but varieties of these thin-skinned gems can be found year-round in supermarkets and produce stores.

4 servings

1 cup water
1 1/2 pounds new potatoes (red-skinned), scrubbed
1/2 pound turkey breast, skin and fat removed, cooked, chopped
4 green onions, washed, ends removed, chopped
1 jar (2 ounces) pimientos, sliced, drained
1 teaspoon fresh dill weed; or 1/2 teaspoon dried
1/4 cup nonfat buttermilk dressing

■ In a large pot, heat the water to boiling. Add the potatoes. Cover and heat to boiling; reduce heat. Cook until tender, 20 to 25 minutes. Remove from the pot and cool slightly. Cut into cubes.

In a large serving bowl, toss together the potatoes, turkey, onion, pimientos, dill weed and dressing. Refrigerate at least 1 hour and serve.

Nutrition Information Per Serving

			% of daily value
Calories	**274**		
Calories from fat	**20**	%	
Fat	**6**	g	9%
Saturated fat	**0.5**	g	3%
Cholesterol	**45**	mg	15%
Sodium	**193**	mg	8%
Carbohydrate	**35**	g	12%
Fiber	**1.5**	g	
Sugar	**2**	g	
Protein	**20**	g	

Diabetic exchange

2 starch, 2 meat

Pasta & Beet Salad

Beets lend a wonderful color and texture to this fresh-from-the-garden pasta salad. And the 2 teaspoons of horseradish give it a real kick.

8 servings

1 quart water
2 uncooked beets, scrubbed
8 ounces pasta shells or twists, cooked according to package directions, omitting salt and fat
3 tablespoons nonfat Italian dressing
2 celery stalks, washed, ends removed, sliced
1 apple, cored, seeded and sliced
1/4 cup low-fat mayonnaise
3 tablespoons nonfat plain yogurt
2 tablespoons skim milk
2 teaspoons prepared horseradish
4 cups raw spinach, washed, stems trimmed
1 ripe avocado, peeled, pitted and cut into 16 slices

■ In a medium saucepan, boil the water. Add the beets and boil until just tender, about 20 minutes. Drain, cool, peel and chop, then set aside.

In a large bowl, toss the cooked pasta with the nonfat Italian dressing. Add the beets, celery, green onion and apple. In a small bowl stir together the low-fat mayonnaise, nonfat plain yogurt, skim milk and horseradish and mix with pasta. Chill at least 1 hour.

Line the plates with spinach and pile the salad in the center. Place 2 slices of avocado on top of each salad.

Nutrition Information Per Serving

			% of daily value
Calories	**197**		
Calories from fat	**27**	%	
Fat	**6**	g	9%
Saturated fat	**0.5**	g	3%
Cholesterol	**31**	mg	10%
Sodium	**66**	mg	3%
Carbohydrate	**29**	g	10%
Fiber	**3.5**	g	
Sugar	**4**	g	
Protein	**7**	g	

Diabetic exchange

1 starch, 2 vegetable, 1 fat

15

Sweet Potato Salad

This recipe offers a delicious, low-fat way to prepare sweet potatoes. The chopped walnuts add a crunchy texture to every bite.

4 servings

2 cups cooked, cubed sweet potato
1/2 cup chopped green pepper
1/2 cup chopped celery
3 green onions, sliced thin
2 tablespoons chopped walnuts
2 tablespoons low-fat mayonnaise
1/4 cup nonfat yogurt
Zest and lemon juice from 1 whole lemon (about 3 tablespoons)
1/8 teaspoon ginger

■ Place the sweet potato, green pepper, celery, green onion and walnuts in a salad bowl.

Stir the mayonnaise, nonfat yogurt, lemon zest, lemon juice and ginger together in a separate bowl.

Combine with the sweet potato mixture.

Nutrition Information Per Serving

			% of daily value
Calories	**135**		
Calories from fat	**28**	%	
Fat	**4**	g	6%
Saturated fat	**trace**	g	1%
Cholesterol	**3**	mg	1%
Sodium	**52**	mg	2%
Carbohydrate	**22**	g	7%
Fiber	**4**	g	
Sugar	**2**	g	
Protein	**4**	g	

Diabetic exchange

1/2 vegetable, 1 1/2 starch, 1 fat

Sweet Bunny Salad

Nonfat yogurt provides a good base for creamy dressings. The dressing used in this Sweet Bunny Salad can be served over a green salad with fruit or over a mixed fruit cup.

6 servings

Dressing:
1/3 cup honey
1 tablespoon distilled vinegar
1/2 to 1 cup nonfat plain yogurt
1 teaspoon dry yellow mustard
2 teaspoons onion juice or minced onion
2 teaspoons poppy seeds

Salad:
1 large bunch romaine lettuce, washed, torn into bite-size pieces
2 kiwifruit, sliced
1 can (11 ounces) mandarin orange segments, drained
2 tablespoons slivered almonds, toasted

Cook's note:

When buying low-fat dressings, choose those that contain less than 2 grams of fat and 300 mg of sodium per 2-tablespoon serving.

■ To prepare the dressing: In a blender or food processor, combine the honey, vinegar, 1/2 cup nonfat plain yogurt, yellow mustard, onion juice or minced onion, and poppy seeds. Blend or process until evenly mixed. Add more yogurt if a thicker dressing is desired. Chill the dressing at least 1/2 hour.

Just before serving, combine the lettuce, kiwifruit and mandarin orange segments in a large salad bowl. Evenly divide the salad among 6 serving plates. Drizzle 1 to 2 tablespoons of dressing over the salad and sprinkle with almonds.

Nutrition Information Per Serving

			% of daily value
Calories	112		
Calories from fat	16	%	
Fat	2	g	3%
Saturated fat	trace	g	1%
Cholesterol	0	mg	0%
Sodium	34	mg	2%
Carbohydrate	24	g	8%
Fiber	3	g	
Sugar	19	g	
Protein	3	g	

Diabetic exchange

1 1/4 fruit, 1 vegetable, 1/2 fat

15

Tuna Pasta Salad

This old favorite blends two familiar ingredients — tuna and pasta — to make a versatile salad that can be served either hot or cold. For a zippier version, omit the sugar and add 1/4 teaspoon cumin, 1/4 teaspoon poultry seasoning and ground red pepper to taste.

6 servings

8 ounces rotini, cooked according to package directions, omitting salt and fat, drained and rinsed
1 can (6 1/2 ounces) water-packed tuna, drained
1 cup frozen peas, rinsed with lukewarm water
1/4 cup finely diced onion
1/2 cup thinly sliced celery
1/4 teaspoon black pepper
3/4 cup low-fat buttermilk
3/4 cup nonfat sour cream
1 1/2 tablespoons sugar
1 1/2 teaspoons prepared mustard
2 tablespoons light mayonnaise

■ In a large bowl, combine the cooked rotini, tuna, peas, onion, celery and pepper.
In a separate bowl, whisk together the buttermilk, sour cream, sugar, mustard and mayonnaise until smooth.
Pour the dressing over the pasta mixture and toss to coat.
Serve warm or cool.

Nutrition Information Per Serving

			% of daily value
Calories	**306**		
Calories from fat	**26**	%	
Fat	**9**	g	14%
Saturated fat	**0.5**	g	3%
Cholesterol	**16**	mg	5%
Sodium	**203**	mg	8%
Carbohydrate	**38**	g	13%
Fiber	**trace**	g	
Sugar	**5**	g	
Protein	**16**	g	

Diabetic exchange

1 1/2 starch, 2 meat

Waldorf Salad

This lovely salad of vivid colors and distinctive flavors has a long history. The original version — created in the 1890s by the chefs at the Waldorf-Astoria Hotel in New York City — contained only mayonnaise, celery and apples served on a bed of lettuce. Chopped walnuts were added later to give this crunchy salad even more flavor and, unfortunately, more fat. This recipe calls for fewer nuts — only 2 tablespoons — and nonfat mayonnaise.

8 servings

1 tablespoon lemon juice
1/2 cup nonfat mayonnaise
1 cup diced celery
1/2 cup raisins
2 tablespoons chopped walnuts
3 cups pared and diced favorite apple (about 3 medium apples)
8 romaine lettuce leaves, washed, dried

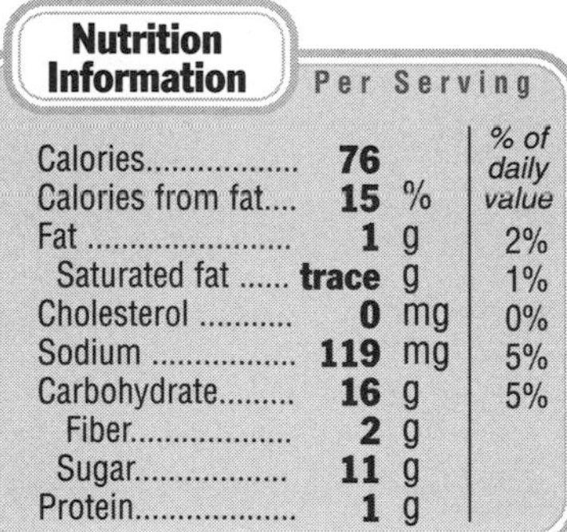

Nutrition Information Per Serving

			% of daily value
Calories	76		
Calories from fat	15	%	
Fat	1	g	2%
Saturated fat	trace	g	1%
Cholesterol	0	mg	0%
Sodium	119	mg	5%
Carbohydrate	16	g	5%
Fiber	2	g	
Sugar	11	g	
Protein	1	g	

■ In a medium-size bowl, mix the lemon juice with the mayonnaise. Add the celery, raisins and walnuts, and mix thoroughly. Add the diced apple immediately to avoid browning.

Line each serving plate with lettuce leaves. Place 1/2 cup of the salad on top of the lettuce and serve.

Diabetic exchange

1 fruit, 1/2 fat

15

Zucchini & Corn Salad

Tired of hearing about foods you shouldn't eat? Don't count corn among them. It's very low in fat, high in complex carbohydrates and loaded with fiber. This Zucchini and Corn Salad is an excellent way to use two vegetables that are abundant and affordable in mid- to late summer.

4 servings

2 small zucchini, washed, ends removed, sliced
1 package (12 ounces) frozen whole kernel corn, defrosted
1/4 cup chopped green onion
1 tablespoon vegetable oil
2 teaspoons cider vinegar
1 teaspoon lemon juice
1 clove garlic, peeled, ends removed, crushed
1/2 teaspoon chili powder
1/4 teaspoon dry mustard
1/8 teaspoon ground cumin
1/8 teaspoon salt

■ In a medium-size bowl, combine the zucchini, corn and green onion; set aside.

In a small bowl, combine the oil, cider vinegar, lemon juice, garlic, chili powder, dry mustard, cumin and salt. Whisk together until blended.

Pour the dressing over the zucchini mixture and toss to coat. Cover and refrigerate, or serve immediately.

Nutrition Information Per Serving

			% of daily value
Calories	**111**		
Calories from fat	**25**	%	
Fat	**4**	g	6%
Saturated fat	**trace**	g	1%
Cholesterol	**0**	mg	0%
Sodium	**73**	mg	3%
Carbohydrate	**20**	g	7%
Fiber	**3**	g	
Sugar	**3**	g	
Protein	**3**	g	

Diabetic exchange

1 starch, 1 vegetable, 1 fat

Pastas & Rice

Brown Rice Pilaf

Wild rice is low in fat and high in complex carbohydrates. This Heart Smart® recipe for Brown Rice Pilaf combines 3/4 cup of wild rice with long-grain brown rice. Although the pilaf can be prepared with just brown rice, you will find that the wild rice adds a unique flavor and texture.

12 servings

3 cups canned chicken broth, defatted
3/4 cup wild rice, well rinsed in warm water and drained
3/4 cup long-grain brown rice, uncooked
1 tablespoon vegetable oil
3/4 cup fresh mushrooms, sliced
1/2 cup red bell pepper, chopped
1/2 cup yellow bell pepper, chopped
1/4 cup thinly sliced carrot
1/4 teaspoon curry powder
1/4 teaspoon pepper
1/8 teaspoon ground cumin
2 cloves garlic, peeled, ends removed, minced

■ In a large saucepan, bring the chicken broth to a boil. Stir in the wild and brown rice. Cover, reduce heat and simmer 55 minutes or until tender and the liquid is absorbed. Remove from the heat and set aside.

Heat the oil in a large nonstick skillet over medium heat until hot. Add the mushrooms, red and yellow pepper, carrot, curry powder, pepper, cumin and garlic. Saute until crisp-tender. Add to the rice mixture; toss gently. Serve warm.

Cook's note:

American Indians grew wild rice in the Great Lakes area because, like white rice, it grows in the water. The Chippewas in the Lake Superior area once had the largest natural fields of wild rice in the Great Lakes region.

Nutrition Information Per Serving

			% of daily value
Calories	83		
Calories from fat	21	%	
Fat	2	g	3%
Saturated fat	0.5	g	3%
Cholesterol	0	mg	0%
Sodium	197	mg	8%
Carbohydrate	14	g	5%
Fiber	1.5	g	
Sugar	1	g	
Protein	1	g	

1 starch, 1/2 fat

30

Chicken & Pasta

Chicken, broccoli, Parmesan cheese and either linguine or spaghetti team up to form a complete, balanced meal. This is true comfort food.

4 servings

8 ounces linguine or spaghetti, broken
1 package (10 ounces) frozen cut broccoli
1 tablespoon vegetable oil
1/4 cup chopped onion
1 can (10 3/4 ounces) condensed chicken broth
1 tablespoon dried minced onion
1/2 teaspoon dried minced garlic or garlic powder
1/2 teaspoon pepper
1 tablespoon cornstarch
1 tablespoon cold water
3 cups cooked chicken breast, diced
6 tablespoons Parmesan cheese

■ In a large pot of boiling water, cook the linguine or spaghetti for 5 minutes. Add the broccoli and return to a boil. Cook for 4 to 5 minutes more, or until the broccoli is crisp-tender. Drain in a colander.

In a medium-size skillet, heat the oil and saute the onion until soft. Add the chicken broth, dried minced onion, garlic or garlic powder, and pepper. Bring to a boil. Reduce the heat, cover and simmer for 5 minutes.

In a small bowl, mix together the cornstarch and water. Stir into the broth mixture. Cook and stir until thickened and bubbly. Stir in the diced chicken and heat through.

In a large bowl, toss the broth mixture with the cooked pasta and broccoli until coated. Sprinkle with Parmesan cheese and serve.

Nutrition Information Per Serving

			% of daily value
Calories	**470**		
Calories from fat	**21**	%	
Fat	**11**	g	17%
Saturated fat	**3**	g	15%
Cholesterol	**80**	mg	27%
Sodium	**502**	mg	21%
Carbohydrate	**50**	g	17%
Fiber	**3**	g	
Sugar	**1**	g	
Protein	**42**	g	

Diabetic exchange

4 lean meat, 3 starch, 1 vegetable

Curried Rice

Like chili powder, curry powder is a blend of pulverized spices that add flavor and color to any dish. One of these spices is turmeric, which gives curry dishes their characteristic yellow-orange color and distinctive fragrance. Turmeric is made from the ground roots of a tropical plant related to ginger. In some Middle Eastern cultures it is used to make perfume.

6 servings

1 tablespoon margarine
1 tablespoon onion, peeled, ends removed, finely chopped
1/2 to 1 teaspoon curry powder
1/4 teaspoon pepper
3 cups hot cooked regular or brown rice

■ In a small skillet over medium heat, melt the margarine and saute the onion until tender. Stir in the curry powder and pepper.

Stir in the rice.

Nutrition Information Per Serving

		% of daily value
Calories	**128**	
Calories from fat	**20** %	
Fat	**3** g	5%
Saturated fat	**0.5** g	3%
Cholesterol	**0** mg	0%
Sodium	**23** mg	1%
Carbohydrate	**23** g	8%
Fiber	**1.5** g	
Sugar	**0** g	
Protein	**2** g	

Diabetic exchange

1 1/2 starch, 1/2 fat

15

Rice with Black Beans

Looking for a quick, tasty meal? This entree can be prepared in less than 20 minutes from start to finish — and is it good! Add a tossed salad, a glass of milk and some fruit for dessert for a nutritious meal.

4 servings

Vegetable oil cooking spray
1 medium onion, peeled, ends removed, chopped
2 cloves garlic, peeled, ends removed, minced
1 can (15 ounces) black beans, rinsed and drained
1 can (14 1/2 ounces) stewed tomatoes
1 can (17 ounces) corn, drained
2/3 cup water
1/2 teaspoon dried oregano leaves
1 1/2 cups instant brown rice, uncooked

■ Spray a large skillet with the cooking spray. Add the onion and garlic; cook and stir until tender but not browned, about 5 minutes.

Stir in the black beans, stewed tomatoes, corn, water and oregano. Bring the mixture to a boil. Stir in the uncooked brown rice. Return to a boil.

Reduce the heat to low; cover and simmer for 5 minutes. Remove from the heat. Let stand for 5 minutes before serving.

Nutrition Information Per Serving

			% of daily value
Calories	305		
Calories from fat	6	%	
Fat	2	g	3%
Saturated fat	0.5	g	3%
Cholesterol	0	mg	0%
Sodium	773	mg	32%
Carbohydrate	64	g	21%
Fiber	3.5	g	
Sugar	7	g	
Protein	12	g	

Diabetic exchange
3 1/2 starch, 2 vegetable

Low-Fat Angel Hair Pesto

With low-fat and fat-free products, it's getting easier to follow the American Heart Association's guidelines of eating less than 30 percent of each day's calories from fat. But fat-free does not mean calorie-free. Many low-fat and fat-free items have as many calories as their counterparts. For example, 2 tablespoons of reduced-fat peanut butter has nearly as many calories as regular peanut butter. So remember, a low-fat diet, particularly one low in saturated fat, may help in the fight against heart disease, but calories still count when trying to lose weight.

6 servings

2 cups tightly packed fresh basil leaves
1 to 2 cloves garlic, peeled, ends removed
1/2 cup grated fat-free Parmesan cheese
2 tablespoons lemon juice
1 tablespoon olive oil
12 ounces angel hair pasta, cooked according to package direction, omitting salt and oil (reserve 1/2 cup of the cooking liquid)
2 tomatoes, washed, cored, cut in wedges
Black pepper to taste

■ To make the pesto: In a blender or a food processor fitted with a metal blade, combine the basil leaves, garlic and Parmesan cheese. With the processor running, add the lemon juice and olive oil. Combine until well blended.

Place the pasta in a medium-size sauce pot. Add the pesto and toss.

Add the reserved liquid from the pasta, 1/4 cup at a time, until the sauce reaches the desired consistency.

Add the tomato wedges and pepper to taste. Cover and warm the mixture over medium heat for 5 minutes. Remove from the heat and serve immediately.

Nutrition Information Per Serving

			% of daily value
Calories	286		
Calories from fat	11	%	
Fat	3	g	5%
Saturated fat	0.5	g	3%
Cholesterol	0	mg	0%
Sodium	156	mg	7%
Carbohydrate	50	g	17%
Fiber	1.5	g	
Sugar	1	g	
Protein	12	g	

3 starch, 1/2 lean meat

Sauces, Relishes & Dips

Apple Chutney

This is a great way to use green tomatoes that did not have a chance to ripen. Chutneys were first used in Indian cuisine as relishes or sauces. In this country, we think of them as sweetened fruit relishes. They rarely contain fat and are low in sodium. They are, however, high in calories if prepared with large amounts of sugar. A typical mango chutney contains 300 calories per 1/2-cup serving. But because chutneys are so easy to prepare, the amount of sugar can be controlled.

32 servings

4 medium green tomatoes (1 pound), cored
1 medium sweet red pepper
2 medium apples
3/4 cup chopped onion
3/4 cup sugar
1 teaspoon salt
1/2 teaspoon black pepper
1/2 teaspoon ground cinnamon
1/4 teaspoon ground cloves
1/2 teaspoon ground ginger

Nutrition Information Per Serving

			% of daily value
Calories	**28**		
Calories from fat	**2**	%	
Fat	**trace**	g	1%
Saturated fat	**0**	g	0%
Cholesterol	**0**	mg	0%
Sodium	**69**	mg	3%
Carbohydrate	**7**	g	2%
Fiber	**0.5**	g	
Sugar	**5**	g	
Protein	**trace**	g	

■ Wash, trim and quarter the tomatoes and peppers, removing the seeds and membranes from the peppers. Quarter and core the apples; do not pare. Put the tomatoes, peppers, apples and onion in a food processor with the steel blade in place, or place in the food grinder using the coarse blade; process until finely chopped. Drain, discarding the liquid.

Combine the vegetable-fruit mixture, sugar, salt, black pepper, cinnamon, cloves and ginger in a large soup pot or Dutch oven. Heat to boiling; reduce the heat and simmer, covered, for 30 minutes, stirring occasionally.

Place the finished relish in an airtight container, and store it in the refrigerator for up to 2 to 3 weeks.

Makes 2 pints (2-tablespoon serving).

1/2 fruit

15

Fruit Relish

Whether you are serving a turkey burger, a lean hamburger or a low-fat hot dog, it is fun to have different relishes to accompany them. Most relishes contain as much as 200 mg of sodium per tablespoon, so try your hand at making your own Heart Smart® version. This Fruit Relish contains 1 mg of sodium per tablespoon and can make the lowliest hot dog a gourmet treat.

24 servings

8 ounces crushed pineapple, undrained, in natural juice
1/4 cup brown sugar
2 tablespoons white wine vinegar
1/2 teaspoon curry powder
1/8 teaspoon garlic powder
1/2 cup raisins

■ In a medium-size saucepan, combine the pineapple, brown sugar, vinegar, curry powder and garlic powder. Bring to a boil over high heat and add the raisins. Reduce heat to low and simmer uncovered for 6 to 8 minutes. Cool to room temperature.

Store the relish in a tightly covered container in the refrigerator for up to 2 months. Serve with meat or poultry.

Makes 1 1/2 cups.

Nutrition Information Per Serving

			% of daily value
Calories	21		
Calories from fat	1	%	
Fat	trace	g	1%
Saturated fat	0	g	0%
Cholesterol	0	mg	0%
Sodium	1	mg	1%
Carbohydrate	6	g	2%
Fiber	0	g	
Sugar	5	g	
Protein	trace	g	

Diabetic exchange

1/2 fruit

Pesto Sauce

Pesto is an Italian sauce often tossed with hot pasta. Traditional pesto is made by grinding fresh basil, nuts, garlic and salt into a paste. Sharp, dry cheese is pounded in, and olive oil is beaten in with a wooden spoon or whisk. Basil is the most popular type of pesto, but you can experiment with cilantro, mint, sage or parsley. You can use a blender to make the pesto, but be careful not to overwork it.

24 servings

2 cups tightly packed basil leaves, washed, dried
1 to 2 cloves garlic, peeled, ends removed
1/2 cup grated fat-free Parmesan cheese
2 tablespoons lemon juice
1 tablespoon extra virgin olive oil
1 teaspoon lightly toasted pine nuts, optional
1 tablespoon water or as needed, optional

■ In a food processor fitted with a metal blade or in a blender, process the basil leaves, garlic and Parmesan cheese. With the machine running, add the lemon juice, olive oil and, if desired, pine nuts until a smooth paste-like consistency forms. Add the water if the mixture is too thick.

Makes 1 1/2 cups (1-tablespoon serving).

Nutrition Information Per Serving

		% of daily value
Calories	**18**	
Calories from fat	**35** %	
Fat	**1** g	2%
Saturated fat	**0** g	0%
Cholesterol	**0** mg	0%
Sodium	**37** mg	2%
Carbohydrate	**2** g	1%
Fiber	**0** g	
Sugar	**0** g	
Protein	**1** g	

Diabetic exchange

free food

15

Turkey Gravy

Baste your turkey with a mixture of wine and chicken broth, which will keep the turkey moist without adding fat. Then you can use the defatted drippings and chicken broth to make a delicious, low-fat gravy.

8 servings

2 cups mixture of clear chicken broth and defatted turkey drippings from roasting pan
1/4 cup cold water
2 tablespoons cornstarch
Freshly ground black pepper

Nutrition Information Per Serving

			% of daily value
Calories	**18**		
Calories from fat	**19**	%	
Fat	**trace**	g	1%
Saturated fat	**0**	g	0%
Cholesterol	**trace**	mg	1%
Sodium	**194**	mg	8%
Carbohydrate	**2**	g	1%
Fiber	**0**	g	
Sugar	**0**	g	
Protein	**1**	g	

■ Measure the defatted turkey drippings and add chicken broth to make 2 cups. Pour into a saucepan. Heat to boiling.

Combine the water and cornstarch, beating until smooth, or shake the mixture in a tightly capped jar. Gradually add this mixture to the chicken broth and turkey drippings. Cook over medium heat, stirring constantly until thick. Add pepper.

Cook's note:

To eliminate even more fat when using canned broth, cool the can in the refrigerator, remove the lid, then scrape off any fat on top. If you use low-sodium chicken broth, the sodium level drops to 1 mg.

Diabetic exchange

free food

Vegetables

Arabian Spinach

This recipe for Arabian Spinach can be served as part of a meatless meal. The chickpeas — a good source of protein and iron — are teamed with spinach — an excellent source of vitamin C — to provide a winning combination of taste and nutrition.

4 servings

2 teaspoons olive oil
1 whole onion, peeled, ends removed, sliced
2 large garlic cloves, peeled, ends removed, crushed
1 teaspoon cumin seeds
14 ounces fresh spinach, stems removed, washed and torn
1 can (15 ounces) chickpeas, drained
White pepper to taste

■ In a large frying pan or wok, heat the oil and saute the onion until softened. Add the garlic and cumin seeds.

Add the spinach in stages, stirring until the leaves begin to wilt. Stir in the chickpeas and pepper. Reheat until just bubbling. Serve hot.

Nutrition Information Per Serving

			% of daily value
Calories	**155**		
Calories from fat	**23**	%	
Fat	**4**	g	6%
Saturated fat	**0.5**	g	3%
Cholesterol	**0**	mg	0%
Sodium	**402**	mg	17%
Carbohydrate	**23**	g	8%
Fiber	**3.5**	g	
Sugar	**1**	g	
Protein	**8**	g	

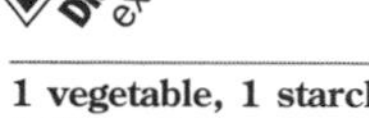

1 vegetable, 1 starch, 1/2 meat

45 minutes

Baked Tomatoes with Spinach Stuffing

Adding more fruits and vegetables to your diet provides your body with potassium as well as other needed vitamins and minerals. This recipe for Baked Tomatoes with Spinach Stuffing provides 436 mg of potassium and offers another delicious meatless choice.

4 servings

4 large tomatoes, washed
Vegetable oil cooking spray
2 garlic cloves, peeled, ends removed, minced
2 tablespoons finely chopped shallots
1 package (10 ounces) frozen chopped spinach, thawed and squeezed dry
1/4 cup bread crumbs
1/4 cup grated Parmesan cheese
2 tablespoons fresh parsley, washed, dried, chopped

Nutrition Information Per Serving

			% of daily value
Calories	**105**		
Calories from fat	**26**	%	
Fat	**3**	g	5%
Saturated fat	**1.5**	g	8%
Cholesterol	**5**	mg	2%
Sodium	**236**	mg	10%
Carbohydrate	**16**	g	5%
Fiber	**3.5**	g	
Sugar	**4**	g	
Protein	**7**	g	

■ Preheat the oven to 350 degrees.

Cut a 1/2-inch slice from the top of each tomato; discard the tops. Scoop out the pulp and discard the seeds. Coarsely chop the pulp. Set aside.

Spray a medium skillet with the cooking spray. Add the garlic and shallots to the pan and cook on medium high for 4 minutes, stirring. Stir in the spinach and tomato pulp. Cook for 2 minutes.

Spoon the spinach mixture into tomatoes. Arrange the stuffed tomatoes in a 9-inch pie plate. Top with bread crumbs, Parmesan cheese and parsley. Bake, uncovered, for 10 to 15 minutes or until heated through. Remove from the oven and serve.

Diabetic exchange

2 vegetable, 1/2 starch, 1/2 meat

Creamed New Potatoes with Peas & Onions

Research published in the European Journal of Clinical Nutrition found that some foods may do a better job of filling you up than others. Compared with white bread, which researchers assigned a rating of 100, potatoes were three times as filling, and apples, oranges, oatmeal and fish were two times as filling. Croissants, cakes, doughnuts and candy bars were found to be between one-half to one-third as filling. In other words, eating oatmeal instead of a doughnut for breakfast not only saves calories but also makes you feel more satisfied. Try looking for foods high in fiber and low in fat, which will fill you up with fewer calories. This recipe for Creamed New Potatoes with Peas and Onions has more than 3 grams of fiber per serving.

6 servings

12 small new potatoes (about 1 1/4 pounds), scrubbed, peeled if desired
Boiling water
3 tablespoons green onions, finely sliced
1 package (10 ounces) frozen peas
1 tablespoon tub margarine
1 tablespoon all-purpose flour
1 cup skim milk
1/4 teaspoon salt, optional
1/8 teaspoon white pepper
Dash of ground nutmeg

■ Cook the potatoes in boiling water for 15 to 20 minutes or until tender. Drain well. Set aside on a serving dish and keep warm.

Cook the green onion and peas in a small amount of water according to the package instructions, omitting the salt. Drain and set aside.

Meanwhile, in a medium-size saucepan or skillet, melt the margarine over low heat. Stir in the flour, mixing until smooth (mixture will be dry); cook 1 minute, stirring constantly. Gradually whisk in the skim milk until smooth. Increase the heat to medium and cook, stirring constantly until the mixture is thick and bubbly.

Stir in the salt (if desired), white pepper, nutmeg, and the peas and onion mixture. Cook until thoroughly heated. Pour the creamed peas and onions over the warmed potatoes and serve.

Nutrition Information Per Serving

			% of daily value
Calories	**154**		
Calories from fat	**13**	%	
Fat	**2**	g	3%
Saturated fat	**0.5**	g	3%
Cholesterol	**trace**	mg	1%
Sodium	**99**	mg	4%
Carbohydrate	**28**	g	9%
Fiber	**3.5**	g	
Sugar	**2**	g	
Protein	**6**	g	

Diabetic exchange

2 starch

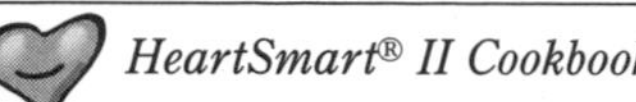

60

Garden Salad Baked Potatoes

Part salad, part side dish, this variation on the baked potato is a sure pleaser. The flavors of the blended root vegetables — green onions, carrots and radishes — complement the taste of the hot, soft potato. No need for added butter here.

6 servings

6 baking potatoes, washed, eyes removed
1 teaspoon beef-flavored instant bouillon
1 cup low-fat cottage cheese
2 teaspoons lemon juice
1/4 cup green onions, washed, ends removed, sliced fine
1/4 cup carrots, peeled, shredded
1/4 cup radishes, washed, tops and ends removed, shredded
1 cup alfalfa sprouts, rinsed

■ Preheat the oven to 350 degrees. Wrap each potato in foil if desired. Bake 45 to 60 minutes until tender.

Meanwhile, mix the bouillon, cottage cheese and lemon juice in a blender or food processor until smooth. Add the green onions, carrots and radishes, and mix gently. When the potatoes are done, make a slice in each and squeeze open. Divide the garden mix into 6 portions and stuff into each of the potatoes. Top with alfalfa sprouts and serve.

Nutrition Information Per Serving

			% of daily value
Calories	252		
Calories from fat	3	%	
Fat	1	g	2%
Saturated fat	0.5	g	3%
Cholesterol	2	mg	1%
Sodium	305	mg	13%
Carbohydrate	53	g	18%
Fiber	5.5	g	
Sugar	5	g	
Protein	10	g	

Diabetic exchange

3 starch, 1 vegetable

15

Glazed Carrots

Despite the rich, satisfying taste of these Glazed Carrots, they contain only 1 gram of fat per serving. By cutting the carrots into julienne strips, you provide more surface area for the carrots to soak up the sugar and ginger glaze — a difference your family will notice at mealtime.

4 servings

6 medium carrots, peeled, ends removed, julienned about 4 inches long and 1/4 inch wide
1 1/2 cups boiling water
2 teaspoons low-fat soft margarine
2 teaspoons brown sugar
1/2 teaspoon fresh minced ginger root

Nutrition Information Per Serving

			% of daily value
Calories	**64**		
Calories from fat	**15**	%	
Fat	**1**	g	2%
Saturated fat	**trace**	g	1%
Cholesterol	**0**	mg	0%
Sodium	**60**	mg	3%
Carbohydrate	**13**	g	4%
Fiber	**3.5**	g	
Sugar	**9**	g	
Protein	**1**	g	

■ Steam the carrots above boiling water in a vegetable steamer until crisp-tender, about 5 minutes. Meanwhile, melt the margarine in a small saucepan; stir in the brown sugar and ginger and cook over medium-low heat, stirring constantly, until the sugar dissolves, about 5 minutes. Add the carrots and stir gently, until well-coated.

Cook's note:

If you don't have a vegetable steamer, improvise by placing the carrots in a heat-proof bowl and set the bowl in a saucepan with the boiling water. Cook, covered, for about 5 minutes.

2 vegetable

90

Harvest Casserole

Using vegetables readily available in the fall and early winter, this Harvest Casserole blends citrus juices and honey to give the dish a warm, tangy flavor. It's perfect for those crisp evenings in late autumn.

8 servings

1 1/2 pounds sweet potatoes, peeled, cubed
1 pound acorn squash, peeled, cleaned, cubed
1 medium apple, cored, seeded, cubed
1/2 cup raisins
2 tablespoons water
1/2 cup chopped onion
1/3 cup orange juice
2 tablespoons honey
1 teaspoon lemon juice
1/8 teaspoon salt
1/8 teaspoon cinnamon
1/8 teaspoon ground allspice
Dash pepper

■ Preheat the oven to 375 degrees. In a 1 1/2 quart baking dish, combine the sweet potatoes, squash, apple and raisins. Set aside.

In a small saucepan, bring the water to a boil and steam the onion until tender. Stir often. Add the orange juice, honey, lemon juice, salt, cinnamon, allspice and pepper. Bring to a boil over high heat. Pour over the vegetables and fruits.

Cover and bake 45 minutes or until the vegetables are tender. Remove the cover. Stir the vegetables until coated with sauce. Bake 10 minutes more. Remove from the oven and serve.

Nutrition Information Per Serving

			% of daily value
Calories	**142**		
Calories from fat	**1**	%	
Fat	**trace**	g	1%
Saturated fat	**0**	g	0%
Cholesterol	**0**	mg	0%
Sodium	**56**	mg	2%
Carbohydrate	**35**	g	12%
Fiber	**4.5**	g	
Sugar	**16**	g	
Protein	**2**	g	

Diabetic exchange

1/2 fruit, 1 1/2 starch

Garlicky Mashed Potatoes with Olive Oil

Garlic and olive oil make a wonderful team when flavoring food. These Garlicky Mashed Potatoes with Olive Oil are quick and delicious — good enough to be served to dinner guests.

6 servings

2 pounds baking potatoes, preferably Idaho, scrubbed
5 large unpeeled garlic cloves
1/2 cup skim milk
1 tablespoon extra-virgin olive oil
1 teaspoon freshly ground pepper
3 teaspoons chives

Nutrition Information Per Serving

			% of daily value
Calories	162		
Calories from fat	13	%	
Fat	2	g	3%
Saturated fat	0.5	g	3%
Cholesterol	0	mg	0%
Sodium	17	mg	1%
Carbohydrate	32	g	11%
Fiber	2.5	g	
Sugar	4	g	
Protein	4	g	

■ Place the potatoes and the garlic cloves in a medium saucepan and cover with cold water. Bring to a boil over high heat, and reduce the heat to medium.

Simmer until the potatoes are tender, about 45 minutes. Drain the potatoes and garlic, reserving 1/2 cup of the cooking liquid.

Peel the potatoes and squeeze the garlic cloves from their skins. Mash the potatoes and garlic with a potato masher or electric mixer. Beat in the milk, reserved potato water and olive oil. Season with pepper and sprinkle with chives.

Diabetic exchange

2 starch

15

Hot Snow Pea Medley

Chili peppers add a great flavor to vegetables whether they are used whole or crushed, as in this recipe for Hot Snow Pea Medley. This dish comes together quickly as fresh, crunchy ingredients are added to a steamy skillet.

6 servings

1 cup sliced onion
1 garlic clove, peeled, ends removed, minced
1/8 teaspoon crushed red pepper
1/4 cup water
1 package (6 ounces) frozen pea pods, thawed and drained
1 cup cherry tomatoes, washed, stemmed, cut in half
1 can (8 ounces) water chestnuts, drained
1 tablespoon sesame seeds, toasted
1 teaspoon sesame oil
1 teaspoon fresh lemon juice
1/8 teaspoon salt, optional

Nutrition Information Per Serving

			% of daily value
Calories	**50**		
Calories from fat	**28**	%	
Fat	**2**	g	3%
Saturated fat	**trace**	g	1%
Cholesterol	**0**	mg	0%
Sodium	**50**	mg	2%
Carbohydrate	**8**	g	3%
Fiber	**1.5**	g	
Sugar	**2**	g	
Protein	**2**	g	

■ In a medium skillet, steam the onion, garlic and red pepper in water over medium heat.

Cook for approximately 5 minutes, stirring often.

Add the pea pods, tomatoes, water chestnuts, sesame seeds, sesame oil, lemon juice and salt, if desired.

Cook, stirring often, for about 2 minutes or until the vegetables are heated through. Serve hot.

Cook's note:

To toast the sesame seeds, preheat the oven to 350 degrees. Spread the sesame seeds on a shallow baking dish and toast for 5 to 8 minutes or until the seeds are golden. Remove from the oven and let cool.

Diabetic exchange

1 1/2 vegetable, 1/2 fat

Italian Grilled Vegetables

Grilled vegetables act as a colorful companion to a summer meal. Vegetables can be cooked on the grill either in a basket, on a skewer or in a foil packet.

8 servings

3 medium-size ears of corn with husks
3 tablespoons olive oil
1 teaspoon dried oregano leaves
1/4 teaspoon black pepper
1/8 teaspoon garlic powder
3 medium-size zucchini (about 10 ounces each) washed, ends removed
3 medium-size yellow straight-neck squashes (about 10 ounces each) washed, ends removed
1 medium-size green pepper, washed
1 medium-size red pepper, washed
1 medium-size orange pepper, washed
8 jumbo mushrooms (about 3/4 pound) cleaned

■ About one hour before serving, prepare the outdoor grill for barbecuing. Pull the husks away from the corn without separating them from the stalk. Discard the silk from the corn and reposition the husks over the corn. In a 9-by-13-inch glass baking dish, place the corn in their husks and enough water to cover; let the corn soak 10 minutes. Remove and pat the corn husks dry with paper towels.

In a cup, mix the olive oil, oregano, pepper and garlic powder. Cut each zucchini and yellow squash lengthwise in half. Cut each pepper lengthwise in half; discard the seeds. Brush the zucchini, yellow squash, peppers, mushrooms, and corn (not husks) with olive-oil mixture.

Place the corn in their husks and half the vegetables on grill over medium heat; cook, turning occasionally, until the vegetables are browned and tender when pierced with a fork, 15 to 20 minutes. Remove the vegetables to a platter. Repeat with the remaining vegetables.

Nutrition Information Per Serving

			% of daily value
Calories	**108**		
Calories from fat	**32**	%	
Fat	**4**	g	6%
Saturated fat	**0.5**	g	3%
Cholesterol	**0**	mg	0%
Sodium	**11**	mg	1%
Carbohydrate	**17**	g	6%
Fiber	**4.5**	g	
Sugar	**5**	g	
Protein	**4**	g	

Diabetic exchange

2 vegetable, 1/2 starch, 1 fat

15 minutes

Steamed Green Beans & Water Chestnuts

Five daily servings of fruits and vegetables assure that you're getting an adequate amount of potassium in your diet. The body needs potassium to maintain adequate water balance, normal muscle function and cell growth. This recipe uses lots of fresh vegetables, high in potassium.

4 servings

2 teaspoons soft-tub margarine
6 green onions, washed, ends removed, sliced
1/2 pound fresh mushrooms, cleaned, sliced
1/8 teaspoon black pepper
1/8 teaspoon garlic powder
1 cup water, optional
3/4 pound fresh green beans, cleaned
1 can (8 ounces) sliced water chestnuts, drained and rinsed
1 tablespoon lemon juice

■ In a medium-size skillet, melt the margarine and saute the green onions and mushrooms. Add the pepper and garlic powder.

In a vegetable steamer or saucepan with water in the bottom, steam the green beans and water chestnuts. Steam until the beans are bright green, 3 to 5 minutes.

In a large bowl, toss the sauteed and steamed vegetables with lemon juice and serve.

Nutrition Information Per Serving

			% of daily value
Calories	74		
Calories from fat	25	%	
Fat	2	g	3%
Saturated fat	0.5	g	3%
Cholesterol	0	mg	0%
Sodium	42	mg	2%
Carbohydrate	13	g	4%
Fiber	2.5	g	
Sugar	3	g	
Protein	3	g	

Diabetic exchange

2 vegetable, 1/2 fat

60

Sweet Potato Apple Casserole

Sweet potatoes are usually prepared by candying, frying or dousing them in large amounts of butter — not a good idea from the Heart Smart® perspective. This recipe for Sweet Potato Apple Casserole offers a delicious, low-fat way to prepare sweet potatoes while retaining all the flavor.

6 servings

3 to 4 medium sweet potatoes
2 medium tart apples
Vegetable oil cooking spray
2 teaspoons fresh lemon juice, divided
2/3 cup dark brown sugar
1 teaspoon ground cinnamon
2 tablespoon frozen tub margarine, divided

Nutrition Information Per Serving

			% of daily value
Calories	**230**		
Calories from fat	**16**	%	
Fat	**4**	g	6%
Saturated fat	**0.5**	g	3%
Cholesterol	**0**	mg	0%
Sodium	**66**	mg	3%
Carbohydrate	**49**	g	16%
Fiber	**3.5**	g	
Sugar	**36**	g	
Protein	**2**	g	

■ Wash the sweet potatoes. Boil the potatoes in their skins, covered, until nearly tender, about 10 minutes. Drain, cool, peel and slice.

While the sweet potatoes are cooking, wash, core and slice the apples.

Preheat the oven to 350 degrees.

Spray a 3-quart baking dish with the cooking spray. Place half of the sliced sweet potatoes in the baking dish. Cover with half the apples. Drizzle with 1 teaspoon of lemon juice. Sprinkle with half the brown sugar and cinnamon. Dot with half the margarine.

Repeat to make another layer with remaining 1 teaspoon lemon juice and 1 tablespoon margarine. Bake 45 minutes or until the top is brown.

Diabetic exchange

1 fat, 2 starch, 1 fruit

15

Tomatoes & Zucchini

It can be easy to kick the salt habit if you use more herbs and spices. This recipe for Tomatoes and Zucchini uses fresh basil, an intense herb that is especially good in tomato dishes, and parsley as a garnish. But don't underestimate the value of parsley. It contains vitamins A, B and C and calcium and iron.

6 servings

Vegetable oil cooking spray
1 large onion, peeled, ends removed, thinly sliced
1 clove garlic, peeled, ends removed, minced
4 medium tomatoes, peeled, cored, coarsely chopped
2 medium zucchini, washed, ends removed, thinly sliced
1/2 medium green pepper, washed, cored, seeded, chopped
1 1/2 teaspoons fresh basil, washed, dried, finely chopped; or 1/2 teaspoon dried
1/4 teaspoon freshly ground black pepper
2 tablespoons freshly grated Parmesan cheese
2 tablespoons fresh parsley, washed, dried, chopped or 2 teaspoons dried

■ Spray a large skillet with the cooking spray. Add the onion and garlic and saute until the onion is tender but not brown, stirring occasionally, about 3 to 4 minutes.

Stir in the tomatoes, zucchini, green pepper, basil and pepper. Cover and simmer for 10 minutes or until the zucchini is tender, stirring occasionally. Uncover and simmer about 5 minutes, or until most of the liquid evaporates.

Pour into 6 individual serving bowls. Sprinkle with Parmesan cheese. Garnish with parsley and serve.

Cook's note:

Store fresh herbs unwashed in the refrigerator. Rinse and chop them when needed. Storing fresh herbs in a container of water may keep them fresh, but some of the flavor and nutrients will be lost.

Nutrition Information Per Serving

			% of daily value
Calories	48		
Calories from fat	18	%	
Fat	1	g	2%
Saturated fat	0.5	g	3%
Cholesterol	2	mg	1%
Sodium	49	mg	2%
Carbohydrate	7	g	2%
Fiber	2.5	g	
Sugar	4	g	
Protein	3	g	

Diabetic exchange

1 1/2 vegetable

Curried Vegtables with Brown Rice

Rice is a nutritious food that costs about 5 cents per 1-cup serving. But most seasoned-rice mixes cost at least 45 cents per serving. By buying plain long-grain rice and adding your own seasonings, you can save money and provide a delicious Heart Smart® dish.

8 servings

1 tablespoon vegetable oil
1 medium onion, peeled, ends removed, coarsely chopped
1/4 tablespoon curry powder
Freshly ground pepper to taste
1/2 teaspoon cumin
1/2 bay leaf
1/2 cup water
2 medium carrots, peeled, ends removed, thickly sliced on the diagonal
1/2 small cauliflower, washed, separated into florets
1/2 pound broccoli florets
1 green pepper, washed, cored, seeded, cut into large chunks
1 red pepper, washed, cored, seeded, cut into large chunks
6 cups cooked brown rice
1/4 cup cashews
1 cup raisins

■ Heat the vegetable oil in a Dutch oven over medium heat. Add the onion and cook, stirring occasionally, until soft, about 5 minutes.

Stir in the curry powder, pepper, cumin, bay leaf, water, carrot, cauliflower and broccoli. Cover and cook over low to medium heat for 10 minutes, or until the vegetables are crisp-tender, stirring occasionally.

Uncover, then remove and discard the bay leaf.

Add the green and red peppers and cook over medium heat until the peppers are crisp, about 5 to 8 minutes.

Place the cooked brown rice in the bottom of a large, shallow baking dish. Scatter the vegetables over the rice. Sprinkle with cashews and raisins and serve.

Nutrition Information Per Serving

			% of daily value
Calories	292		
Calories from fat	15	%	
Fat	5	g	7%
Saturated fat	1	g	5%
Cholesterol	0	mg	0%
Sodium	23	mg	19%
Carbohydrate	58	g	19%
Fiber	5.5	g	
Sugar	15	g	
Protein	7	g	

Diabetic exchange

3 starch, 2 vegetable, 1 fat

15

Microwave Vegetable-Filled Squash

Autumn's acorn squash is easy to prepare in the microwave. Abundant and inexpensive throughout the winter months, squash can replace potato or rice dishes at the family table for a bit of variety.

4 servings

2 small acorn squash
2 teaspoons margarine, divided
1 cup cooked peas
1/4 cup cooked pearl onions, optional

Nutrition Information Per Serving

			% of daily value
Calories	**169**		
Calories from fat	**11**	%	
Fat	**2**	g	3%
Saturated fat	**0.5**	g	3%
Cholesterol	**0**	mg	0%
Sodium	**32**	mg	1%
Carbohydrate	**37**	g	12%
Fiber	**4.5**	g	
Sugar	**8**	g	
Protein	**5**	g	

■ Split the squash; scoop out the seeds. If the squash is hard to cut, pierce it with a fork or sharp knife in several places and microwave whole for 1 to 2 minutes on high (100 percent power).

Arrange the squash halves in a microwave-safe dish. Cover with wax paper; cook 10 to 12 minutes on high. Rub a 1/2 teaspoon of margarine inside each of the 4 halves. In small bowl, mix together the peas and onion, if desired. Evenly divide the vegetables among the 4 squash halves. Cover with wax paper; microwave on high for 2 to 3 minutes.

Diabetic exchange

2 1/2 starch

Vegetable Stuffed Peppers

Vitamin C plays an important role in the body's ability to fight infection. The adult Recommended Daily Allowance for vitamin C is 60 mg per day. By including fruits and vegetables in your daily diet, it's easy to get plenty of vitamin C without taking supplements. Green peppers, broccoli, citrus fruits, strawberries, melons, tomatoes, raw cabbage and leafy greens are all good sources. One serving of this recipe for Vegetable Stuffed Peppers - a wonderful side dish served with fish or chicken - provides 68 mg of vitamin C.

4 servings

4 quarts water as needed, divided
2 large green, yellow or red peppers, washed, cored, seeded, stems removed, cut in half lengthwise
3 tomatoes, peeled, cored, seeded, chopped
1/4 cup onion, peeled, ends removed, chopped
1/4 cup fresh mushrooms, cleaned, chopped
2 tablespoons chives, washed, chopped
1 clove garlic, peeled, ends removed, minced
1/4 teaspoon black pepper
2/3 cup cooked rice
1/2 cup fresh bread crumbs (1 slice of bread)
1 tablespoon Parmesan cheese
1 1/2 teaspoons margarine, melted

■ Preheat the oven to 350 degrees. In a medium saucepan, add 3 1/2 quarts water, or enough to submerge the peppers, and boil the peppers 3 to 5 minutes. Remove from the water and drain. Place the peppers cut side up in a shallow baking dish.

In a large mixing bowl, combine the tomatoes, onion, mushrooms, chives, garlic, black pepper and rice, and mix well. Divide the mixture among the pepper shells and fill. In a small bowl, mix together the bread crumbs, Parmesan cheese and margarine. Sprinkle the mixture over the filled peppers.

Pour the remaining 1/2 quart water or enough to fill the bottom of the baking dish 1/2 inch. Bake the peppers uncovered for 25 to 30 minutes. Remove from the oven and serve.

Nutrition Information Per Serving

		% of daily value
Calories	**98**	
Calories from fat	**23** %	
Fat	**3** g	5%
Saturated fat	**0.5** g	3%
Cholesterol	**1** mg	1%
Sodium	**85** mg	4%
Carbohydrate	**17** g	6%
Fiber	**2.5** g	
Sugar	**4** g	
Protein	**3** g	

Diabetic exchange

1/2 starch, 2 vegetable, 1/2 fat

30

Whipped Sweet Potatoes

Light and fluffy, these Whipped Sweet Potatoes can be prepared a day ahead to make a meal come together quickly. The minced parsley, lemon peel and nutmeg make a colorful garnish.

12 servings

4 pounds sweet potatoes, peeled, cut into 2-inch pieces
1/4 cup chicken broth
2 tablespoons brown sugar
2 teaspoons grated lemon peel
1 1/2 teaspoons ground nutmeg
1/4 teaspoon white pepper
Garnish: minced parsley, grated lemon peel, ground nutmeg

■ Cook the sweet potatoes in a large pot of boiling water until tender, about 15 minutes. Drain well. Transfer to a large bowl, cool slightly and puree in a mixer or processor in batches. Return to the pot.

Mix in the chicken broth, brown sugar, lemon peel and nutmeg. Season with white pepper.

If prepared ahead, stir the potato mixture over medium heat to rewarm and thicken slightly. Transfer the potatoes to a serving bowl. Top with parsley, lemon and nutmeg.

Nutrition Information Per Serving

			% of daily value
Calories	**96**		
Calories from fat	**1**	%	
Fat	**trace**	g	1%
Saturated fat	**0**	g	0%
Cholesterol	**trace**	mg	1%
Sodium	**49**	mg	2%
Carbohydrate	**22**	g	7%
Fiber	**4**	g	
Sugar	**2**	g	
Protein	**2**	g	

Diabetic exchange

1 1/2 starch

Meatless

Bulgur Chili

Go meatless in this chili recipe and sacrifice none of the flavor. Bulgur consists of wheat kernels that have been steamed and crushed. It provides a chewy texture to this Heart Smart® chili.

8 servings

Vegetable oil cooking spray
2 cloves garlic, peeled, ends removed, chopped
1 cup chopped onion
1 cup chopped sweet green peppers
1 cup chopped sweet red peppers
2 cups sliced mushrooms
1 cup frozen corn
1 can (15 ounces) kidney beans, rinsed, drained
1 can (8 ounces) tomato sauce
1 can (15 ounces) chopped tomatoes, undrained
1/2 cup fine bulgur (uncooked 3 ounces)
1/2 cup water
1 teaspoon dried oregano
1 teaspoon ground cumin
1 teaspoon chili powder
Ground red (cayenne) pepper to taste

■ Spray a large sauce pot with the cooking spray. Add the garlic, onion, green and red peppers, mushrooms and corn. Cook 10 minutes over medium heat, or until the vegetables are tender, stirring occasionally.

Add the kidney beans, tomato sauce, tomatoes, bulgur, water, oregano, cumin, chili powder and red cayenne pepper. Reduce heat to low, cover and cook for 20 to 25 minutes. Stir often while cooking. Remove from the heat and serve.

Nutrition Information Per Serving

			% of daily value
Calories	**147**		
Calories from fat	**6**	%	
Fat	**1**	g	2%
Saturated fat	**trace**	g	1%
Cholesterol	**0**	mg	0%
Sodium	**289**	mg	12%
Carbohydrate	**31**	g	10%
Fiber	**7.5**	g	
Sugar	**3**	g	
Protein	**7**	g	

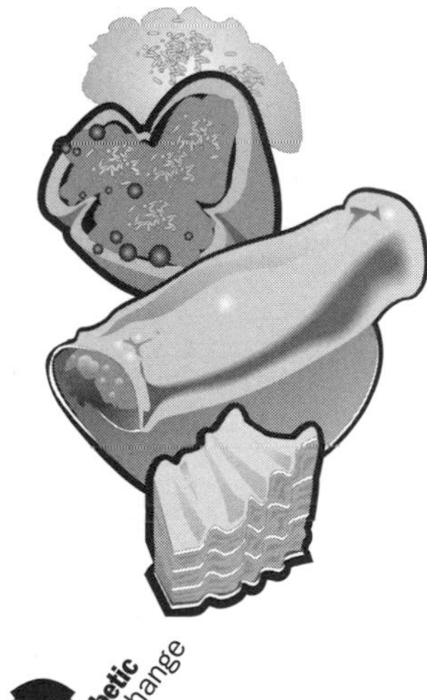

Diabetic exchange

2 starch

90

Cheesy Broccoli-Corn Strudel

The trick to limiting fat yet still having a flaky crust in this strudel is to use phyllo dough. Phyllo dough is prepared with flour, water and salt. Sheets, or leaves, of the dough are then spread with fat, which provides flakiness as the dough bakes. Many recipes call for lavish amounts of butter. But this time we've substituted butter-flavored vegetable oil cooking spray. This dish can be served as either an appetizer or a meatless main course.

6 servings

1 cup part-skim ricotta cheese
2 ounces light cream cheese, softened
1/2 cup (2 ounces) shredded part-skim mozzarella cheese
1 package (10 ounces) frozen chopped broccoli, thawed and drained
1 cup whole kernel corn
4 egg whites, slightly beaten
1/4 cup sliced green onions
2 ounces diced pimiento, drained
1/2 teaspoon dried whole basil
1/4 teaspoon black pepper
24 sheets 9-by-12-inch frozen phyllo pastry, thawed, divided
Butter-flavored vegetable oil cooking spray
1/4 cup toasted wheat germ, divided
1 teaspoon vegetable oil, divided

■ Preheat the oven to 375 degrees. Line a 15-by-10-by-1-inch jelly-roll pan with parchment paper or foil.

In a large bowl combine the ricotta cheese, cream cheese and mozzarella. Add the broccoli, corn, egg whites, green onion, pimiento, basil and black pepper. Mix well and set aside.

Place 4 sheets of phyllo pastry on a work surface (keep the remaining pastry between dampened towels). Coat the phyllo with butter-flavored cooking spray and sprinkle with 1 tablespoon of wheat germ. Top with 4 more phyllo sheets, coat with butter-flavored cooking spray and sprinkle with 1 tablespoon wheat germ. Top with 4 more phyllo sheets; coat with butter-flavored cooking spray.

Spoon half of the cheese mixture lengthwise on the phyllo stack, leaving a 1-inch margin on the long side and 1 1/2-inch margins on the short sides. Turn the ends to encase the filling. Roll in jelly-roll fashion, starting with the filling end. Place the seam side down on the prepared jelly-roll pan.

Repeat the entire procedure with the remaining phyllo sheets. Place alongside the other prepared strudel.

Brush both with vegetable oil. Using a thin, sharp knife, make diagonal slits about 1/4-inch deep, 2 inches apart, across the top of both rolls. Bake 45 minutes or until golden. Remove from the oven and let stand 10 minutes before serving.

Makes 16 appetizer slices; or cut into quarters to make 6 main-course servings.

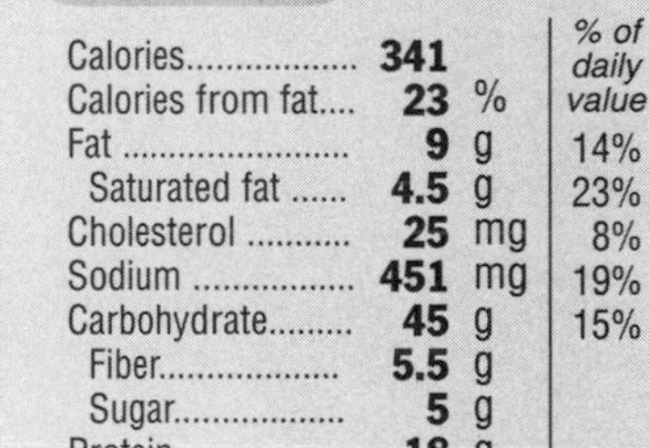

Nutrition Information Per Serving

			% of daily value
Calories	341		
Calories from fat	23	%	
Fat	9	g	14%
Saturated fat	4.5	g	23%
Cholesterol	25	mg	8%
Sodium	451	mg	19%
Carbohydrate	45	g	15%
Fiber	5.5	g	
Sugar	5	g	
Protein	18	g	

1 meat, 2 1/2 starch, 1 1/2 vegetable, 1/2 fat

Creamy Fettuccine with Vegetables

The most effective way to lower the fat in your diet — especially saturated fat — is to limit how much high-fat red meat you eat. When served with a Heart Smart® Oatmeal Carrot Muffin, this fettuccine recipe provides as much protein as 4 ounces of red meat.

4 servings

2 to 3 cups water
1 cup carrots, peeled, ends removed, sliced
1 cup zucchini, washed, ends removed, sliced
1 cup broccoli florets, washed
1 cup fresh green beans, washed, cut in half, or frozen, thawed
8 ounces whole-grain fettuccine noodles
1 1/2 cups low-fat (1 percent) cottage cheese
2/3 cup skim milk
1 teaspoon basil
1/4 cup parsley, washed, dried, chopped
1/4 cup Parmesan cheese

■ In a large saucepan, place 2 inches of water. Steam the carrots, zucchini, broccoli and green beans until tender-crisp. Remove from heat and drain. Place the vegetables in a large serving bowl to cool.

Cook the noodles according to the package directions, omitting salt and fat. Drain the noodles and set aside to cool.

Using a blender or food processor fitted with a metal blade, puree the cottage cheese until smooth. Blend in the skim milk, basil and parsley. Add the noodles and sauce to the cooled vegetables and mix until coated. Sprinkle with Parmesan cheese. Serve at room temperature.

Nutrition Information Per Serving

			% of daily value
Calories	**348**		
Calories from fat	**10**	%	
Fat	**4**	g	6%
Saturated fat	**2**	g	10%
Cholesterol	**9**	mg	3%
Sodium	**509**	mg	21%
Carbohydrate	**54**	g	18%
Fiber	**2.5**	g	
Sugar	**8**	g	
Protein	**24**	g	

Diabetic exchange

3 starch, 2 vegetable, 1 1/2 lean meats.

30

Fettuccine with Artichoke Sauce

It's important to choose your pasta carefully. Macaroni is generally cholesterol-free, but noodles often are made with whole eggs. Egg noodles contain about 50 mg of cholesterol per serving. So look for a macaroni product or yolk-free noodles.

8 servings

1 tablespoon olive oil
1 medium onion, peeled, ends removed, chopped
2 cloves garlic, peeled, ends removed, minced
1/4 cup all-purpose flour
1/2 teaspoon oregano
2 cups plus 4 tablespoons skim milk, divided
1/4 cup grated fat-free Parmesan cheese
1 can (14 ounces) artichoke hearts, drained, cut up
2 tablespoons fresh parsley; or 2 teaspoons dried
8 ounces fettuccine, cooked according to package directions, omitting salt and fat
Snipped parsley, washed, dried, optional
Coarsely ground pepper to taste

■ In a medium-size saucepan, heat the olive oil over medium heat. Add the onion and garlic and cook until tender, about 5 minutes.

Stir in the flour and oregano. Stir in 2 cups of the skim milk.

Cook, stirring constantly, until thick and bubbly. Stir for 1 minute more. Stir in the nonfat Parmesan cheese. (At this point the sauce can be cooled and stored in the refrigerator in a covered container up to 24 hours if desired.)

Stir in the chopped artichoke hearts and parsley. Cook about 5 minutes.

If the sauce is too thick, stir in 2 to 4 more tablespoons of skim milk to reach the desired consistency.

Spoon the sauce over the hot fettuccine. Sprinkle with additional parsley, if desired, and pepper.

Nutrition Information Per Serving

			% of daily value
Calories	**197**		
Calories from fat	**9**	%	
Fat	**2**	g	3%
Saturated fat	**0.5**	g	3%
Cholesterol	**1**	mg	1%
Sodium	**119**	mg	5%
Carbohydrate	**34**	g	11%
Fiber	**0.5**	g	
Sugar	**4**	g	
Protein	**9**	g	

Diabetic exchange

2 starch, 1 vegetable

Garden Vegetable Lasagna

Most people love cheese. But because regular cheese contains nearly 2 teaspoons, or 8 grams, of fat per ounce, many people have eliminated it from their diets. This recipe for Garden Vegetable Lasagna uses fat-free mozzarella and ricotta cheeses, which reduces the fat from 21 grams to 5 grams per serving.

6 servings

1 tablespoon olive oil
1/2 cup diced onion
3 teaspoons minced garlic
1/2 cup sliced mushrooms
1/2 cup chopped broccoli
1/2 cup chopped zucchini
1/2 cup eggplant, peeled, diced
1/2 cup diced celery
1/2 cup diced carrot
1/2 cup diced red pepper
1/2 cup diced green pepper
1 can (28 ounces) whole peeled tomatoes in juice, quartered or crushed, drained, divided, 1/4 cup liquid reserved
1 1/2 teaspoons dry basil leaves
1 1/2 teaspoons dry marjoram leaves
Pepper to taste
1 cup fat-free ricotta cheese
1/8 cup Parmesan cheese
1/4 cup egg substitute
1 tablespoon chopped parsley
1 1/2 cups fat-free mozzarella cheese, divided
6 pieces lasagna noodles, cooked according to package directions, divided

■ Preheat the oven to 350 degrees. In a heavy saucepan, heat the oil and saute the onion until translucent, about 3 minutes. Add the garlic and saute for 2 minutes. Then add the mushrooms, broccoli, zucchini, eggplant, celery, carrot, and red and green peppers, and saute until tender. Add the reserved tomato liquid and bring to a boil, then add the basil, marjoram and 2 1/4 cups tomatoes. Season to taste with pepper, remove from heat and cool.

In a medium bowl, combine the ricotta cheese, Parmesan cheese, egg substitute and parsley; set aside.

Combine 1 1/4 cups mozzarella cheese with the cooled vegetable mixture and set aside.

In a 9-by-6-inch baking pan, layer two cooked noodles on the bottom. Cover with half of the ricotta mixture, half of the vegetable mixture, then repeat using the remaining mixtures and two more noodles. Top with the remaining two noodles. Cover with the remaining 1 cup tomatoes and sprinkle with the remaining 1/4 cup mozzarella cheese.

Bake, covered, for 1 hour. Uncover and bake for an additional 30 minutes. Remove from the oven and let stand for 15 minutes before serving.

Nutrition Information Per Serving

			% of daily value
Calories	233		
Calories from fat	20	%	
Fat	5	g	8%
Saturated fat	0.5	g	3%
Cholesterol	18	mg	6%
Sodium	740	mg	31%
Carbohydrate	34	g	11%
Fiber	1.5	g	
Sugar	6	g	
Protein	25	g	

Diabetic exchange

2 meat, 2 vegetable, 1 1/2 starch

60

Spinach Cheese-Stuffed Shells

When people prepare meatless meals, they often choose cheese to replace meat. Ounce for ounce, cheese provides similar amounts of protein. But it also contains similar amounts of cholesterol and often is higher in fat and sodium. One ounce of cheddar, for example, has 9 grams of fat. When you also consider that this same ounce of cheese contains 30 mg of cholesterol and 176 mg of sodium, you can see that cheese can make a meatless meal unhealthy. Fortunately, many nonfat and low-fat cheeses are available. It is possible to have your cheese and eat it, too. Although the taste is different from full-fat counterparts, several companies have mastered an acceptable product. Try different ones until you find the taste and texture you like.

6 servings

8 ounces fat-free ricotta cheese
1 egg white
1/2 cup plus 1 to 2 tablespoon fat-free Parmesan cheese, divided
2 teaspoons ground or dried basil
2 teaspoons pepper
1 teaspoon garlic powder
1 cup fresh chopped spinach
1 jar (26 ounces) reduced - sodium, low-fat spaghetti sauce, divided
8 ounces large macaroni shells (about 28), cooked according to package directions
Pinch of dry red hot peppers
8 ounces (2 cups) low-fat shredded mozzarella cheese

■ In a medium-size bowl, combine the ricotta cheese, egg white, Parmesan cheese, basil, pepper, garlic powder and spinach. Thoroughly mix all the ingredients.

Coat the bottom of a 9-by-13-inch baking pan with 1/4 of the spaghetti sauce. Preheat the oven to 350 degrees.

Rinse the cooked macaroni shells in cold water and stuff each with 1 heaping teaspoon of the cheese filling. Place the stuffed shells in the spaghetti-sauce-coated baking dish. Pour the remaining 3/4 of the spaghetti sauce over the stuffed shells. Spread a pinch of hot red peppers and, if desired, 1 to 2 tablespoons of the remaining Parmesan cheese over the top.

Cover and bake the shells for 35 to 40 minutes. During the last 5 minutes of baking, sprinkle mozzarella cheese over the shells.

Nutrition Information Per Serving

			% of daily value
Calories	360		
Calories from fat	17	%	
Fat	6	g	9%
Saturated fat	4	g	20%
Cholesterol	21	mg	7%
Sodium	746	mg	31%
Carbohydrate	44	g	15%
Fiber	0	g	
Sugar	7	g	
Protein	28	g	

Cook's note:

When cooking with nonfat cheese, you may notice it does not melt well. One option is to finely shred the cheese and cook it longer at a low temperature. Another option is to use a processed nonfat cheese, designed to melt better.

1 milk, 2 bread, 1 1/2 meat, 1 vegetable

Skillet Pizza

Pizza can be a very nutritious fast food if you choose the right toppings. Select vegetables such as mushrooms, onion and green pepper, and avoid extra cheese, olives, pepperoni, sausage and anchovies.

6 servings

Vegetable oil cooking spray
1 package of 6 refrigerator biscuits
1 teaspoon water
1 can (8 ounces) pizza sauce
1/4 cup broccoli florets, washed, chopped
2 tablespoons carrot, peeled, grated
2 tablespoons mushrooms, cleaned, chopped
1 tablespoon green pepper, washed, seeded, cored, chopped
1 tablespoon onion, peeled, ends removed, chopped
2 ounces part-skim mozzarella cheese, shredded

■ Spray a heavy 10-inch skillet with the cooking spray. Press the biscuits into the bottom and up the sides of skillet.

Moisten the edges of the biscuits with water and pinch to seal the biscuits together. Cook, covered, over medium-low heat for 2 minutes. Check the crust and seal any holes by pressing the biscuits together with a fork. Don't use your fingers!

Spoon the pizza sauce over the crust. Sprinkle with the broccoli, carrot, mushrooms, green pepper, and onion and cook, covered, for 3 minutes. Top with grated mozzarella cheese and cook, covered, over medium-low heat for 2 to 3 minutes, or until the cheese is melted.

Remove from heat and serve at the table right from the skillet.

Nutrition Information Per Serving

			% of daily value
Calories	**136**		
Calories from fat	**33**	%	
Fat	**5**	g	8%
Saturated fat	**2**	g	10%
Cholesterol	**5**	mg	2%
Sodium	**551**	mg	23%
Carbohydrate	**16**	g	5%
Fiber	**1**	g	
Sugar	**0**	g	
Protein	**5**	g	

Diabetic exchange

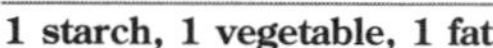

1 starch, 1 vegetable, 1 fat

15

Italian Vegetables & Pasta

Low-fat meals need not take all day to prepare. One way to reduce preparation time is to use frozen vegetables. In winter, when fresh vegetables must be shipped long distances, the frozen varieties may actually contain more vitamins and minerals.

4 servings

6 ounces uncooked linguine (eggless)
Vegetable oil cooking spray
3 tablespoons green onion, washed, ends removed, chopped
3 cups frozen mixed vegetables (broccoli, cauliflower, carrots), thawed
3/4 teaspoon dried thyme
3/4 teaspoon dried oregano
1/2 teaspoon pepper
14 1/2 ounces stewed tomatoes, undrained
4 teaspoons Parmesan cheese, grated

■ Cook the linguine according to the package instructions, omitting salt and fat, and drain.

Spray a large skillet with the cooking spray. Stir-fry the green onion and vegetables for 3 minutes until crisp-tender.

Add the thyme, oregano and pepper. Add the tomatoes and simmer until heated throughout. Spoon the vegetable mixture over linguine and top with Parmesan cheese.

Nutrition Information Per Serving

			% of daily value
Calories	**224**		
Calories from fat	**8**	%	
Fat	**2**	g	3%
Saturated fat	**0.5**	g	3%
Cholesterol	**trace**	mg	1%
Sodium	**363**	mg	15%
Carbohydrate	**44**	g	15%
Fiber	**6**	g	
Sugar	**5**	g	
Protein	**9**	g	

Diabetic exchange

2 starch, 3 vegetable

Linguine & Red Clam Sauce

Clams are high in protein and contain fair amounts of calcium and iron. This recipe pairs clams with tomatoes, giving the dish a rich flavor and chewy texture.

4 servings

8 ounces linguine, cooked according to package directions, omitting salt
1 zucchini (4 ounces) cut in half lengthwise and thinly sliced
1/2 cup carrot, peeled, ends removed, chopped
1/3 cup celery, washed, ends removed, chopped
1/3 cup onion, peeled, ends removed, chopped
2 cloves garlic, peeled, minced
2 teaspoons olive oil
1/2 teaspoon dried marjoram leaves
1/4 teaspoon pepper
1 can (16 ounces) whole tomatoes, cut up and undrained
1 can (6 1/2 ounces) chopped clams, undrained
2 tablespoons tomato paste

■ While the linguine is cooking, combine the zucchini, carrot, celery, onion, garlic, oil, marjoram leaves and pepper in a 2-quart casserole dish, and mix well. Rinse and drain the linguine, cover to keep warm and set aside.

Microwave the vegetables on high for 5 1/2 to 8 minutes, or until the vegetables are tender, stirring once or twice. Add the tomatoes, clams and tomato paste; mix well.

Microwave on high, covered, for 5 to 9 minutes, or until the flavors are blended and the sauce is hot. Serve the sauce over the linguine.

Nutrition Information Per Serving

			% of daily value
Calories	301		
Calories from fat	12	%	
Fat	4	g	6%
Saturated fat	0.5	g	3%
Cholesterol	29	mg	10%
Sodium	304	mg	13%
Carbohydrate	55	g	18%
Fiber	2.5	g	
Sugar	5	g	
Protein	13	g	

Diabetic exchange

3 starch, 2 vegetable, 1/2 fat

90

Manicotti Florentine

The beauty of this recipe is that it can be made in large batches and frozen for a quick meal later. Freezing food does not destroy its nutritive value, but remember that the cold, dry air in the freezer, which normally protects the food, can cause it to deteriorate if it's not packaged properly. If using plastic freezer bags or containers, be sure they are securely sealed. If wrapping in aluminum foil, be certain all the food is covered. Double wrapping is recommended.

5 servings

1 tablespoon olive oil
1/2 cup onion, peeled, ends removed, chopped
1 teaspoon garlic, chopped
1/2 package (10 ounces) frozen chopped spinach, thawed, drained (1 cup)
1/2 cup low-fat (1 percent) cottage cheese
1/2 cup part-skim ricotta cheese
1/4 cup Parmesan cheese, grated
1 egg white
1/4 teaspoon black pepper
Pinch of nutmeg
2 cups tomato sauce, divided
1/4 cup water
10 uncooked jumbo manicotti shells
2 1/4 ounces part-skim mozzarella cheese, shredded

■ Preheat the oven to 375 degrees. In a large skillet, heat the oil. Add the onion and garlic and saute until the onion is translucent, about 3 to 4 minutes.

In a large bowl, combine the spinach, cottage and ricotta cheeses, Parmesan cheese, egg white, black pepper, nutmeg and the sauteed onion and garlic. Mix well until blended.

In an 9-by-13-inch baking dish, mix together 1 cup of the tomato sauce and water. Spread to make an even layer.

Stuff each manicotti shell with an equal amount of the cheese mixture; arrange in the baking dish. Pour the remaining 1 cup tomato sauce evenly over the top.

Cover with foil and bake until the shells are tender, about 50 minutes. Uncover and sprinkle with mozzarella cheese. Return to the oven and bake 10 minutes longer, or until the cheese is melted and bubbly.

Nutrition Information Per Serving

			% of daily value
Calories	**322**		
Calories from fat	**26**	%	
Fat	**9**	g	14%
Saturated fat	**4**	g	20%
Cholesterol	**20**	mg	7%
Sodium	**363**	mg	15%
Carbohydrate	**40**	g	13%
Fiber	**1**	g	
Sugar	**1**	g	
Protein	**19**	g	

Diabetic exchange

2 starch, 2 vegetable, 1 lean meat, 1 fat

Mexican Burrito Bake

This recipe uses both chili powder and cumin for flavor and contains no added salt. Chili powder is not simply ground-up dried chilies. Almost all commercial chili powder is composed of pulverized chilies plus dried garlic, cumin, oregano, cloves, coriander and flaked, dry onion. If you'd like to reduce the sodium content of this recipe even more, use chicken broth, canned tomatoes and cheese low in sodium.

6 servings

3/4 cup uncooked long-grain white rice
1/2 teaspoon dried oregano leaves
1 1/2 cups defatted chicken broth
1/4 cup onion, peeled, ends removed and chopped
1/4 cup green pepper, cored, seeded and chopped
1 clove garlic, peeled and minced
1 1/2 teaspoons chili powder
1 can (8 ounces) whole tomatoes, drained and cut up
2 tablespoons green onion, ends removed and sliced
2 tablespoons canned chopped green chilies
1/2 teaspoon ground cumin
1 can (16 ounces) pinto beans, drained
6 whole-wheat 8-inch soft flour tortillas
1 cup shredded part-skim mozzarella cheese
1/2 cup tomato, cored, seeded and chopped

■ In a 2-quart microwave-safe casserole dish, combine the rice, oregano and broth. Cover. Microwave on high for 5 minutes.

Reduce the power setting to 50 percent or medium, and continue cooking 12 to 16 minutes longer, or until the rice is tender and the liquid is absorbed. Set aside, covered.

In a 1-quart casserole dish, combine the onion, green pepper, garlic, chili powder, tomatoes, green onion, chilies and cumin. Mix well. Cover. Microwave on high for 4 minutes.

Add the pinto beans and microwave for 2 more minutes or until the mixture is hot, stirring once. Spoon the bean mixture down the center of each tortilla. Top with rice mixture. Roll up, enclosing the filling.

Place the tortillas seam-side down in a shallow-sided microwave dish. Sprinkle with cheese and chopped tomato. Microwave on high for 3 to 5 minutes, or until the cheese is melted, rotating the dish once. May be served with salsa.

Nutrition Information Per Serving

			% of daily value
Calories	**320**		
Calories from fat	**17**	%	
Fat	**6**	g	9%
Saturated fat	**2**	g	10%
Cholesterol	**11**	mg	4%
Sodium	**709**	mg	30%
Carbohydrate	**52**	g	17%
Fiber	**2**	g	
Sugar	**2**	g	
Protein	**14**	g	

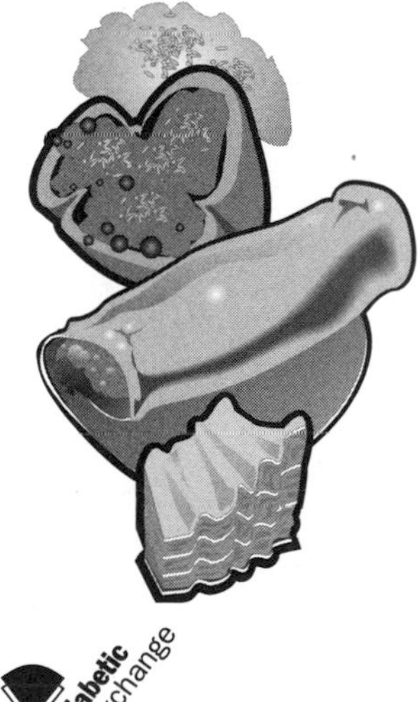

Diabetic exchange

1/2 meat, 3 starch, 1 vegetable

30

Mushroom-Spinach Pasta

Topping your spaghetti with a canned sauce may be quick, but it can translate to a meal high in fat and sodium. Some popular cream sauces can have as many as 80 grams of fat and 1,100 mg of sodium per cup. This tasty recipe for Mushroom-Spinach Pasta is low in both fat and sodium because of the fresh, low-fat and salt-reduced ingredients.

8 servings

2 cups low-fat (1 percent) cottage cheese
6 ounces low-fat cream cheese, softened
Vegetable oil cooking spray
1/2 cup finely chopped onion
1/2 pound fresh mushrooms, cleaned and sliced
1/3 cup dry white wine
1/4 teaspoon dried thyme, crushed
Dash of pepper
1 can (6 1/2 ounces) evaporated skim milk
1 package (10 ounces) frozen chopped spinach, defrosted and well drained
16 ounces spaghetti, cooked according to package directions, omitting salt and fat
1/3 cup freshly grated Parmesan cheese

■ In a food processor fitted with a metal blade, combine the cottage cheese and cream cheese until smooth.

Spray a medium-sized saucepan with the cooking spray.

Add the onion and mushrooms and cook until tender. Add the white wine, thyme and pepper. Stir in the cheese mixture, evaporated skim milk and spinach; heat thoroughly, stirring occasionally.

Place the hot spaghetti on a large platter; top with the sauce and toss gently. Sprinkle with Parmesan cheese.

Cook's note:

For a zestier version, increase the thyme to 1/2 teaspoon and add 1/2 teaspoon garlic powder and a dash of nutmeg. Add these to the recipe with the white wine.

Nutrition Information Per Serving

			% of daily value
Calories	247		
Calories from fat	27	%	
Fat	8	g	12%
Saturated fat	4.5	g	23%
Cholesterol	23	mg	8%
Sodium	454	mg	19%
Carbohydrate	26	g	9%
Fiber	2	g	
Sugar	3	g	
Protein	18	g	

Diabetic exchange

1 1/2 starch, 1 1/2 meat, 1 vegetable

Pepper Mostaccioli

Green bell peppers are in good supply year-round. That's because they ship well and remain firm and fresh for weeks. This filling recipe — with its green strips of color provided by the bell pepper — is best prepared in winter because the ingredients are either dried, canned or abundant when the weather's cold.

4 servings

1 tablespoon olive oil
1 green pepper, washed, cored, seeded, cut into 1/4-inch strips
1 onion, peeled, ends removed, chopped
1 clove garlic, peeled, ends removed, crushed
1 can (14 1/2 ounces) tomatoes
1 teaspoon dried basil leaves
Freshly ground pepper to taste
1 1/2 cups mostaccioli pasta, cooked according to package directions, omitting salt and fat
2 tablespoons Parmesan cheese, grated

■ In a large skillet, heat the oil over medium heat. Saute the green pepper, onion and garlic in oil until tender, about 10 minutes.

Stir in the tomatoes, basil and ground pepper; heat until hot. Toss with the hot mostaccioli and sprinkle with Parmesan cheese.

Nutrition Information — Per Serving

		% of daily value
Calories	**246**	
Calories from fat	**22** %	
Fat	**6** g	9%
Saturated fat	**1** g	5%
Cholesterol	**3** mg	1%
Sodium	**76** mg	3%
Carbohydrate	**42** g	14%
Fiber	**2** g	
Sugar	**5** g	
Protein	**8** g	

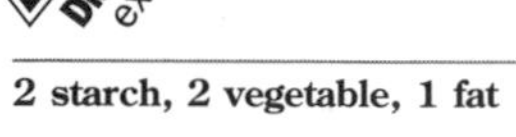

2 starch, 2 vegetable, 1 fat

Spaghetti Verdura

This dish is a wonderful way to use some of summer's fresh produce. Zucchini, bell peppers and basil complement the cheese, spices and pasta. No need to add salt. The anchovy fillets provide plenty of salty flavor.

4 servings

1 tablespoon olive oil
2 small zucchini, washed, ends removed, sliced
2 anchovy fillets, rinsed, patted dry, cut into 2 or 3 pieces
2 large cloves garlic,, unpeeled
2 large red or yellow bell peppers, washed, cored, seeded, coarsely chopped
2 cups canned tomatoes (1 pound can) with juice, coarsely chopped
2 teaspoons capers, drained
2 teaspoons fresh basil, chopped; or 2/3 teaspoon dried
1/4 teaspoon freshly ground black pepper
1 pound spaghetti, cooked according to package directions, omitting salt and fat
1/3 cup freshly grated Romano or Parmesan cheese

■ In a large skillet, heat the olive oil over medium heat. Add the zucchini, anchovies and garlic cloves. Saute, stirring occasionally, 2 to 3 minutes. When the zucchini is soft, add the peppers, tomatoes with juice, capers and basil. Stir well.

Bring to a simmer, cover and cook over medium heat, stirring occasionally, for 10 minutes or until the peppers are tender. Remove the garlic cloves from the vegetable sauce and discard. Stir in the pepper. Serve over cooked spaghetti. Top with cheese.

Nutrition Information Per Serving

			% of daily value
Calories	**308**		
Calories from fat	**20**	%	
Fat	**7**	g	11%
Saturated fat	**1.5**	g	8%
Cholesterol	**9**	mg	3%
Sodium	**486**	mg	20%
Carbohydrate	**52**	g	17%
Fiber	**4.5**	g	
Sugar	**6**	g	
Protein	**12**	g	

Diabetic exchange

2 starch, 4 vegetable, 1 fat

Veggie Pasta Mix

This Veggie Pasta Mix can be prepared with domestic mushrooms or with any of the wild varieties. Either way, this low-fat dish — only 13 percent of its calories come from fat — is packed with vitamins and minerals. When served with zesty French bread, the meal provides ample protein and is a delicious meatless treat.

4 servings

Vegetable oil cooking spray
1 cup broccoli florets, washed
1 cup carrots, peeled, ends removed, thinly sliced
1 cup zucchini, sliced
1/4 cup onion, peeled, ends removed, sliced
1 sweet yellow pepper, cut into thin strips
1 sweet green pepper, cut into thin strips
1/2 cup fresh mushrooms, cleaned, sliced
4 cups spaghetti, cooked and drained
1 small tomato, cut into wedges
2 tablespoons dry vermouth
1/4 cup plus 2 tablespoons grated Parmesan cheese
1 tablespoon fresh parsley, minced
1/4 teaspoon sweet red pepper flakes, optional

Cook's note:

Mushrooms contain only 21 calories per cup and are virtually free of fat and sodium.

■ Spray a large nonstick skillet with cooking spray and place over medium heat until hot. Add the broccoli, carrots, zucchini and onion and saute for 4 minutes. Add the yellow pepper strips, green pepper strips and mushrooms and saute 4 minutes.
Add the cooked pasta, tomato, vermouth and toss gently. Cook until thoroughly heated. Sprinkle with Parmesan cheese, parsley and pepper flakes, if desired, and toss gently. Serve immediately.

Nutrition Information Per Serving

			% of daily value
Calories	**287**		
Calories from fat	**13**	%	
Fat	**4**	g	6%
Saturated fat	**2**	g	10%
Cholesterol	**7**	mg	2%
Sodium	**197**	mg	8%
Carbohydrate	**50**	g	17%
Fiber	**5**	g	
Sugar	**6**	g	
Protein	**13**	g	

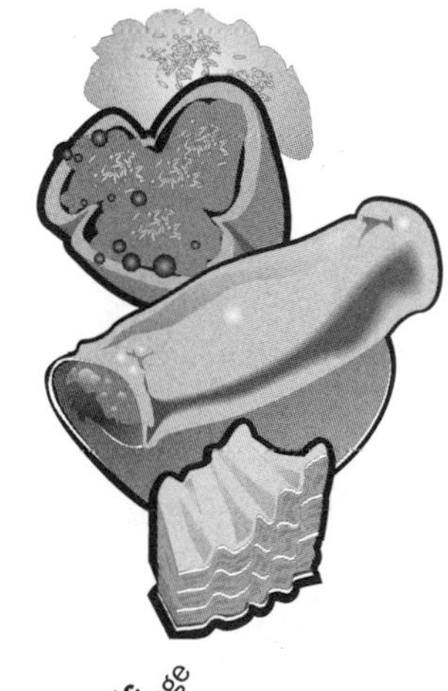

Diabetic exchange

3 starch, 2 vegetable

15

Wild Mushroom Stroganoff

Wild mushrooms take the place of meat in this stroganoff. The meaty texture and woodsy taste of mushrooms are a nutritional bargain. They have only 20 calories per cup and less than 1 gram of fat. They also provide nearly 25 percent of an adult's daily niacin and riboflavin needs.

4 servings

1 tablespoon vegetable oil
4 cups thinly sliced wild mushrooms, such as shiitake, chanterelles, crimini, enoki
1 large onion, peeled, ends removed, chopped
1 clove garlic, peeled, ends removed, minced
1 tablespoon tomato paste
1/4 cup flour
1 1/4 cups beef stock or beef broth
1 cup fat-free sour cream
2 tablespoons cooking sherry
1 tablespoon Worcestershire sauce
1 1/2 pounds yolk-free noodles, cooked according to package directions

■ In a large skillet, heat the oil over medium heat. Add the mushrooms, onion and garlic. Saute 3 to 4 minutes, or until the onion is barely tender.

Add the tomato paste to the skillet and blend in the flour. Slowly add the beef stock or broth and cook, stirring constantly until the mixture thickens.

Stir in the sour cream, sherry and Worcestershire sauce. Heat briefly and serve over the cooked noodles.

Cook's note:

Mushrooms have a long history in cooking. The ancients believed they were created by thunderbolts, perhaps because there were so many mushrooms after it rained. The Egyptian pharaohs decreed mushrooms a royal food.

Nutrition Information Per Serving

			% of daily value
Calories	421		
Calories from fat	11	%	
Fat	5	g	8%
Saturated fat	0.5	g	5%
Cholesterol	4	mg	1%
Sodium	371	mg	15%
Carbohydrate	75	g	25%
Fiber	2	g	
Sugar	3	g	
Protein	16	g	

Diabetic exchange

2 vegetable, 4 starch, 1/4 milk

Baked Ziti

This is a meatless meal everyone will love. Use the marinara sauce for other noodles too, such as spaghetti or colored rotini. You may freeze the sauce for up to 6 months.

8 servings

Vegetable oil cooking spray
1 1/2 cups chopped onion
1/2 cup finely sliced carrots
1/2 tablespoons chopped garlic
4 cups canned tomatoes
Freshly ground pepper to taste
1 tablespoon freshly chopped basil; or 1 teaspoon dried
1/2 tablespoon fresh oregano; or 1/2 teaspoon dried
1/2 tablespoon fresh rosemary; or 1/2 teaspoon dried
1/4 cup fresh chopped parsley; or 1/2 teaspoon dried
1/2 cup fat-free ricotta cheese
1/4 teaspoon crush red pepper flakes
1 pound ziti pasta, cooked according to package directions omitting salt, well drained
3 tablespoons fat-free Parmesan cheese

■ Spray a large heavy skillet with the cooking spray. Over medium-high heat, sauce the onion and carrots until the onion is translucent and golden, about 8 minutes. Add the garlic and tomatoes; cover and simmer for 20 minutes.

Add the pepper, basil, oregano and rosemary. Cover and continue simmering for 30 minutes.

Remove from the heat and stir in the parsley. Allow the mixture to cool. Add the ricotta cheese and red pepper flakes. Preheat the oven to 350 degrees.
In a food processor fitted with a metal blade or blender, process the sauce for 2 minutes or until smooth.

Place the cooked ziti in a 13-by-9-by-2-inch baking dish. Add the processed sauce and stir to combine. Sprinkle with the Parmesan cheese. Bake for 30 minutes or until heated through.

Nutrition Information Per Serving

			% of daily value
Calories	**273**		
Calories from fat	**5**	%	
Fat	**1**	g	2%
Saturated fat	**0**	g	0%
Cholesterol	**1**	mg	1%
Sodium	**294**	mg	12%
Carbohydrate	**53**	g	18%
Fiber	**1.5**	g	
Sugar	**4**	g	
Protein	**12**	g	

Diabetic exchange

3 starch, 1 vegetable

120 minutes

Stuffed Cabbage Leaves

One serving of this meatless entree provides more than 30 percent of the Recommended Dietary Allowance for folic acid. Adequate amounts of folic acid in the diet can decrease the risk for heart disease by decreasing the amount of homocysteine in the blood. Other choices rich in folic acid include orange juice, beets, broccoli, dried beans, peas, wheat germ, spinach and other leafy green vegetables.

6 servings

1 medium cabbage
Boiling water
1 tablespoon vegetable oil
1 medium onion, peeled, ends removed, chopped
1 green bell pepper, washed, cored, seeded, chopped
4 large cloves garlic, peeled, ends removed, minced
1 can (15 ounces) low-sodium tomato sauce
1 can (15 ounces) regular tomato sauce
1 pound light, firm tofu, squeezed dry and crumbled
5 egg whites, lightly beaten
1 cup cooked rice
1/4 cup raisins
1/2 teaspoon paprika
1/2 teaspoon black pepper, divided
Vegetable oil cooking spray
1 medium green bell pepper, washed, cored, sliced into rings
1 medium onion, peeled, ends removed, sliced into rings or half-rings
1/4 cup water

■ Remove the core from the cabbage. Place the whole cabbage in boiling water and steam for 5 minutes. Remove the cabbage and carefully peel off 8 to 12 outer leaves. Set aside.

To prepare the filling: Heat the vegetable oil in a large skillet over medium heat. Add the onion, bell pepper and garlic and cook until tender, about 5 minutes. Meanwhile, in a small bowl, mix together the low-sodium and regular tomato sauce.

Remove the onion mixture from the heat and stir in the tofu, half of the tomato sauce mixture, egg whites, rice, raisins, paprika and 1/4 teaspoon of the black pepper.

Spray a 5-quart casserole dish with the cooking spray. Preheat the oven to 350 degrees.

Place a 1/2 cup of the filling in the center of either 1 large or 2 smaller overlapping cabbage leaves. Fold the ends of the leaf in and roll it around the filling to encase the filling. Repeat the process with the remaining cabbage leaves. Place the stuffed cabbage close together in the prepared casserole dish. For garnish, spread the bell pepper and onion rings evenly over the stuffed cabbage.

To prepare the sauce: In a medium bowl, mix together the remaining tomato sauce, 1/4 teaspoon black pepper and water. Stir in any remaining filling.

Pour the sauce over the stuffed cabbage. Cover and bake for 1 hour. Remove from the oven and serve.

Nutrition Information — Per Serving

			% of daily value
Calories	211		
Calories from fat	6	%	
Fat	2	g	3%
Saturated fat	0	g	0%
Cholesterol	0	mg	0%
Sodium	563	mg	23%
Carbohydrate	38	g	13%
Fiber	5	g	
Sugar	7	g	
Protein	12	g	

1/2 starch, 6 vegetable

Meats

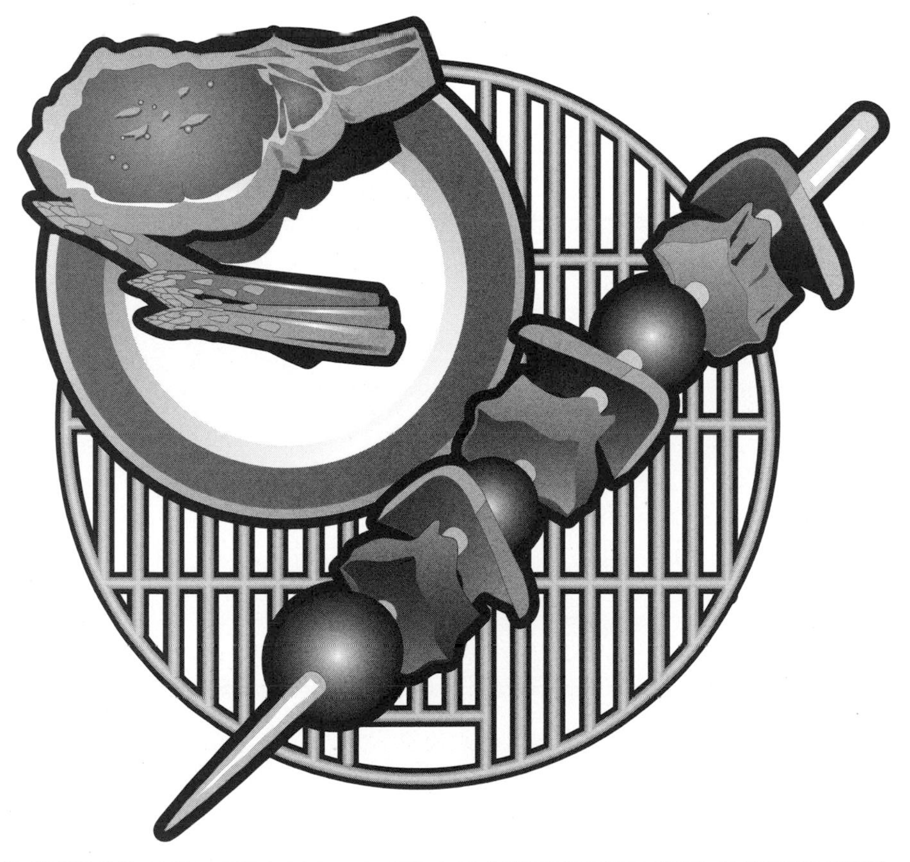

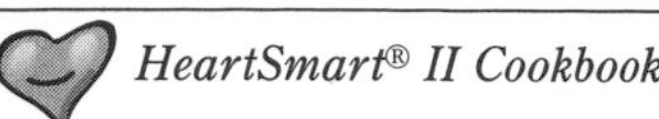

Angel Hair Pork Pasta

The key to choosing Heart Smart® pork is to pay careful attention to the cut of meat you select. Pork tenderloin is the leanest cut, with less than 30 percent of its calories from fat. Stir-frying allows this Angel Hair Pork Pasta to be prepared quickly while preserving all the wonderful flavors of the fresh ingredients.

4 servings

1 tablespoon vegetable oil
3/4 pound pork tenderloin, cut crosswise into 1/8-inch strips
2 medium yellow peppers, washed seeded, cored, ends removed, cut into 1/2-inch strips
1 small zucchini, washed, ends removed, julienned 2 inches long
1 cup mushrooms, cleaned, sliced
1 small onion, peeled, ends removed, diced
8 cherry tomatoes, stemmed, halved
1/2 cup water
1 teaspoon chicken-flavored instant bouillon granules
1/4 teaspoon crushed thyme
1/8 teaspoon ground black pepper
4 ounces fresh angel hair pasta (capellini), cooked according to package directions, omitting salt and fat

■ In a large skillet or wok, heat the vegetable oil over high heat. Add the pork and cook, stirring constantly, 2 to 3 minutes, until the pork is no longer pink. Remove the pork from the skillet and set aside.

Add the pepper strips, zucchini, mushrooms and onion to the skillet. Stir frequently for 3 minutes or until crisp-tender.

Add the tomatoes, water, bouillon, thyme and black pepper to the vegetable mix and bring to a boil. Reduce heat, cover and simmer for 3 minutes. Add the pork and the pasta, tossing until coated with the sauce.

Serve immediately.

Nutrition Information Per Serving

			% of daily value
Calories	205		
Calories from fat	29	%	
Fat	7	g	11%
Saturated fat	1	g	5%
Cholesterol	55	mg	18%
Sodium	233	mg	10%
Carbohydrate	19	g	6%
Fiber	2.5	g	
Sugar	3	g	
Protein	18	g	

Cook's note:

People on a low-fat diet should avoid sausage, bacon and high-fat cuts of pork such as ribs, blade and shoulder.

1 starch, 2 lean meat, 1 vegetable

45

Beef & Vegetable Kabobs

You can include red meat occasionally as part of a Heart Smart® meal plan by choosing lean cuts and limiting portions to 3 ounces. Lean cuts, which are less tender than well-marbled ones, can be tenderized by marinating the meat in an acidic liquid such as lemon juice, vinegar or wine.

4 servings

1/2 cup nonfat Italian dressing
2 tablespoons red wine vinegar
2 teaspoons minced garlic
1/4 teaspoon cumin
1 tablespoon dried hot red pepper flakes
Freshly ground black pepper to taste
1 pound 1/2-inch-thick top round beef, trimmed and cut into 1- inch pieces
16 large cherry tomatoes, washed, stems removed
16 large mushrooms, cleaned
1 green pepper, washed, cored, seeded, cubed into 16 pieces
1 large onion, peeled, ends removed, cubed into 16 chunks

■ To prepare the marinade, combine the Italian dressing, vinegar, garlic, cumin, red pepper flakes and black pepper in a shallow dish or pie plate.

Reserve and set aside a few tablespoons of the marinade to be used in basting.

Place the beef in the marinade, turning to coat thoroughly. Let the beef marinate, covered, in the refrigerator for at least 4 hours or overnight.

Drain the beef and discard the marinade.

Preheat the grill.

Thread the beef and vegetables, alternating them, onto eight 10-inch skewers. Brush the kabobs with the reserved marinade and grill them on a rack set 5 to 6 inches over glowing coals.

Baste them for the first 5 minutes with reserved marinade and turn for 10 to 15 minutes, or until beef is cooked through but still juicy. Discard the remaining marinade.

Nutrition Information Per Serving

			% of daily value
Calories	176		
Calories from fat	22	%	
Fat	4	g	6%
Saturated fat	1.5	g	8%
Cholesterol	54	mg	18%
Sodium	95	mg	4%
Carbohydrate	12	g	4%
Fiber	2.5	g	
Sugar	5	g	
Protein	22	g	

Cook's note:

To prevent bacterial contamination, always marinate meats in the refrigerator and, after draining the meat, throw away the marinade.

Diabetic exchange

3 lean meat, 2 vegetable

Cajun Pork Fried Rice

All meats — including poultry and fish — contain 20 to 25 mg of cholesterol per ounce. Cholesterol remains even after meat is trimmed of all visible fat. In a Heart Smart® diet, use meats in small quantities, as a flavoring for foods.

4 servings

1 tablespoon olive oil
6 ounces cooked lean pork center loin, cubed
1 medium onion, peeled, ends removed, chopped
1 package (10 ounces) frozen cut okra, thawed, drained
2 cups mushrooms, cleaned, thinly sliced
2 stalks celery, washed, ends removed, thinly sliced
1/4 cup red pepper, seeded, cored, chopped
1 clove garlic, peeled, ends removed, minced
2 teaspoons Worcestershire sauce
1/2 teaspoon paprika
1/4 teaspoon ground ginger
1/4 teaspoon dry mustard
1/4 teaspoon Tabasco sauce
1/8 teaspoon thyme, crushed
Dash ground red (cayenne) pepper
3 cups cooked rice, preferably cold
4 egg whites, lightly beaten
2 tablespoons parsley, washed, finely chopped

■ In a large skillet or wok, heat the oil over medium-high heat. Add the pork to the oil and cook, stirring, about 3 minutes until lightly browned.

Add the onion, okra, mushrooms, celery, red pepper and garlic. Cook, stirring occasionally for 5 to 8 minutes until the onion is tender. Stir in Worcestershire sauce, paprika, ginger, mustard, Tabasco, thyme and ground red pepper.

Add the rice. Cook, stirring, until the rice is lightly browned, about 4 minutes.

Push the mixture to the edges of skillet or wok, leaving a space in the center. Add the egg whites to the center. Cook, stirring, until the egg is lightly scrambled. Stir the rice into the eggs.

Sprinkle with parsley.

Nutrition Information Per Serving

			% of daily value
Calories	**356**		
Calories from fat	**15**	%	
Fat	**6**	g	9%
Saturated fat	**1**	g	5%
Cholesterol	**30**	mg	10%
Sodium	**131**	mg	5%
Carbohydrate	**56**	g	19%
Fiber	**4**	g	
Sugar	**4**	g	
Protein	**20**	g	

Pork contains many valuable nutrients such as zinc, iron and B vitamins — especially thiamine.

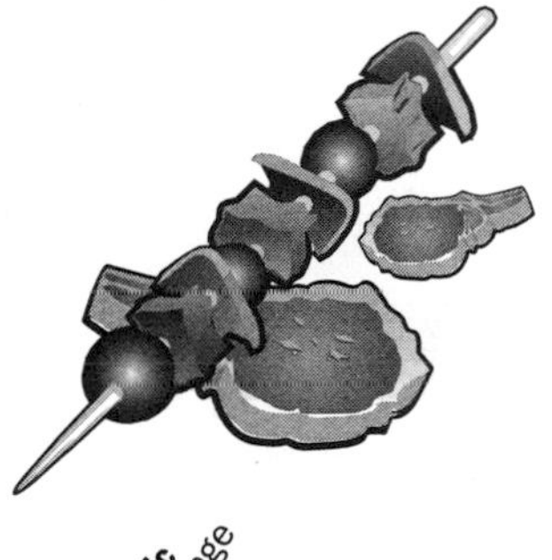

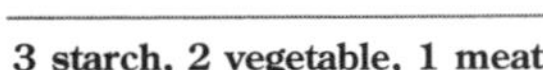

3 starch, 2 vegetable, 1 meat

15 (clock)

Heart Smart® Burgers

It's hard to imagine that something as greasy and full of fat as hamburgers could be included in a Heart Smart® diet. The difference here, of course, is not to use only ground beef in the recipe. By mixing in a half-portion of ground turkey, the amount of fat per serving drops significantly.

4 servings

1/2 pound ground round beef
1/2 pound ground turkey breast
1/4 cup diced green onions, including green tops
1/4 cup diced green pepper, seeded
1/4 teaspoon Mrs. Dash seasoning
2 egg whites, beaten
1 tablespoon Worcestershire sauce
1 teaspoon prepared mustard
8 onion slices
4 tomato slices
1 cup alfalfa sprouts
4 whole-wheat hamburger buns

Nutrition Information Per Serving

			% of daily value
Calories	273		
Calories from fat	35	%	
Fat	11	g	17%
Saturated fat	3.5	g	18%
Cholesterol	42	mg	14%
Sodium	365	mg	15%
Carbohydrate	24	g	8%
Fiber	1.5	g	
Sugar	4	g	
Protein	19	g	

■ Prepare the charcoal grill. Mix the ground round and the ground turkey in a large bowl. Add the green onion, green pepper, Mrs. Dash seasoning, egg whites, Worcestershire sauce and mustard and mix thoroughly.

Divide the mixture into 4 portions and form into patties.

Cook the patties over the grill until well-done — at least 8 to 10 minutes — because the turkey needs to be cooked thoroughly. Watch carefully and move the burgers away from the coals if necessary to allow them to cook all the way through. Flip only once when the juice emerges from the upper side of the burger.

Serve on a whole-wheat hamburger bun with 2 slices of onion, 1 slice of tomato and about 1/4 cup of alfalfa sprouts for each burger.

Diabetic exchange

2 starch, 2 meat

Heart Smart® Meat Loaf

Most of us gain weight because our metabolisms slow as we age. But much of that slowdown can be attributed to a decrease in activity. Stay active and adjust your caloric intake so you are not gaining that pound or two each year. This recipe for Heart Smart® Meat Loaf will help in your battle with the bulge and still satisfy your craving for this traditional favorite.

8 servings

Vegetable oil cooking spray
1 medium onion, peeled, ends removed, finely diced
1 medium green pepper, washed, cored, seeded, finely diced
1 large celery rib, washed, ends removed, finely diced
1 teaspoon thyme
1 pound ground turkey breast or extra-lean ground turkey breast
1 pound lean ground beef
1/2 cup rolled oats
2/3 cup ketchup, divided
2 egg whites
1 1/2 teaspoons freshly ground pepper

■ Spray a large skillet with the cooking spray.

Saute the onion, green pepper, celery and thyme over medium heat for 5 to 10 minutes; add water if the pan becomes dry. Remove from the heat and cool.

Meanwhile, preheat the oven to 350 degrees.

In a large bowl, combine the onion mixture, turkey and beef. Add the rolled oats, 1/3 cup of ketchup, the egg whites and pepper; mix well.

Spray a 9-by-13-inch shallow baking dish with the cooking spray. Spoon the mixture into the baking dish and shape it into a flat loaf about 2 inches high. Smooth the top with the back of a spoon and spread the remaining 1/3 cup of ketchup on top.

Bake for 45 minutes to 1 hour, or until the loaf is just cooked through and shows no trace of pink, or until a meat thermometer registers 145 degrees in the loaf's center.

Remove from the oven and let stand 10 minutes before slicing.

Nutrition Information Per Serving

			% of daily value
Calories	221		
Calories from fat	34	%	
Fat	8	g	12%
Saturated fat	3	g	15%
Cholesterol	65	mg	22%
Sodium	330	mg	14%
Carbohydrate	10	g	3%
Fiber	0.5	g	
Sugar	0.5	g	
Protein	28	g	

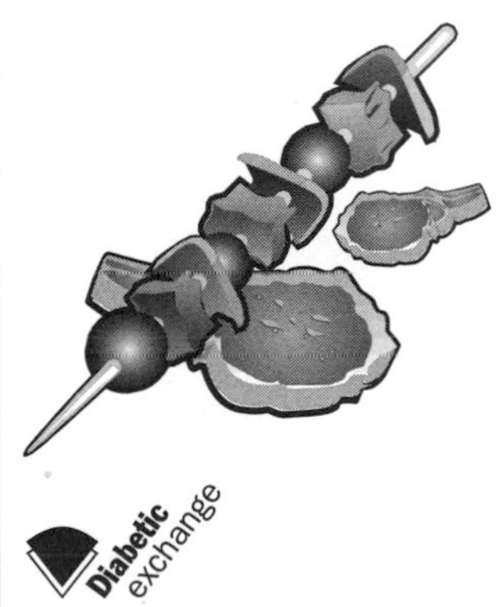

Diabetic exchange

1/2 starch, 4 lean meat

15 minutes

Herbed Flank Steak

When grilling, be sure to preheat the coals. A light gray coating of ash on the coals assures a consistent heat that will cook the Herbed Flank Steak evenly, preserving all the flavorful juices.

6 servings

1 1/2 pounds flank steak
3/4 cup dry red wine
2 tablespoons cooking oil
1/4 cup lemon juice
1/4 cup minced onion
1 to 2 tablespoons cracked black pepper
2 teaspoons crushed dried thyme
1 teaspoon crushed dried marjoram

Nutrition Information Per Serving

			% of daily value
Calories	**199**		
Calories from fat	**35**	%	
Fat	**8**	g	12%
Saturated fat	**2**	g	10%
Cholesterol	**72**	mg	24%
Sodium	**54**	mg	2%
Carbohydrate	**2**	g	1%
Fiber	**0.5**	g	
Sugar	**0**	g	
Protein	**27**	g	

■ Score the steak by making very thin slashes, about 1-inch apart, diagonally across the grain. Set aside.

To prepare the marinade: In a plastic sealable bag or shallow baking dish, combine the red wine, oil, lemon juice, onion, pepper, thyme and marjoram. Add the steak and seal the bag or cover the baking dish. Marinate in the refrigerator at least 6 hours or overnight, turning several times.

At serving time, preheat the grill or broiler. Remove the steak from the marinade and discard the marinade. To grill, place the steak on an uncovered grill directly over medium coals for 5 minutes. To broil, place the steak on the broiler pan fitted with a rack 6 inches from the heat for 5 minutes. For either preparation, turn and grill the steak to desired doneness about 3 minutes on the second side.

Cook's note:

Be sure to grill meat thoroughly. The meat juices should run clear and the flesh should not be pink. Thick cuts, such as steaks, should reach 160 degrees on a meat thermometer; poultry should reach 180 degrees.

Diabetic exchange

4 meat

Lamb Kabobs with Couscous

These quick and easy kabobs use marinated lamb instead of beef paired with vegetables. Served with couscous, a granular semolina, these kabobs will be a hit with your backyard barbecue guests.

4 servings

1/4 cup low-calorie Italian dressing
1/4 cup lemon juice
2 tablespoons finely chopped onion
1 clove garlic, peeled, ends removed, minced
1/2 teaspoon marjoram
1/2 teaspoon thyme
1/2 teaspoon pepper
1 pound lean boneless lamb, cut into 1-inch chunks
8 to 12 large mushroom caps
1/2 medium zucchini, cut into 1/2-inch chunks
1 red bell pepper, cut into squares
2 cups couscous, cooked according to package directions, omitting salt and fat
8 wooden skewers

■ In a plastic sealable bag or medium bowl, combine the Italian dressing, lemon juice, onion, garlic, marjoram, thyme and pepper.

Place the lamb in the plastic bag or bowl with the marinade. Refrigerate for 1 hour. Remove the lamb from the marinade, reserving the marinade. Preheat the grill or broiler.

To assemble the kabobs: Evenly divide the lamb, mushroom caps, zucchini and red bell peppers onto the skewers. Brush the kabobs with reserved marinade. Grill or broil 4 inches from the heat source for 6 to 10 minutes, turning once.

Serve the kabobs with couscous.

Nutrition Information Per Serving

			% of daily value
Calories	**315**		
Calories from fat	**29**	%	
Fat	**10**	g	15%
Saturated fat	**3**	g	15%
Cholesterol	**79**	mg	26%
Sodium	**192**	mg	8%
Carbohydrate	**27**	g	9%
Fiber	**6**	g	
Sugar	**2**	g	
Protein	**29**	g	

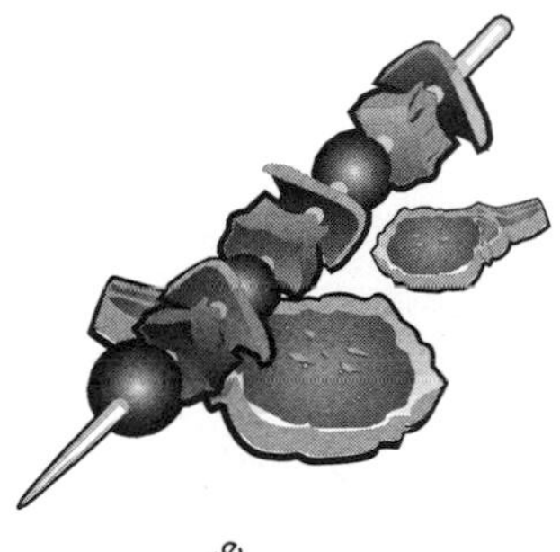

3 lean meat, 1 1/2 starch, 1 vegetable

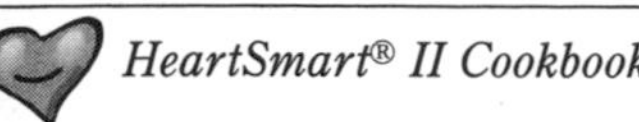

Orange Lamb Stuffed with Spinach & Mint

When cooking lamb, the American Lamb Council recommends the following herbs and spices to best enhance the meat's distinctive flavor: parsley, rosemary, basil, marjoram, thyme, oregano, mustard, mint, coriander, caraway, garlic, curry, allspice and cloves.

10 servings

6 cloves garlic, peeled, ends removed, divided
Vegetable oil cooking spray
1 pound spinach, rinsed well, cooked according to package directions, well drained and squeezed dry
1 1/2 to 2 cups coarsely chopped mint leaves
Grated zest of two oranges (about 3 tablespoons)
1 teaspoon dried thyme leaves
1 teaspoon freshly ground black pepper
1/4 teaspoon cinnamon
2 egg whites, well beaten
1 cup fresh orange juice
1 cup dry white wine
1 tablespoon Dijon mustard
1 tablespoon crumbled, dried rosemary
1 teaspoon coarsely ground black pepper
1 leg of lamb, butterflied (about 5 pounds total weight after the bone is removed and the fat is trimmed)
8 to 10 sprigs mint, washed, dried, optional

■ Preheat the oven to 400 degrees.

Finely chop four cloves of the garlic.

Spray a small nonstick skillet with the cooking spray. Add the garlic and saute over low heat, about 5 minutes.

Transfer the garlic to a medium-size bowl and add the cooked and well-drained spinach, mint leaves, orange zest, thyme, pepper and cinnamon.

Pour in the egg whites and blend well. Set the stuffing aside.

Mince the remaining two garlic cloves.

In a medium-size bowl, combine the minced garlic with the orange juice, wine, mustard, rosemary and black pepper. Mix thoroughly and set the marinade aside.

Lay the lamb out on a flat surface. With a narrow spatula or knife, spread the stuffing over the lamb. Carefully roll the lamb up lengthwise, forming a long, thin roast. Tie it at intervals with kitchen string.

Place the lamb, seam side down, in a shallow roasting pan. Pour the orange juice marinade over the lamb.

Roast for 20 minutes.

Reduce the heat to 350 degrees and roast another 40 minutes for medium-rare. Baste the meat with the pan juices several times during roasting. Remove the lamb from the oven and let it rest, loosely covered with foil, for 15 minutes.

Cut the lamb into 1/2- to 3/4-inch-thick slices. Place on serving plates and garnish each serving with a mint sprig.

Cook's note:

You can generally tell the age of a lamb by the weight of its leg. The leg of a spring lamb weighs 4 to 7 pounds; a winter leg is older and weighs up to 9 pounds.

Nutrition Information Per Serving

			% of daily value
Calories	260		
Calories from fat	32	%	
Fat	9	g	14%
Saturated fat	3	g	15%
Cholesterol	101	mg	34%
Sodium	126	mg	5%
Carbohydrate	5	g	2%
Fiber	1.5	g	
Sugar	2	g	
Protein	34	g	

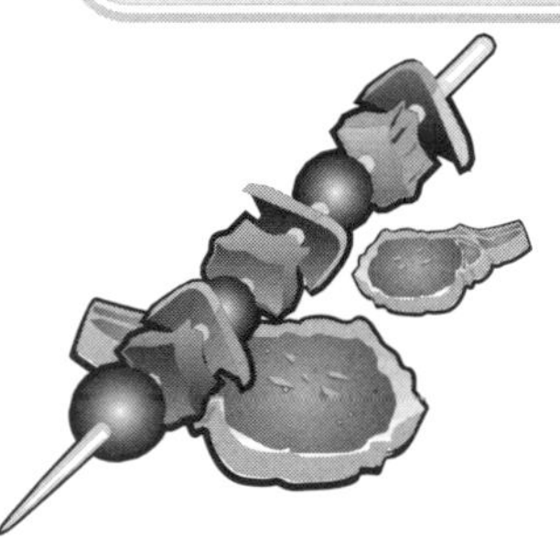

4 1/2 lean meat, 1 vegetable

Beef & Asparagus Salad

To save time, purchase lean roast beef at a deli for this recipe.

6 servings

1/4 cup red wine vinegar
1 1/2 tablespoons water
1 tablespoon Dijon mustard
2 teaspoons olive oil
1 cup asparagus, cleaned, woody ends removed, sliced diagonally into 1-inch pieces
1 quart boiling water
1 quart ice water
4 cups torn salad greens, washed, dried
1 cup mushrooms, cleaned, sliced
1 cup sweet red pepper, washed, cored, seeded, julienned
1 cup red onion, peeled, ends removed, sliced
3/4 pound lean roast beef, sliced into thin shreds

■ In a jar with a tight-fitting lid, combine the red wine vinegar, water, Dijon mustard and olive oil. Shake well.

Steam the asparagus in boiling water for 3 to 5 minutes. Remove from the heat and drain. Immediately place the drained asparagus into ice water. Drain well.

To serve, arrange the greens, asparagus, mushrooms, red pepper and red onion on a platter or individual serving dishes. Place the roast beef on top. Drizzle with the salad dressing.

Nutrition Information Per Serving

			% of daily value
Calories	**152**		
Calories from fat	**30**	%	
Fat	**5**	g	8%
Saturated fat	**1**	g	5%
Cholesterol	**46**	mg	15%
Sodium	**246**	mg	10%
Carbohydrate	**8**	g	3%
Fiber	**2**	g	
Sugar	**2**	g	
Protein	**15**	g	

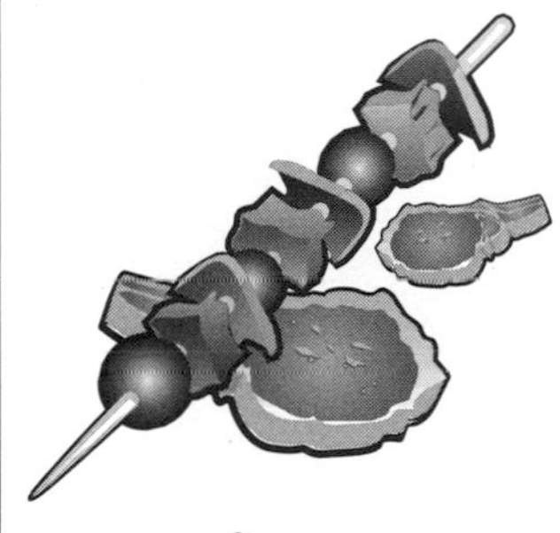

2 lean meat, 2 vegetable

30

Pepper Steak

Using the freezer to quick-chill the round steak in this recipe makes slicing it into strips and trimming away fat much easier. This preparation method lets all the flavor from the meat come through without too much fat.

4 servings

- *1 pound boneless top round steak, completely trimmed and partially frozen for easy slicing (about 30 to 45 minutes in the freezer)*
- *2 cloves garlic, minced*
- *2 tablespoons reduced-sodium soy sauce*
- *2 teaspoons cornstarch*
- *1 teaspoon dry sherry*
- *1 tablespoon vegetable oil*
- *2 medium red or green bell peppers, seeded and cut into 1/2-inch squares*
- *1 teaspoon fresh ginger root, minced*
- *2 cups hot cooked white or brown rice*

■ Remove the round steak from the freezer and slice diagonally across the grain to make 1/4-inch strips; set aside. In a medium-size bowl, combine the garlic, soy sauce, cornstarch and sherry. Add the steak slices and toss to coat well. Cover and refrigerate for up to 6 hours.

Heat the oil in a wok or heavy skillet over high heat for 1 minute. Reduce the heat to moderate. Add the pepper squares and stir-fry for 2 to 3 minutes. Remove the peppers from the pan and set aside. Add the ginger, stir for a few seconds, then add the steak mixture. Stir-fry for 3 minutes, or until the meat is no longer pink. Stir in the peppers and serve immediately with rice.

Nutrition Information Per Serving

			% of daily value
Calories	**280**		
Calories from fat	**24**	%	
Fat	**8**	g	12%
Saturated fat	**1.5**	g	8%
Cholesterol	**54**	mg	18%
Sodium	**321**	mg	13%
Carbohydrate	**27**	g	9%
Fiber	**1**	g	
Sugar	**1**	g	
Protein	**23**	g	

Diabetic exchange

3 lean meat, 1 1/2 starch, 1 vegetable

Salisbury Steak with Vegetable Sauce

Being Heart Smart® does not mean eliminating red meat from your diet. It does mean using lean cuts and small portions. Salisbury steak is a great winter meal. Trim down the fat content by using lean ground beef and lean ground turkey. Stretch the meat by adding onion, celery, apples and bread crumbs.

6 servings

Meat mixture:

Vegetable oil cooking spray
1 1/2 cups onion, peeled, ends removed, chopped
1 1/2 cups celery, washed, ends removed, minced
2 apples (about 1 pound), cored, unpeeled, cut into 1/2-inch cubes
1 pound lean ground beef
1/2 pound ground turkey breast
3 egg whites
2 to 3 cloves garlic, peeled, ends removed, crushed or finely chopped (about 1 teaspoon)
1/2 teaspoon freshly ground pepper
1 1/2 cups fresh bread crumbs (2 to 3 slices firm, fresh bread)

Sauce:

2 medium-size carrots, peeled, ends removed
1 medium to large onion, peeled, ends removed
2 cups water
1 tablespoon light soy sauce
1/4 teaspoon freshly ground black pepper
1 1/2 tablespoons tomato paste
1/4 teaspoon Tabasco sauce

■ Spray a large skillet with the cooking spray. Add the onion and celery and saute for 4 to 5 minutes over medium heat, until the vegetables are translucent. Add the apples to celery-onion mixture and set aside. Place the ground beef and turkey in a large bowl. Add the celery-onion mixture, egg whites, garlic and pepper. Mix well.

Add the bread crumbs to the meat mixture and mix well.

Dampen your hands with water and form the meat mixture into 6 large patties, each weighing approximately 4 ounces. Arrange in a large skillet so there is a little space between the patties and cook 20 minutes, turning once.

To prepare the sauce: Using a food processor or by hand, chop the carrots and onion. You should have 2 cups total. Transfer the vegetables to a medium saucepan and add the water, soy sauce, pepper, tomato paste and Tabasco. Bring to a boil, reduce heat and boil gently for 5 minutes.

When the patties have cooked for 20 minutes, drain the fat. Spoon the sauce over and around the patties and cook at medium heat for 10 minutes. Serve warm.

Nutrition Information Per Serving

			% of daily value
Calories	360		
Calories from fat	27	%	
Fat	11	g	17%
Saturated fat	4	g	20%
Cholesterol	71	mg	24%
Sodium	328	mg	14%
Carbohydrate	40	g	13%
Fiber	6	g	
Sugar	24	g	
Protein	29	g	

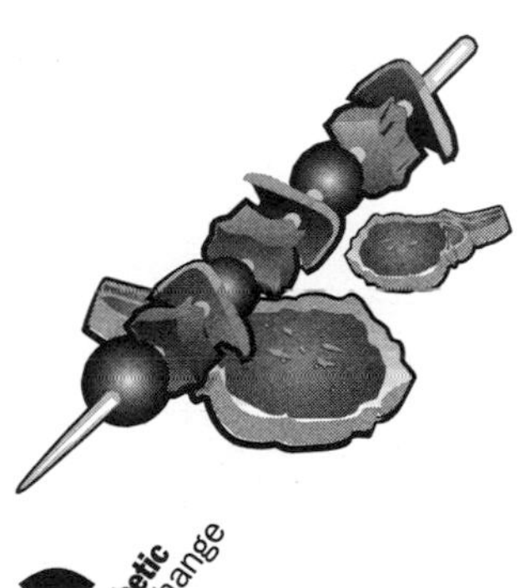

Diabetic exchange

3 lean meat, 2 starch, 1 vegetable

30

Sloppy Joes

Nothing could be simpler than cooking up some lean ground beef and turkey and preparing this children's favorite. Portions go a long way with all the added flavorful ingredients.

8 servings

8 ounces ground turkey breast
8 ounces lean ground beef
1 small onion, peeled, ends removed, chopped
1 stalk celery, washed, ends removed, chopped
6 ounces tomato paste
1/4 cup ketchup
1 tablespoon prepared mustard
1 tablespoon vinegar
1 tablespoon sugar
10 3/4 ounces chicken gumbo soup concentrate
1 tablespoon barbecue sauce
8 hamburger buns

■ In a large skillet over medium heat, brown the ground turkey and the ground beef. Drain the fat.

Add the onion and celery to the meat mixture and cook until soft, about 5 minutes.

Add the tomato paste, ketchup, mustard, vinegar, sugar, chicken gumbo soup concentrate and barbecue sauce.

Bring to a boil. Reduce the héat and simmer 5 to 10 minutes.

Serve on hamburger buns.

Nutrition Information Per Serving

			% of daily value
Calories	**253**		
Calories from fat	**28**	%	
Fat	**8**	g	14%
Saturated fat	**2.5**	g	13%
Cholesterol	**31**	mg	10%
Sodium	**778**	mg	32%
Carbohydrate	**31**	g	10%
Fiber	**2.5**	g	
Sugar	**6**	g	
Protein	**15**	g	

Diabetic exchange

1 1/2 meats, 1/2 vegetable, 2 starch

Hawaiian Ginger Pork

The Polynesian traders had a great influence on the cuisine of Hawaii. They brought ginger, guavas, papayas and Hawaii's most famous crop, pineapples, to the islands. They also brought pigs and possibly chickens because there was no native game.

4 servings

1 tablespoon vegetable oil
3/4 pound pork tenderloin, trimmed, sliced 1/2-inch thick
1 can (20 ounces) pineapple chunks in their own juice, drained, liquid reserved
2 tablespoons brown sugar
1/4 teaspoon ginger
2 medium carrots, peeled, ends removed, sliced
1 medium green pepper, washed, cored, cut into 1-inch pieces
1 tablespoon cornstarch

Nutrition Information Per Serving

		% of daily value
Calories	**292**	
Calories from fat	**24** %	
Fat	**8** g	12%
Saturated fat	**2** g	10%
Cholesterol	**79** mg	26%
Sodium	**75** mg	3%
Carbohydrate	**31** g	10%
Fiber	**4** g	
Sugar	**9** g	
Protein	**25** g	

■ In a large skillet, heat the oil over medium-high heat until hot. Add the pork slices and cook 2 to 3 minutes on each side or until browned. Remove the pork from the skillet.

Add 1/2 cup of the reserved pineapple liquid, brown sugar and ginger to the skillet; blend well.

Add the carrots to the skillet, turn to coat with liquid. Add the pork slices.

Bring to boil; reduce heat to low. Cover, simmer for 15 minutes, or until the carrots are tender. Stir in the green pepper and pineapple chunks. Cover and simmer an additional 5 minutes. Transfer the pork to warm platter.

In a small bowl, stir the cornstarch into the remaining pineapple liquid until dissolved. Gradually stir into the mixture in the skillet.

Cook and stir over medium-high heat until the sauce is bubbly and thickened, at least 3 minutes. Spoon the sauce over the pork.

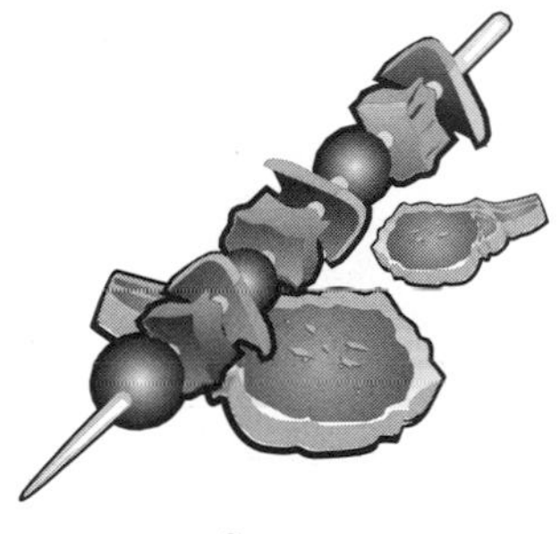

3 lean meat, 1 1/2 fruit, 1 1/2 vegetable

60

Stuffed Pork Tenderloin

Even though it contains more saturated fat than poultry, a 4-ounce serving of pork easily can be included in a low-fat diet. This Stuffed Pork Tenderloin is elegant enough for a gourmet, yet only has 237 calories, 23 percent of those from fat.

4 servings

1 teaspoon olive oil
1/4 pound mushrooms, cleaned, chopped
1/4 cup onion, peeled, ends removed, finely chopped
3/4 pound pork tenderloin, trimmed of fat
1/2 teaspoon ground black pepper
10 ounces frozen spinach, thawed, drained
1 tablespoon fresh marjoram, washed, dried, chopped; or 1 teaspoon dried
1 cup defatted chicken broth
1 cup dry white wine, divided
2 tablespoons fresh lemon juice
1 teaspoon cornstarch

■ Preheat the oven to 375 degrees.

In a large skillet, heat the oil. Add the mushrooms and onion and cook over medium heat, stirring frequently, until almost all of the moisture evaporates.

Cut the tenderloin cylinder almost in half lengthwise, stopping 1/2 inch before it's cut through. Then open the pork and place it, cut side down, on the work surface. Cover with a piece of plastic wrap and pound it with a wooden mallet until the pork has a rectangular shape and is about 1/2-inch thick.

Spread the mushroom mixture over the pork, leaving about 1/4 inch clear on all sides. Sprinkle with pepper evenly over the mushroom mixture. Arrange the spinach on top and sprinkle marjoram over the spinach.

Roll up the pork from a long side and tie it with kitchen string. Place the pork in a roasting pan and pour the broth over it, along with 1/2 cup of the wine and the lemon juice. Roast the pork for 45 minutes, basting several times with the cooking juices.

Remove the pork from the oven. Place it on a serving plate and keep it warm. Pour the cooking liquid into a separator. Let the fat rise, then discard it. Place the defatted liquid into a medium-size saucepan and simmer it over medium heat.

In a small bowl, mix the cornstarch with the remaining 1/2 cup of wine and stir it into the simmering liquid. Cook, stirring, for 2 minutes. Serve in a gravy boat.

Put the pork on a cutting board, cut away the string and slice the pork into rounds. Arrange the slices on a heated serving plate and serve with the sauce.

Cook's note:

Because of changes in the breeding and feeding of hogs, many cuts of pork have 50 percent less fat than they did 25 years ago. The leanest is pork tenderloin, which has less than 30 percent of its calories from fat.

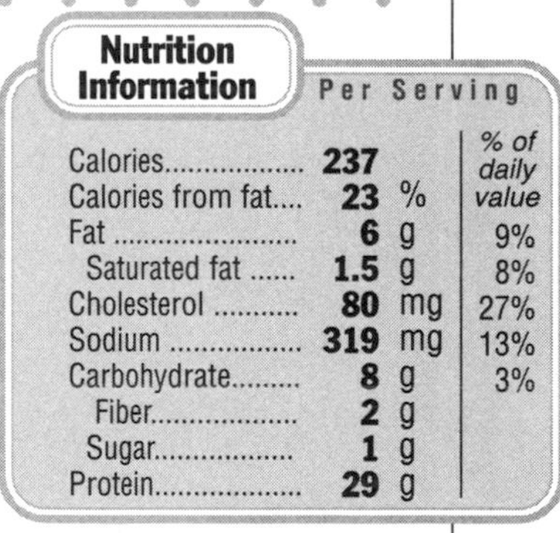

Nutrition Information Per Serving

			% of daily value
Calories	**237**		
Calories from fat	**23**	%	
Fat	**6**	g	9%
Saturated fat	**1.5**	g	8%
Cholesterol	**80**	mg	27%
Sodium	**319**	mg	13%
Carbohydrate	**8**	g	3%
Fiber	**2**	g	
Sugar	**1**	g	
Protein	**29**	g	

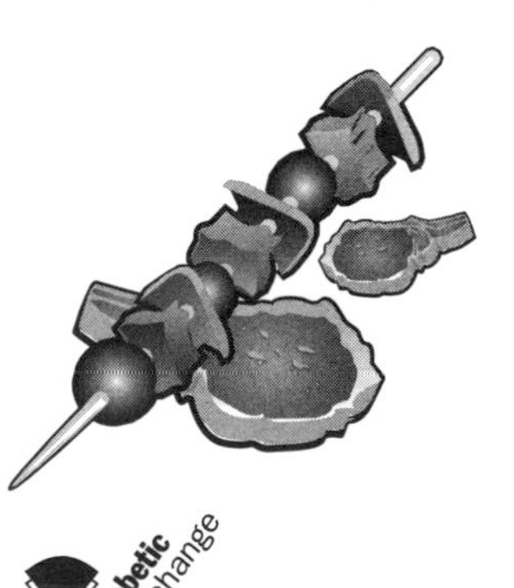

4 lean meat, 1/2 vegetable

Teriyaki Pork Chops

Pork chops are a good Heart Smart® choice because the portions generally are small, the presence of a bone guarantees a strong meat flavor, and it's easy to trim off the extra fat along the edges. Other lean cuts of pork include the center loin, fresh pork leg and lean ham.

4 servings

1/3 cup light soy sauce
2 1/2 tablespoons honey
1 teaspoon fresh ginger, peeled, end removed, grated; or 1/2 teaspoon ground ginger
2 tablespoons dry sherry
1 clove garlic, peeled, ends removed, minced or pressed
2 green onions (including tops), washed, ends removed, thinly sliced
4 thinly cut pork chops (4 ounces each), trimmed

■ In a plastic sealable bag or baking dish, combine the soy sauce, honey, ginger, sherry, garlic and green onion. Mix well. Add the pork chops. Seal the bag or cover the dish and refrigerate, turning occasionally, for 4 hours or overnight.

Just before serving, preheat the grill or broiler.

Grill the pork chops over medium-hot coals for 3 to 4 minutes. Or place the marinated pork chops on the rack of a broiler pan and broil for 3 to 4 minutes. Turn the chops and grill or broil for 3 to 4 minutes on the other side or until the meat is no longer pink. Remove from the grill or broiler and serve.

Nutrition Information Per Serving

			% of daily value
Calories	**226**		
Calories from fat	**34**	%	
Fat	**9**	g	14%
Saturated fat	**3**	g	15%
Cholesterol	**59**	mg	20%
Sodium	**788**	mg	33%
Carbohydrate	**13**	g	4%
Fiber	**trace**	g	
Sugar	**11**	g	
Protein	**19**	g	

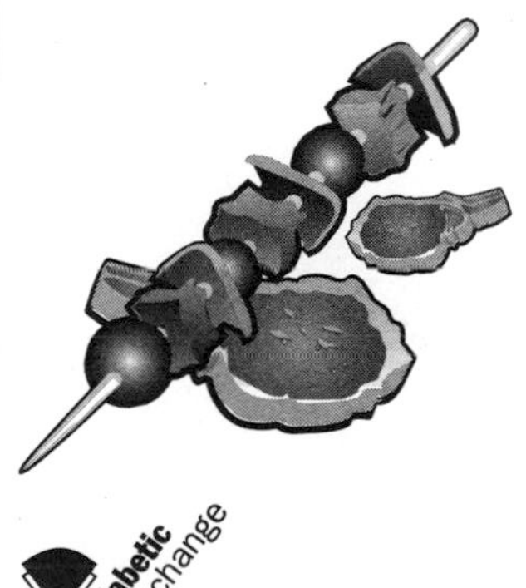
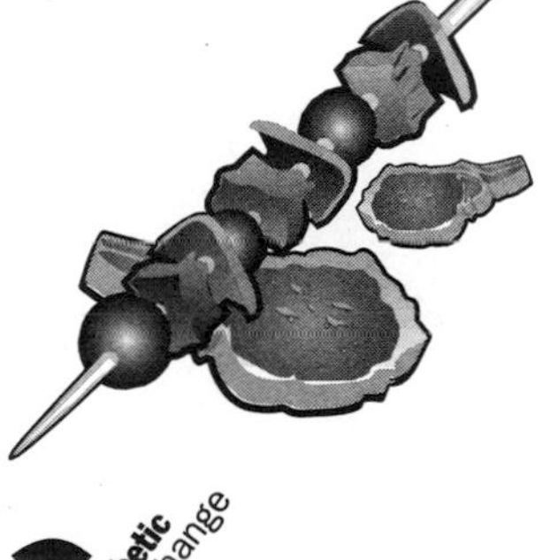

Diabetic exchange

2 1/2 meat, 1 starch

45

Veal Marengo

For most people, following a low-fat diet is the best way to keep cholesterol under control. That means limiting animal products, such as red meat, poultry, whole milk and whole-milk cheeses. Even if these animal foods are low in fat, they still contain cholesterol. So the American Heart Association recommends no more than 6 ounces of red meat, poultry or fish per day.

4 servings

1 pound veal steak, partially frozen and cut diagonally into thin strips
1/4 cup unsifted flour
1 tablespoon vegetable oil
2 medium carrots, peeled, ends removed, thinly sliced
2 medium onions, peeled, ends removed, quartered
2 cups sliced mushrooms
3/4 cup tomato juice
1/4 cup dry white wine
1 teaspoon beef-flavored instant bouillon
1/2 teaspoon dried thyme
1/8 teaspoon pepper
1 bay leaf
2 cups cooked rice (2/3 cup raw)

■ In a plastic sealable bag, combine the veal and flour. Seal the bag and shake to coat.

In a large skillet, heat the vegetable oil over medium heat. Brown the floured veal. Add the carrots and onion. Cook over medium heat, stirring until the onion is tender. Add the mushrooms, tomato juice, wine, bouillon, thyme, pepper and bay leaf.

Cover and simmer 30 minutes. Remove the bay leaf and serve. Serve with 1/2-cup cooked rice.

Nutrition Information Per Serving

			% of daily value
Calories	384		
Calories from fat	21	%	
Fat	9	g	14%
Saturated fat	2.5	g	13%
Cholesterol	89	mg	30%
Sodium	472	mg	20%
Carbohydrate	44	g	15%
Fiber	4.5	g	
Sugar	6	g	
Protein	28	g	

Cook's note:

Cholesterol is a fat-like substance found in the cells of all animals. It is essential for life, but the body makes all we require. Elevated blood cholesterol is associated with an increased risk of heart disease.

Diabetic exchange

2 1/2 meat, 2 starch, 2 vegetable

Seafood

Asparagus, Shrimp & Penne with Saffron Sauce

This is the perfect dish to welcome a long-awaited spring. Light and filling, it takes advantage of fresh spring asparagus.

8 servings

2/3 cup dry white wine
1/4 teaspoon saffron threads
3 cups water
2 pounds medium asparagus, washed, trimmed, cut diagonally into 1-inch pieces
1 tablespoon vegetable oil
1 pound medium shrimp, peeled, deveined
1/4 cup shallots, peeled, ends removed, minced
1 tablespoon cornstarch
1 1/2 cups evaporated skim milk
3/4 cup chicken broth or canned low-sodium chicken broth
Freshly ground black pepper to taste
1 pound penne macaroni or other pasta, cooked according to package directions, drained
1/4 cup fresh chives or fresh chervil, washed, dried, minced

■ In a small bowl, combine the white wine and saffron threads. Let steep for 20 minutes. In a medium skillet, bring the water to a boil. Add the asparagus pieces, cover and cook just until fork tender, about 3 minutes.

Drain well.

Heat the oil in a large skillet. Add the shrimp and cook over moderately high heat. As the shrimp turns opaque, about 1 1/2 minutes, turn and cook the other side, about 1 1/2 minutes. Transfer the shrimp to a plate.

To the same skillet, add the saffron-flavored wine, shallots and cornstarch. Whisk until lump-free. Bring to a boil. Stir in the milk and broth; simmer over moderate heat, stirring occasionally, about 7 minutes.

Stir in the asparagus and shrimp; simmer for 2 minutes. Season with pepper, add the cooked pasta and toss to combine. Garnish with chives or chervil and serve hot.

Nutrition Information Per Serving

			% of daily value
Calories	**342**		
Calories from fat	**11**	%	
Fat	**4**	g	6%
Saturated fat	**1**	g	5%
Cholesterol	**111**	mg	37%
Sodium	**242**	mg	10%
Carbohydrate	**49**	g	16%
Fiber	**trace**	g	
Sugar	**1**	g	
Protein	**24**	g	

Diabetic exchange

2 1/2 starch, 1 vegetable, 1 1/2 lean meat, 1/2 milk

90 minutes

Broiled Swordfish with Passion Fruit Sauce

Passion fruit has a flavor that can be enjoyed anytime, because it is produced and shipped year-round. It can be eaten by itself; added to ice milk, yogurt, salad dressing or fruit salad; or seeded and used to flavor other foods. You'll know that passion fruit is ripe if it's wrinkled but not cracked or mushy.

4 servings

2 to 3 passion fruits (to yield 1/4 cup juice)
1 teaspoon cornstarch
1/8 teaspoon ground red (cayenne) pepper, or to taste
1/4 cup fresh orange juice
3 tablespoons diced red onion
1 tablespoon light rum
1/2 teaspoon sugar, or to taste
1 1/4 pounds swordfish steaks, cut into 4 equal portions, washed, patted dry
Vegetable oil cooking spray
2 tablespoons water
2 small Kirby (pickling) cucumbers, ends removed, skin peeled in alternating strips, sliced
1 bunch watercress, trimmed, washed and dried (about 2 cups)
1 teaspoon balsamic vinegar
1 teaspoon vegetable oil

■ Cut the tops from the passion fruits, and scrape out the pulp into the bowl of a food processor fitted with a metal blade. Process the pulp until liquefied, then strain through a sieve to remove the seeds. Or work the pulp through a sieve, pressing hard with the back of a spoon to separate the pulp from the seeds.

Set the juice and seeds aside.

In a medium bowl or plastic sealable bag, combine the cornstarch and ground red pepper. Gradually stir in orange juice, onion, rum and 1/4 cup of the passion fruit juice. Add the sugar and additional ground red pepper to taste. Make sure the sauce is lump-free.

Set the swordfish steaks in a shallow dish or plastic sealable bag and cover with the passion fruit mixture. Cover the dish or seal the bag. Marinate in the refrigerator for 20 to 30 minutes, occasionally spooning the liquid over the steaks.

Preheat the grill or broiler. Remove the swordfish from the marinade, reserving the marinade. Spray the grill or broiler with the cooking spray. Grill the swordfish on each side until the flesh is opaque, about 3 to 4 minutes, basting each side once with a little of the reserved marinade.

Meanwhile, in a small saucepan combine the rest of the marinade and water. Bring to a simmer over medium heat. Cook, stirring, until thickened slightly, about 1 minute. Remove from the heat and season to taste with ground red pepper. If desired, stir a spoonful or two of the passion fruit seeds back into the sauce for crunch.

Just before serving, toss the cucumbers and watercress in a large bowl with the balsamic vinegar and vegetable oil. Transfer the greens to a platter, set the swordfish on top and spoon the sauce over the swordfish.

Nutrition Information Per Serving

			% of daily value
Calories	230		
Calories from fat	29	%	
Fat	7	g	11%
Saturated fat	1.5	g	8%
Cholesterol	55	mg	18%
Sodium	139	mg	6%
Carbohydrate	9	g	3%
Fiber	3	g	
Sugar	4	g	
Protein	29	g	

4 meat, 1/2 fruit

Cajun-Style Orange Roughy

Cajun seasoning is boldly flavored and sassy. It most often contains garlic, onion, chilies, celery, black pepper and mustard. Its bite stimulates the taste buds and compliments the flavor of seafood.

6 servings

1 can (10 ounces) stewed tomatoes
1 celery stalk washed, ends removed, chopped
1 small onion, peeled, ends removed, chopped
1/4 clove garlic, peeled, ends removed, minced
1/4 medium green pepper, washed, ends removed, cored, seeded, chopped
1/2 bay leaf
1/4 teaspoon ground thyme
1/2 teaspoon ground black pepper
1/2 teaspoon hot sauce, or to taste
Vegetable oil cooking spray
6 orange roughy fillets (six-ounces each), washed, patted dry
2 tablespoons corn oil
2 ounces fresh parsley, washed, dried, chopped

■ In a heavy-bottomed saucepan over medium heat, combine the tomatoes, celery, onion, garlic, green pepper, bay leaf, thyme, black pepper and hot sauce. Bring to a boil, then reduce heat and simmer. Simmer the sauce until the vegetables are cooked and the sauce reduces, about 20 minutes.

Meanwhile, preheat the oven to 400 degrees. Spray a shallow 11-by-15-inch baking pan with the cooking spray. Place the orange roughy in the baking pan and brush lightly with corn oil. Bake for 8 to 12 minutes, or until the fish is firm and flaky. Remove the bay leaf and spoon the sauce over the cooked fish fillets. Sprinkle with parsley for garnish.

Nutrition Information Per Serving

			% of daily value
Calories	209		
Calories from fat	26	%	
Fat	6	g	9%
Saturated fat	1	g	5%
Cholesterol	74	mg	25%
Sodium	224	mg	9%
Carbohydrate	7	g	2%
Fiber	1.5	g	
Sugar	2	g	
Protein	31	g	

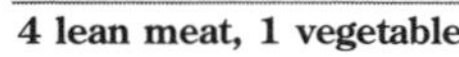

4 lean meat, 1 vegetable

60

Chili-Marinated Swordfish with Pineapple Salsa

Making your own salsa allows you to control the amount of salt. For example, a 1/2-cup serving of this Pineapple Salsa contains only 3 mg of sodium.

4 servings

1 tablespoon chili powder
1 tablespoon red onion, peeled, ends removed, chopped
2 teaspoons garlic, peeled, ends removed, minced
1/4 cup fresh cilantro, washed, dried, chopped
2 teaspoons oregano
1 teaspoon ground cumin
1/4 cup lime juice
1 tablespoon olive oil
1/8 teaspoon black pepper
4 swordfish steaks (6 ounces each), washed, patted dry
Vegetable oil cooking spray
Pineapple Salsa (recipe follows)

■ In a shallow dish or a plastic sealable bag, mix together the chili powder, red onion, garlic, cilantro, oregano, cumin, lime juice, olive oil and black pepper. Add the swordfish steaks. Cover the dish or seal the bag, and refrigerate for 1 to 2 hours.

Preheat the grill or broiler. Spray the grill rack with the cooking spray. Remove the swordfish steaks from the marinade. Grill or broil the steaks for 5 minutes, then turn and cook until done but still juicy inside, about 5 minutes longer. Serve with Pineapple Salsa.

Pineapple Salsa

Most salsas are very low in calories – less than 100 calories per cup – with virtually no fat or cholesterol.

1 small to medium pineapple, peeled, cored, coarsely chopped
3/4 cup red onion, peeled, ends removed, minced
3/4 cup fresh cilantro, washed, dried chopped.
1 tablespoon white wine vinegar
1/4 teaspoon ground cayenne pepper

■ Place the pineapple in a colander and set over a large bowl to drain for about 5 minutes. Discard the liquid. Transfer the pineapple to a bowl. Add the onion, cilantro, vinegar and pepper. Chill for at least one hour. Makes four 1/2-cup servings.

Nutrition Information Per Serving

			% of daily value
Calories	274		
Calories from fat	29	%	
Fat	9	g	14%
Saturated fat	2.5	g	13%
Cholesterol	66	mg	22%
Sodium	170	mg	7%
Carbohydrate	14	g	5%
Fiber	2	g	
Sugar	7	g	
Protein	34	g	

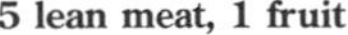

5 lean meat, 1 fruit

Poached Salmon with Dill Sauce

This flavorful salmon is a cinch to prepare, and the dill weed adds a distinct nuance to the sauce.

4 servings

1 medium onion, peeled, ends removed, sliced
1 cube chicken bouillon
1 1/2 cups water
1 tablespoon lemon juice
4 salmon steaks (6 to 7 ounces each)

Sauce:
1 tablespoon tub margarine
1 tablespoon finely chopped onion
2 tablespoons flour
1 teaspoon dill weed
1/8 teaspoon white pepper
1 cup skim milk

■ In a skillet large enough to hold fish in a single layer, combine the onion, bouillon, water and lemon juice. Heat to a boil over high heat. Add the salmon steaks and simmer, tightly covered, about 10 minutes or until the fish flakes easily with a fork.

In small saucepan, melt the margarine over medium heat and saute the chopped onion until tender, about 3 minutes. Stir in the flour, dill weed and pepper. Add the milk, mixing well. Heat until the mixture boils and thickens, stirring constantly, about 2 minutes.

Remove the salmon to a platter. Pour the dill sauce over the salmon and serve.

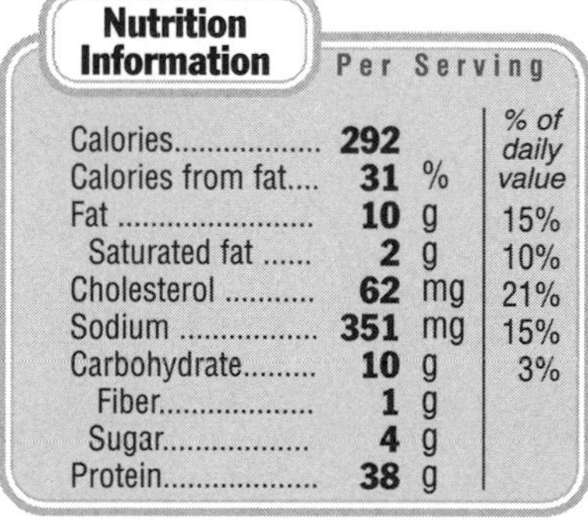

Nutrition Information Per Serving

			% of daily value
Calories	**292**		
Calories from fat	**31**	%	
Fat	**10**	g	15%
Saturated fat	**2**	g	10%
Cholesterol	**62**	mg	21%
Sodium	**351**	mg	15%
Carbohydrate	**10**	g	3%
Fiber	**1**	g	
Sugar	**4**	g	
Protein	**38**	g	

(Using low-sodium chicken bouillon reduces the sodium content of this dish to 182 mg per serving.)

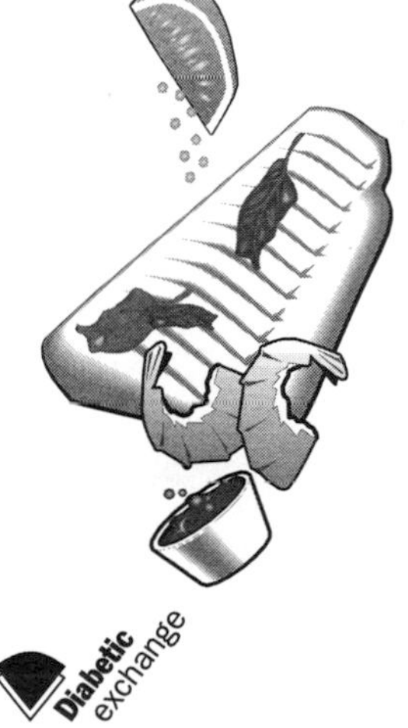

Diabetic exchange

5 meat, 1/4 milk

15 minutes

Salmon Fillets with Mustard Sauce

Vitamin and mineral supplements often are promoted as cure-alls. But good health begins with eating a varied, well-balanced diet, including nutritious foods like this dish, which is loaded with important vitamins and minerals.

6 servings

1 tablespoon olive oil
2 tablespoons fresh celery leaves, washed, dried, chopped
2 tablespoons fresh parsley, washed, dried, chopped
1 tablespoon chopped onion
1/4 teaspoon dried thyme
1/4 teaspoon marjoram
1/4 teaspoon paprika
1 1/2 pounds salmon fillets

■ Preheat the grill or broiler. Pour the olive oil in a small bowl.

Add the celery leaves, parsley, onion, thyme, marjoram and paprika. Brush the mixture over the salmon fillets. Grill or broil the fillets for 6 minutes on each side or until the fish flakes. Serve topped with Mustard Sauce.

Mustard Sauce

1/2 cup nonfat mayonnaise
3/4 teaspoon wine vinegar
1 1/2 teaspoons Dijon mustard
1 1/2 teaspoons fresh parsley washed, dried, chopped
2 teaspoons finely chopped green onion
1/2 teaspoon mustard seed, crushed

■ To make the mustard sauce, mix together the ingredients in a small bowl. Cover and chill for 2 hours.

Nutrition Information Per Serving

			% of daily value
Calories	174		
Calories from fat	31	%	
Fat	6	g	9%
Saturated fat	1.5	g	8%
Cholesterol	42	mg	14%
Sodium	304	mg	13%
Carbohydrate	3	g	1%
Fiber	0	g	
Sugar	0	g	
Protein	23	g	

Diabetic exchange

3 lean meat, 1/2 vegetable

Salmon Burgers

Regardless of how lean your ground beef is, the fat remaining is mostly saturated. For a good alternative, try a salmon burger on the grill. You will have a delicious, moist burger, and you will get a healthy dose of those "good for you" fatty acids that research shows help to protect you from heart disease.

6 servings

Vegetable oil cooking spray
1/2 cup chopped onion
1/3 cup skim milk
1/2 cup unseasoned bread crumbs
4 egg whites
1/4 cup chopped fresh parsley, washed, dried, ends removed
1 teaspoon powdered mustard
1 can (14 3/4-ounces) salmon, drained
1/2 cup seasoned bread crumbs
1/3 cup light mayonnaise
1 tablespoon chopped sweet pickle
6 hamburger rolls

Nutrition Information Per Serving

			% of daily value
Calories	**374**		
Calories from fat	**28**	%	
Fat	**12**	g	18%
Saturated fat	**2**	g	10%
Cholesterol	**44**	mg	15%
Sodium	**793**	mg	33%
Carbohydrate	**42**	g	14%
Fiber	**2**	g	
Sugar	**6**	g	
Protein	**23**	g	

■ Spray a small skillet with the cooking spray. Saute the onion until tender, about 3 minutes. Transfer to a mixing bowl.

Add the skim milk, unseasoned bread crumbs, egg whites, parsley and mustard. Mix well. Add the salmon, breaking it up and mixing well.

Shape the mixture into 6 burgers. Roll each burger in seasoned bread crumbs. Place the burgers on a tray or serving plate. Cover and refrigerate for at least 1 hour.

Preheat the grill or broiler. Spray the grill with the cooking spray. Grill the burgers about 4 inches from hot coals for 3 minutes. Turn carefully and grill for 3 to 4 minutes longer, or until brown.

In a small bowl combine the light mayonnaise and the pickle. Place the burgers on rolls. Use 1 tablespoon of the mayonnaise mixture as topping for each burger and serve.

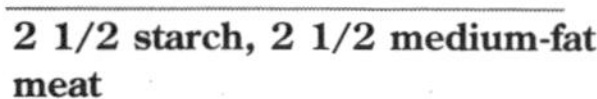

Diabetic exchange

2 1/2 starch, 2 1/2 medium-fat meat

45

Seafood Vegetable Pasta Salad

This dish is great for summer picnics and meals on the go. It provides lots of energy from complex carbohydrates, and the ginger and soy sauce give it an Asian touch.

8 servings

1/3 cup nonfat mayonnaise
1/3 cup plain nonfat yogurt
1 tablespoon light soy sauce
1 teaspoon sugar
1/2 teaspoon ground ginger
Dash of red pepper sauce
8 ounces uncooked spaghetti or vermicelli, broken in half, cooked according to package directions, omitting salt and fat
1 pound shrimp, cooked
1 pound scallops, cooked
1/2 cup water chestnuts, coarsely chopped
1/4 cup snipped cilantro or parsley
2 medium carrots, peeled, ends removed, shredded (about 1 cup)
1 package (10 ounces) frozen pea pods, thawed or fresh

■ To prepare the dressing: In a small bowl, mix together the mayonnaise, yogurt, soy sauce, sugar, ground ginger and red pepper sauce.

To assemble the salad: In a large bowl, place the cooked pasta, seafood, water chestnuts, cilantro or parsley, carrots and pea pods.

Pour the dressing over the salad and toss gently. Serve immediately.

Nutrition Information Per Serving

			% of daily value
Calories	**247**		
Calories from fat	**7**	%	
Fat	**2**	g	3%
Saturated fat	**trace**	g	1%
Cholesterol	**117**	mg	39%
Sodium	**456**	mg	19%
Carbohydrate	**30**	g	10%
Fiber	**1**	g	
Sugar	**2**	g	
Protein	**28**	g	

Diabetic exchange

3 lean meat, 1 1/2 starch, 1 vegetable

Shrimp, Avocado & Spinach Salad

Spinach will not give you Popeye-like strength, but it can add many vitamins and minerals to your summer salad. Spinach and other dark greens are exceptionally high in beta carotene and folacin. Beta carotene plays an important role in decreasing the risk of certain cancers; folacin helps build red blood cells. Although spinach is also high in iron and calcium, it contains oxalic acid, which does not allow these minerals to be absorbed well by the body.

4 servings

2 teaspoons sugar
1/2 teaspoon dried tarragon, crumbled
1/4 teaspoon dry mustard
1/4 teaspoon seasoned pepper
6 tablespoons red wine vinegar
1 1/2 teaspoons olive oil
8 cups fresh spinach, washed well, stemmed, torn into bite-size pieces
1/2 avocado, peeled, pit removed, cut into 3/4-inch pieces
1/2 pound cooked shrimp, patted dry
6 medium mushrooms, cleaned, sliced 1/4-inch thick
1/2 medium Maui, Vidalia or red onion, peeled, ends removed, thinly sliced and separated into rings

■ In a small bowl or jar with a tight-fitting lid, combine the sugar, tarragon, mustard and pepper. Add the red wine vinegar and olive oil, then whisk, or cover the jar with the lid and shake, until the sugar is dissolved. Refrigerate until ready to use.

In a large salad bowl, combine the spinach, avocado, shrimp, mushrooms and onion. Remove the dressing from the refrigerator, whisk or shake again, and pour over the salad. Toss gently to coat. Serve immediately.

Nutrition Information Per Serving

			% of daily value
Calories	**163**		
Calories from fat	**32**	%	
Fat	**6**	g	9%
Saturated fat	**1**	g	5%
Cholesterol	**111**	mg	37%
Sodium	**218**	mg	9%
Carbohydrate	**13**	g	4%
Fiber	**4.5**	g	
Sugar	**3**	g	
Protein	**16**	g	

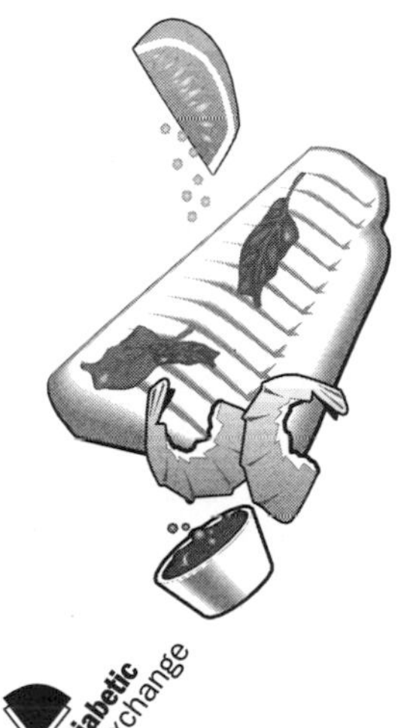

Diabetic exchange

2 meat, 2 vegetable

30

Spaghetti with Tuna Sauce

Good heart health isn't easy to achieve, but lifestyle improvements and medical advances have produced a noticeable decline in heart disease.
According to the most recent research:
- **A diet with 30 percent or less of its calories from fat is recommended for everyone over the age of 2.**
- **Dropping dietary fat to 20 percent or less may be better for those who still have high cholesterol.**
- **A diet with only 10 percent fat, combined with a reduction in stress and moderate exercise, may reverse the buildup of plaque or cholesterol in arteries.**

4 servings

1 tablespoon olive oil
1 onion, peeled, ends removed, diced
2 cloves garlic, peeled, ends removed, finely chopped
1 can (1 pound) stewed, sliced or crushed tomatoes
1 teaspoon dried oregano
1 tablespoon capers, rinsed
1/2 tablespoon green olives, pitted and roughly chopped
1/2 tablespoon black olives, pitted and roughly chopped
2 cans (6 1/2 ounces each) low-sodium water-packed tuna, drained, broken up roughly
Freshly ground black pepper to taste
1 tablespoon fresh parsley, washed, dried, chopped
8 ounces dry spaghetti, cooked according to package directions, omitting salt and fat

■ In a large skillet, heat the olive oil and saute the onion and garlic until the onion is translucent. Add the tomatoes and oregano, cover and simmer on a low heat for about 10 minutes.

Add the capers, green and black olives and tuna to the tomato sauce and heat through. Season with pepper and parsley.

Divide the cooked spaghetti onto 4 serving plates and pour the sauce over.

Nutrition Information Per Serving

	Amount		% of daily value
Calories	400		
Calories from fat	15	%	
Fat	7	g	11%
Saturated fat	1	g	5%
Cholesterol	32	mg	11%
Sodium	390	mg	16%
Carbohydrate	52	g	17%
Fiber	1.5	g	
Sugar	3	g	
Protein	34	g	

Diabetic exchange

3 starch, 1 vegetable, 3 lean meat

Tuna Casserole

Truly one of the great comfort foods, tuna casserole is both easy to prepare and delightfully satisfying. Low-sodium water-packed tuna keeps the sodium content of this dish at acceptable levels.

4 servings

8 ounces uncooked macaroni
Vegetable oil cooking spray
1 can (10 ounces) low-fat, reduced-sodium condensed cream of mushroom soup
1/2 onion, peeled, ends removed, chopped
1/8 teaspoon pepper
1 package (10 1/2 ounces) frozen mixed vegetables
1 can (6 1/2 ounces) low-sodium water-packed tuna, drained
1 tablespoon Parmesan cheese
1 tablespoon unseasoned bread crumbs

Nutrition Information Per Serving

			% of daily value
Calories	**378**		
Calories from fat	**10**	%	
Fat	**4**	g	6%
Saturated fat	**1.5**	g	8%
Cholesterol	**23**	mg	8%
Sodium	**390**	mg	16%
Carbohydrate	**61**	g	20%
Fiber	**3**	g	
Sugar	**5**	g	
Protein	**24**	g	

■ Preheat the oven to 350 degrees.

Cook the macaroni according to the package directions, omitting salt. Drain; set aside.

Spray a 2-quart casserole dish with the cooking spray; set aside.

In a large bowl combine the cream of mushroom soup, onion, pepper, frozen mixed vegetables and tuna. Mix well. Stir in the cooked macaroni.

Pour the mixture into the prepared casserole dish.

In a small bowl, combine the Parmesan cheese and bread crumbs. Sprinkle the top with the Parmesan cheese and bread-crumb mixture.

Bake for 30 to 35 minutes, or until the sauce is bubbly and the crumb topping is golden. Remove from the oven and serve.

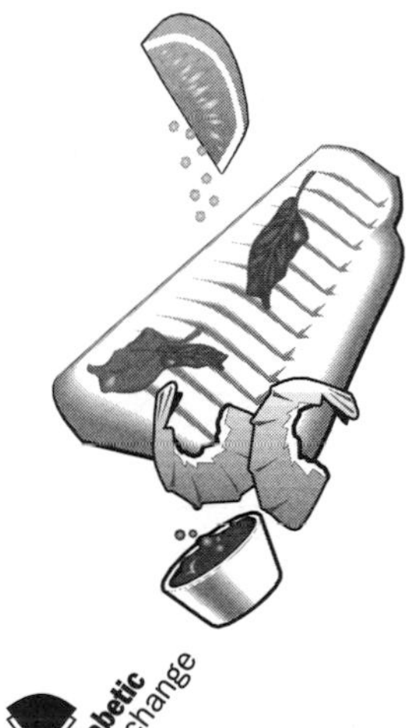

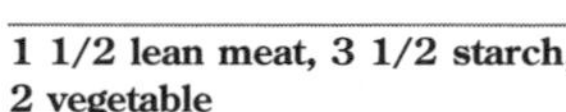

1 1/2 lean meat, 3 1/2 starch, 2 vegetable

15

Vegetable Shrimp Kabobs

Quick and easy, these special gifts from the grill use the complex flavors of herbs to bring out the best taste from the seared shrimp and vegetables.

6 servings

1/4 cup vegetable oil
1/2 cup white wine vinegar
2 tablespoons lemon juice
2 teaspoons reduced-sodium soy sauce
1/2 teaspoon garlic powder
1/2 teaspoon thyme
1/2 teaspoon pepper
1/2 teaspoon rosemary
1/4 teaspoon tarragon
1/4 teaspoon dry mustard
18 jumbo shrimp, (about 1 pound) or 1 pound scallops
18 cherry tomatoes, washed, stems removed
1 green bell pepper, washed, cored, seeded, cut into 1-inch pieces
2 medium yellow onions, peeled, ends removed, quartered
12 mushrooms, cleaned

■ In a plastic sealable bag or a medium deep bowl, combine the oil, white wine vinegar, lemon juice, soy sauce, garlic powder, thyme, pepper, rosemary, tarragon and dry mustard. Mix well. Add the shrimp or scallops. Seal the bag or cover the bowl with plastic wrap and marinate in the refrigerator for at least 1 hour or overnight.

Preheat the broiler or grill.

Thread the marinated seafood, cherry tomatoes, green pepper, onion and mushrooms on 6 skewers. Discard the remaining marinade. Place on the broiler pan or grill 4 inches from heat. Cook for 8 to 10 minutes, turning occasionally. Remove the shrimp and vegetables from the skewers to serve.

Nutrition Information Per Serving

			% of daily value
Calories	145		
Calories from fat	33	%	
Fat	6	g	9%
Saturated fat	1	g	5%
Cholesterol	116	mg	39%
Sodium	172	mg	7%
Carbohydrate	11	g	3%
Fiber	2	g	
Sugar	4	g	
Protein	14	g	

Cook's note:

If using bamboo skewers, first place the wooden skewers in a 9-by-13-inch pan filled with water. Place a dinner plate on top to keep the skewers submerged for 5 minutes. This will keep skewers from burning when broiling or grilling.

Diabetic exchange

2 lean meat, 2 vegetable

Seafood Gumbo

Nutrition research has yet to pinpoint a perfect food. To maintain good health, you need a variety of foods at each meal. Serve Seafood Gumbo with whole grain bread for a complete, healthy meal.

8 servings

1 clove garlic, peeled, ends removed, chopped
1 cup onion, peeled, ends removed, chopped
1/2 cup celery, washed, ends removed, chopped
1 tablespoon vegetable oil
3 tablespoons flour
3 cups water
1 can (28 ounces) tomatoes, with liquid
4 teaspoons chicken-flavored bouillon
1/8 teaspoon ground red (cayenne) pepper
8 ounces washed, trimmed and sliced fresh okra; or 1 package (10 ounces) frozen, sliced okra
1 pound medium raw shrimp, peeled and deveined
1 can (8 ounces) whole oysters, drained
1/4 cup parsley
3 cups cooked rice
Hot pepper sauce, optional

■ In a medium-size soup pot, cook the garlic, onion and celery in the oil until tender. Stir in the flour. Cook and stir until the flour is dark brown, about 15 to 20 minutes.

Add the water, tomatoes, chicken bouillon and ground red pepper. Bring to a boil. Reduce the heat and simmer uncovered for 30 minutes.

Add the okra; simmer for 5 minutes. Add the shrimp and oysters; simmer for 4 to 6 minutes, or until the shrimp turns opaque.

Pour into serving bowls and garnish with parsley.

Serve with rice and hot pepper sauce if desired.

Nutrition Information Per Serving

			% of daily value
Calories	**203**		
Calories from fat	**18**	%	
Fat	**4**	g	6%
Saturated fat	**1**	g	5%
Cholesterol	**105**	mg	35%
Sodium	**333**	mg	14%
Carbohydrate	**25**	g	8%
Fiber	**4**	g	
Sugar	**8**	g	
Protein	**19**	g	

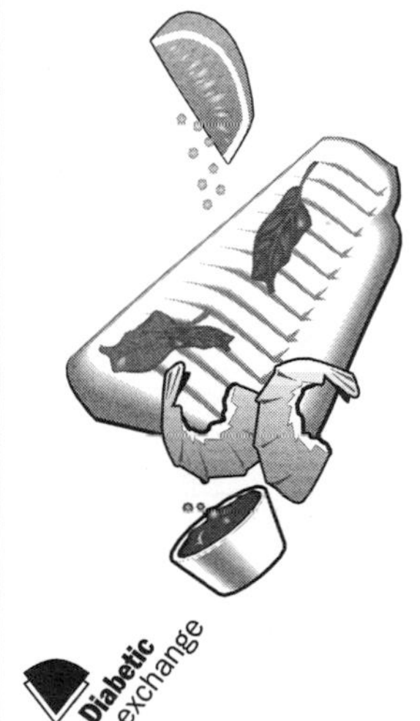

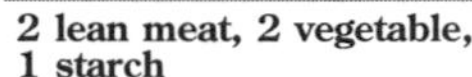

Diabetic exchange

2 lean meat, 2 vegetable, 1 starch

60

Red Snapper & Black Bean Salsa

Salsas are the '90s way to replace fattening cream sauces and gravies. Salsa means sauce in Spanish, but to most of us it is a chunky tomato sauce made spicy by hot peppers. Although almost all prepared salsas are low in fat, they can be high in sodium. Making your own salsa allows you to control the salt shaker. This healthy Red Snapper and Black Bean Salsa is good enough to impress guests at a dinner party.

8 servings

1 1/2 cups diced tomatoes
1 cup canned black beans, rinsed and drained
1/2 cup coarsely chopped fresh cilantro
3 tablespoons red wine vinegar
Dash of Tabasco sauce
1 jalapeno pepper, washed, stem and seeds removed, finely minced
2 pounds red snapper fillets
Juice and zest of 2 to 3 limes
Freshly ground pepper to taste

Nutrition Information Per Serving

			% of daily value
Calories	**155**		
Calories from fat	**11**	%	
Fat	**2**	g	3%
Saturated fat	**trace**	g	1%
Cholesterol	**42**	mg	14%
Sodium	**210**	mg	9%
Carbohydrate	**8**	g	3%
Fiber	**1.5**	g	
Sugar	**1**	g	
Protein	**26**	g	

■ In a medium-size mixing bowl, combine the diced tomato, black beans, cilantro, red wine vinegar, jalapeno, Tabasco sauce and pepper. Mix well. Set aside at room temperature for 30 minutes, stirring occasionally.

Preheat the oven to 375 degrees.

Place each red snapper fillet on a piece of aluminum foil large enough to enclose it. Sprinkle each fillet with lime juice and season with pepper.

Close the packages by folding the foil over the fish and tightly sealing the edges. Set the packages on a baking sheet and bake for 25 to 35 minutes. Open the packets to see that the fish is opaque and flakes easily when pierced with a fork. Remove from the oven.

Place each fillet on a dinner plate and top with a generous portion of the salsa.

Diabetic exchange

3 1/2 meat, 1 vegetable

Salmon-Stuffed Manicotti

Pasta's reputation has gone from fattening food to diet wonder and back again, leaving many people wondering whether they should eat it. The answer is a definite yes. Pasta is not only low in fat but also inexpensive, easy to make and nutritious. When cooking pasta, use 1 gallon of water for every pound of pasta. Cook no more than 2 pounds at one time because the water must be boiling rapidly while cooking. Pasta is done when it is firm yet tender, with just a tiny chalky-white center. As long as you stir the pasta while it is cooking, there is no need to add oil or salt to the water. In this Salmon-Stuffed Manicotti recipe, you can stuff the noodles the night before, then make the sauce and stick it in the microwave for a quick entree the next day.

8 servings

1 can (15 1/2 ounces) of salmon, drained and flaked
1 cup nonfat cottage cheese
1/2 cup plus 1 tablespoon snipped fresh parsley, divided
1/4 cup sliced green onions
3 tablespoons fat-free Parmesan cheese, divided
1/4 teaspoon grated lemon peel
1/4 teaspoon dried dill
1/8 teaspoon pepper or to taste
12 manicotti shells, cooked al dente to package directions, drained and rinsed in cold water

Sauce:
1 cup nonfat cottage cheese
1/3 cup nonfat plain yogurt
1 tablespoon skim milk
1/4 teaspoon dried dill
1/8 teaspoon garlic powder

■ In a medium-size bowl, mix the salmon, cottage cheese, 1/2 cup parsley, green onion, 2 tablespoons Parmesan cheese, lemon peel, dill and pepper.

Stuff each cooked manicotti shell with about 1/4 cup of the salmon mixture.

Arrange the stuffed shells in a 10-square-inch casserole. Cover with plastic wrap and set aside.

In a small bowl, mix the remaining tablespoon of parsley and tablespoon of Parmesan cheese. Set aside.

To prepare the sauce, combine all its ingredients in a food processor fitted with a metal blade or in a blender. Process the sauce until smooth, then set aside.

Microwave the stuffed shells on 100 percent (high) power for 5 minutes. Remove the casserole from the microwave and spoon the sauce over the shells.

Recover and reduce the power to 50 percent (medium); microwave for 4 to 6 minutes longer, rotating the dish once, until the dish is heated through.

Remove the shells to a serving platter with a slotted spoon and sprinkle the parsley-Parmesan mixture on top.

Nutrition Information Per Serving

			% of daily value
Calories	**378**		
Calories from fat	**14**	%	
Fat	**6**	g	9%
Saturated fat	**1.5**	g	8%
Cholesterol	**44**	mg	15%
Sodium	**482**	mg	20%
Carbohydrate	**46**	g	15%
Fiber	**0.5**	g	
Sugar	**1**	g	
Protein	**33**	g	

3 starch, 4 lean meat

30

Crab Cakes

Have you tried the Cabbage Soup Diet, the Zone Diet or the Fit for Life Diet? Don't be lured into following any of the fad diets. They are characterized by their reliance on particular foods, unusual combinations of foods, foods eaten in a particular order, or an excess of carbohydrates or proteins. None will provide the health benefits of a well-balanced diet.

5 servings

2 slightly beaten egg whites
1/2 cup plain nonfat yogurt, divided
2 tablespoons fat-free mayonnaise
1 tablespoon snipped fresh parsley
2 teaspoons Worcestershire sauce
1 teaspoon prepared mustard
1/4 teaspoon paprika
1/8 teaspoon pepper
Ground red (cayenne) pepper to taste
1 tablespoon chopped chives
1 pound crabmeat, drained, flaked and cartilage removed
1/4 cup crushed saltine crackers
Vegetable oil cooking spray
1 medium tomato, washed, cored, sliced
Lemon wedges, optional

■ In a medium-size mixing bowl, combine the egg whites, 1/4 cup of the yogurt, the mayonnaise, parsley, Worcestershire sauce, mustard, paprika, pepper, ground red pepper and chives. Stir in the crabmeat and cracker crumbs.

Preheat the broiler. Spray a shallow baking dish with the cooking spray.

Shape the crab mixture into 5 patties and arrange them on the baking dish.

Broil 4 to 6 inches from the heat for 10 to 15 minutes or until lightly browned. Do not turn the patties during broiling.

Remove the patties from the broiler and serve them on tomato slices with the remaining 1/4 cup yogurt. Garnish the plates with lemon wedges.

Nutrition Information Per Serving

			% of daily value
Calories	192		
Calories from fat	23	%	
Fat	5	g	8%
Saturated fat	0.5	g	3%
Cholesterol	65	mg	22%
Sodium	723	mg	30%
Carbohydrate	11	g	4%
Fiber	1	g	
Sugar	3	g	
Protein	25	g	

Diabetic exchange

3 meat, 1/2 starch, 1/2 vegetable

Poultry

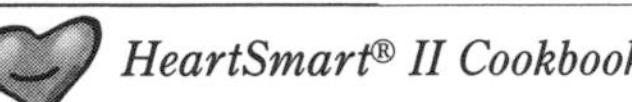

Almond Chicken

With just 9 grams of fat per serving, this dish is rare among recipes that use nuts. The trick is to use a small amount of slivered almonds, which deliver the satisfying crunch without all the fat.

6 servings

6 boneless and skinless chicken breast halves, (4 ounces each) washed, patted dry
Black pepper to taste
Paprika to taste
1/4 cup slivered almonds
1 tablespoon vegetable oil
1/2 cup chopped onion
4 ounces fresh mushrooms, cleaned, sliced
1 tablespoon lemon juice
1/4 cup sherry
3 cups cooked rice
Parsley for garnish, optional

■ Preheat the oven to 325 degrees. Place the chicken pieces in a 9-by-13-inch baking dish and sprinkle with black pepper and paprika.

Place the almonds on a shallow-side baking dish or jelly-roll pan and bake for 6 minutes. Stlr, watch carefully and bake another 4 minutes until brown. Remove from the oven and set aside. Increase the oven temperature to 350 degrees.

In a large skillet, heat the oil over medium heat and saute the onion and mushrooms for 3 minutes. Add the lemon juice, sherry and almonds, stirring well. Spoon the mixture over the chicken pieces.

Cover with foil and bake for 1 hour and 15 minutes. Remove from the oven. Serve with rice, garnish with parsley if desired, and serve.

Nutrition Information Per Serving

			% of daily value
Calories	346		
Calories from fat	22	%	
Fat	8	g	12%
Saturated fat	1.5	g	8%
Cholesterol	73	mg	24%
Sodium	68	mg	3%
Carbohydrate	33	g	11%
Fiber	2	g	
Sugar	2	g	
Protein	31	g	

4 lean meat, 2 starch

30

Breast of Chicken Raspberry

Raspberry vinegar and red wine provide a marvelous marinade for the skinless chicken breasts in this recipe. Be sure to plan for at least an hour of preparation so the chicken has enough time to soak in the rich red juices.

4 servings

2 tablespoons olive oil
1/2 cup raspberry vinegar
1/2 cup red wine
1/4 cup lemon juice
1/4 cup honey
1/4 teaspoon dried tarragon
1/2 teaspoon Dijon mustard
1/8 teaspoon white pepper
Dash of ground red (cayenne) pepper
4 boneless, skinless chicken breasts (6 ounces each), washed, patted dry
Vegetable oil cooking spray
2 ounces fresh parsley, washed, dried, chopped

■ In a large plastic sealable bag, combine the olive oil, raspberry vinegar, red wine, lemon juice, honey, dried tarragon, Dijon mustard, white pepper and ground red pepper. Mix well. Place the chicken breasts in the plastic bag and marinate for one hour.

At serving time, preheat the broiler. Spray a broiler pan and rack with the cooking spray. Place the chicken breasts on the rack of the broiler pan. Broil the chicken breasts 6 inches below the heat source for 5 to 8 minutes per side, basting with the marinade after turning. Cook until done.

Sprinkle with parsley for garnish.

Nutrition Information Per Serving

			% of daily value
Calories	**254**		
Calories from fat	**23**	%	
Fat	**6**	g	9%
Saturated fat	**1.5**	g	8%
Cholesterol	**109**	mg	36%
Sodium	**101**	mg	4%
Carbohydrate	**6**	g	2%
Fiber	**0.5**	g	
Sugar	**4**	g	
Protein	**41**	g	

5 1/2 lean meat, 1/2 fruit

Citrus Chicken Fajitas

The blend of citrus juices and grated lime peel in these Heart Smart® fajitas provides a tropical taste and adds a healthy dose of vitamin C.

4 servings

1 cup grapefruit juice
2 tablespoons plus 1 teaspoon fresh lime juice, divided
1 tablespoon Dijon mustard
1 teaspoon granulated sugar
8 ounces skinless, boneless chicken breast, washed, patted dry, sliced in thin strips
Vegetable oil cooking spray
1 medium red bell pepper, washed, seeded, cored, thinly sliced
1 cup green onions, peeled, ends removed, chopped
1/4 cup nonfat plain yogurt
1 tablespoon grated lime peel
4 flour tortillas (6 inch), heated
Lime wedges, optional
Cilantro, optional

■ In a medium-size glass bowl or gallon plastic sealable bag, mix the grapefruit juice, 2 tablespoons lime juice, mustard and sugar. Add the chicken strips. Refrigerate for 1 to 2 hours, turning the chicken occasionally. Drain and reserve the marinade.

Spray a large skillet with the cooking spray. Saute the chicken for 4 to 5 minutes until it's no longer pink. Remove from the skillet. Add the reserved marinade, and simmer uncovered for 8 to 10 minutes to reduce liquid. Add the pepper and green onion. Cook, stirring frequently, for 2 to 3 minutes, until the vegetables are tender.

Add the chicken and reheat 1 minute. In a small bowl, combine the yogurt, lime peel and remaining 1 teaspoon of lime juice.

Divide the chicken and vegetables evenly among 4 warm tortillas. Top each with lime and cilantro. Serve the yogurt mixture on the side.

Nutrition Information Per Serving

			% of daily value
Calories	**216**		
Calories from fat	**15**	%	
Fat	**4**	g	6%
Saturated fat	**0.5**	g	3%
Cholesterol	**36**	mg	12%
Sodium	**94**	mg	4%
Carbohydrate	**28**	g	9%
Fiber	**1.5**	g	
Sugar	**6**	g	
Protein	**17**	g	

1 starch, 1 1/2 lean meat, 2 vegetable

75 minutes

Turkey Divan Stuffed Potato

Stuffed potatoes are a wonderful way to enjoy a filling meal loaded with vitamins and minerals. In this recipe, turkey and broccoli team up with mozzarella cheese to provide a simple yet delicious filling for the potato.

1 servings

1 medium potato
2/3 cup broccoli, cooked
2 ounces light meat turkey, cubed
2 ounces part-skim mozzarella cheese, shredded
1 tablespoon chopped chives,
Paprika to taste
Dash of salt-free seasoning blend

Nutrition Information Per Serving

			% of daily value
Calories	**408**		
Calories from fat	**25**	%	
Fat	**11**	g	17%
Saturated fat	**6.5**	g	33%
Cholesterol	**71**	mg	24%
Sodium	**334**	mg	14%
Carbohydrate	**71**	g	24%
Fiber	**6.5**	g	
Sugar	**4**	g	
Protein	**37**	g	

■ Preheat the oven to 425 degrees. Scrub the potato; pierce the skin with a fork. Bake 40 to 60 minutes until done. Or scrub, pierce and bake in the microwave on high for 4 to 6 minutes, turning the potato over once. Set aside.

If you use frozen broccoli, cook in oven or microwave according to the package directions, omitting salt and fat. If you use fresh broccoli, steam it in the microwave covered with plastic wrap at the full setting for 2 to 3 minutes. Or cook in a vegetable steamer for 10 to 15 minutes or in a covered saucepan in 1/2-inch of water for 10 to 15 minutes over moderate heat.

Split open the cooked potato lengthwise and add the cubes of cooked turkey. (Turkey can be leftovers or salt-free turkey luncheon meat.) Sprinkle with shredded mozzarella, chives, paprika and seasoning blend; reheat briefly in the microwave, about 2 minutes on high, or in the regular oven, 5 minutes at 425 degrees.

Diabetic exchange

4 starch, 1 vegetable, 3 lean meat

Chicken Paella

Among seasonings, saffron is king. It's the world's most expensive spice, derived from the yellow-orange stigmata of a small purple crocus. Each stigma must be handpicked and dried, and it takes 14,000 of them to make an ounce of saffron. It doesn't take much of this fine spice to add a unique color and flavor to this low-fat adaptation of the traditional Spanish dish.

4 servings

1 tablespoon olive oil
2 whole chicken breasts, (1 pound) skinless, boneless, washed, patted dry, cut into 2-inch pieces
Black pepper to taste
2 cups low-sodium chicken broth, divided
2 medium onions, peeled, ends removed, diced
1 medium green pepper, washed, seeded, cored, cut into fairly large pieces
1 cup mushrooms, cleaned, sliced
1/2 cup parsley, washed, dried, chopped
1 clove garlic , peeled, ends removed, sliced; or garlic to taste
4 medium tomatoes, skinned, cored and cut in quarters, seeded if desired
2 pinches saffron
1 cup uncooked long-grain rice
1/2 cup frozen peas, thawed

■ In a large nonstick skillet, heat the oil.

Saute the chicken pieces on all sides over high heat and season lightly with pepper. Remove from the pan and set aside.

Add 1/4 cup chicken broth to the pan. Gently steam the onion and pepper about 5 minutes. Add the mushrooms, parsley and garlic; saute for 5 minutes. Add the tomatoes.

Sprinkle with saffron and the remaining broth. Add the rice, chicken and peas to the vegetables.

In a medium saucepan, bring the remaining broth to a boil. Pour this broth over the paella and cook, covered, over low heat for 30 to 45 mintues.

Nutrition Information Per Serving

			% of daily value
Calories	417		
Calories from fat	16	%	
Fat	7	g	11%
Saturated fat	1.5	g	8%
Cholesterol	74	mg	25%
Sodium	108	mg	5%
Carbohydrate	53	g	18%
Fiber	4	g	
Sugar	5	g	
Protein	34	g	

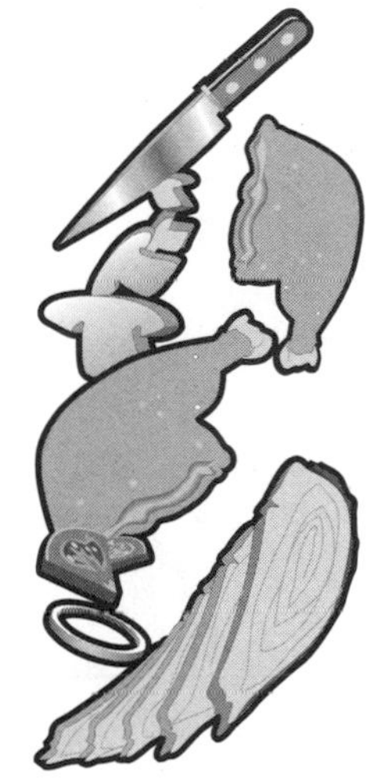

3 lean meat, 3 starch, 2 vegetable

120

Chicken & Vegetable Provencale

Dishes named Provencale are cooked in the style of the Provence region of France. This recipe for chicken and vegetables uses the fresh herbs and produce typical of the region. Generally, these dishes are prepared in olive oil. To trim the fat, we bake the chicken and vegetables in defatted chicken broth.

4 servings

3 cups frozen mixed vegetables (cauliflower, broccoli and carrots)
2 large ripe tomatoes, washed, cored, sliced
1 large onion, peeled, ends removed, thinly sliced
3 tablespoons parsley, washed, dried, chopped, divided
3 teaspoons dried leaf basil, divided
1/4 teaspoon black pepper
1/2 cup defatted chicken broth
2 cloves garlic, peeled, ends removed, minced
3 tablespoons lemon juice
2 whole chicken breasts, (1 pound) washed, patted dry, skinned and split

■ Preheat the oven to 350 degrees.

In a large, shallow baking dish, combine the mixed vegetables, tomatoes and onion. Sprinkle with 1 tablespoon parsley, 2 teaspoons basil and the black pepper. Pour the chicken broth over the vegetables.

In a small bowl combine the remaining 2 tablespoons parsley, 1 teaspoon basil, garlic and lemon juice to form a paste. This can be done by using a mortar and pestle or by chopping the parsley and garlic finely and mixing with the lemon juice and basil in a small cup or bowl with the back of a spoon. Spread the paste over each chicken breast.

Place the chicken over the vegetables in the baking dish. Cover with foil. Bake for 1 1/2 hours. Uncover and brown. Baste the chicken occasionally with pan juice during baking. Remove from the oven and serve.

Nutrition Information Per Serving

			% of daily value
Calories	208		
Calories from fat	16	%	
Fat	4	g	6%
Saturated fat	1	g	5%
Cholesterol	73	mg	24%
Sodium	216	mg	9%
Carbohydrate	15	g	5%
Fiber	7	g	
Sugar	9	g	
Protein	30	g	

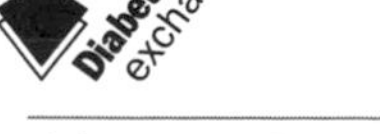

4 lean meat, 3 vegetable

Chicken Manicotti with Chive Cream Sauce

It's fun to pack manicotti noodles with your favorite ingredients. But to make the stuffing go smoothly, make sure the noodles are not overcooked. Too-tender manicotti tears easily and lacks the chewy texture that makes this recipe so delicious.

6 servings

1 package (8 ounces) manicotti shells (about 12)
Vegetable oil cooking spray
8 ounces fat-free cream cheese, softened
1 tablespoon chopped chives
1 tablespoon chopped onion
2/3 cup skim milk
1/4 cup grated fat-free Parmesan cheese
2 cups diced cooked chicken breast
1 package (10 ounces) frozen chopped broccoli, thawed and drained
1 jar (4 ounces) pimientos, drained and chopped
1/4 teaspoon ground black pepper
Paprika to taste

■ Cook the manicotti shells according to the package directions, until tender but slightly firm. Drain the shells, rinse with cold water and drain again.

Preheat the oven to 350 degrees. Spray a large baking dish with the cooking spray. In a small saucepan, combine the cream cheese, chives and onion over medium-low heat until the cheese is melted. Slowly add the milk in a steady stream, stirring until smooth. Stir in the Parmesan cheese and keep warm.

In a large mixing bowl, combine 3/4 cup of the warm cream sauce, the chicken, broccoli, pimiento and black pepper. Using a small spoon, carefully stuff each manicotti shell with about 1/3 cup of the filling.

Arrange the filled shells in a large baking dish. Pour the remaining sauce (about 1/2 cup) over the stuffed shells.

Sprinkle with paprika. Cover and bake for 25 to 30 minutes.

Nutrition Information Per Serving

			% of daily value
Calories	380		
Calories from fat	10	%	
Fat	4	g	6%
Saturated fat	1	g	5%
Cholesterol	45	mg	15%
Sodium	334	mg	14%
Carbohydrate	52	g	17%
Fiber	2	g	
Sugar	2	g	
Protein	31	g	

3 lean meat, 3 starch, 1 vegetable

30 minutes

Chicken Paprikash

It's the paprika that makes this chicken dish sizzle. Most commercial supplies of this spice come from South America, California, Spain and Hungary, with the Hungarian variety considered the best. Search out ethnic markets for the most pungent paprika.

4 servings

1 tablespoon vegetable oil
2 whole chicken breasts, (1 pound) skinless, boneless, washed and patted dry, cut into chunks
1 medium onion, peeled, ends removed, sliced and separated into rings
2 teaspoons paprika
1/8 teaspoon black pepper
3/4 cup chicken broth, defatted
2/3 cup plain nonfat yogurt
2 tablespoons all-purpose flour
1 tablespoon tomato paste
4 ounces eggless noodles, cooked according to package directions, omitting fat and salt
2 tablespoons fresh parsley, washed, dried, snipped

■ In a large skillet, heat the oil over medium heat. Add the chicken and cook until cooked through, about 10 minutes.

Add the onion rings and cook for 3 minutes until the rings are tender but not brown. Carefully stir in the paprika, pepper and chicken broth.

In a small bowl, combine the yogurt, flour and tomato paste; stir this mixture into the skillet. Cook and stir until thick and bubbly.

Cook and stir 1 minute more.

Toss the parsley with the hot cooked noodles. Arrange the noodles on a large serving platter. Spoon the chicken mixture over the noodles and serve.

Nutrition Information Per Serving

			% of daily value
Calories	337		
Calories from fat	20	%	
Fat	7	g	11%
Saturated fat	1.5	g	8%
Cholesterol	74	mg	25%
Sodium	275	mg	11%
Carbohydrate	31	g	10%
Fiber	1	g	
Sugar	3	g	
Protein	35	g	

Diabetic exchange

4 lean meat, 2 starch

Cranturkey Pocket

This is a great way to use leftover turkey and cranberry sauce from holiday feasts.

15

Poultry

4 servings

- *2 pita rounds (6-inch), halved, divided*
- *4 tablespoons nonfat cream cheese, softened, divided*
- *8 ounces thinly sliced roasted turkey breast, divided*
- *1 small cucumber, peeled, ends removed, sliced, divided*
- *1/4 cup cranberry sauce or cranberry relish, divided*
- *1 cup alfalfa sprouts, divided*

■ Spread the inside of each pita half with 1 tablespoon nonfat cream cheese. Layer equal amounts of the turkey and cucumber into each pita half.

Spread 1 tablespoon of the cranberry sauce or relish over the turkey. Evenly divide the alfalfa sprouts among the pita halves and serve.

Nutrition Information Per Serving

			% of daily value
Calories	**182**		
Calories from fat	**4**	%	
Fat	**1**	g	2%
Saturated fat	**trace**	g	1%
Cholesterol	**50**	mg	17%
Sodium	**224**	mg	9%
Carbohydrate	**21**	g	7%
Fiber	**1.5**	g	
Sugar	**1**	g	
Protein	**22**	g	

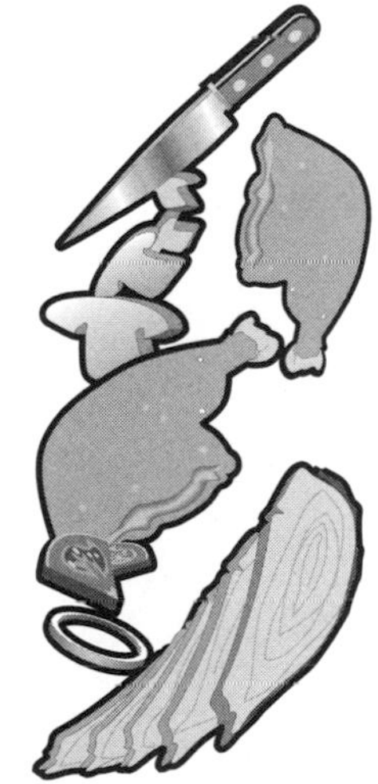

1 starch, 2 1/2 lean meat, 1 vegetable

45

Curried Turkey Pilaf

The curry powder in this dish adds flavor and color to the rice. Curry powder is a blend of up to 20 herbs and spices. Among those most commonly used are chilies, cinnamon, coriander, cumin, fennel, cloves, nutmeg, cayenne and black pepper.

6 servings

1/4 cup slivered almonds
1 tablespoon olive oil
3 green onions, washed, ends removed, chopped
1 red pepper, washed, cored, seeded, sliced
1 1/4 cups uncooked white rice
1 bay leaf
1 tablespoon curry powder
1 teaspoon ground cumin
1/8 teaspoon paprika
2 1/2 cups defatted chicken stock or canned broth
1/2 pound green beans, trimmed, sliced
2 carrots, peeled, ends removed, sliced
4 cups cooked turkey, cubed into 1/2- to 1-inch pieces
1/4 cup dried apricots, chopped
3 tablespoons lemon juice

■ In a large skillet, toast the almonds over medium heat, stirring frequently until golden, about 5 minutes. Remove from the skillet and set aside.

In the same skillet, heat the oil over medium heat. Add the green onion and red pepper; cook 2 minutes, stirring occasionally.

Add the rice, bay leaf, curry powder, cumin and paprika. Cook 2 minutes, stirring. Add the chicken stock or broth, green beans and carrots. Increase heat to high and bring to a boil. Reduce heat to low; cover and simmer for 15 minutes.

Remove the rice from heat. Stir the turkey, almonds and apricots into the rice; add the lemon juice. Return to heat, cover and simmer until the rice is tender and the turkey is heated through, about 5 minutes. Remove and discard the bay leaf.

Nutrition Information Per Serving

			% of daily value
Calories	409		
Calories from fat	24	%	
Fat	11	g	17%
Saturated fat	2.5	g	13%
Cholesterol	72	mg	24%
Sodium	407	mg	17%
Carbohydrate	42	g	14%
Fiber	3.5	g	
Sugar	5	g	
Protein	35	g	

Diabetic exchange

4 lean meat, 2 starch, 1 vegetable, 1/2 fruit

Grilled Chicken Breasts with Peach Chutney

If you're looking for something new to liven up your diet, try serving a unique chutney with grilled fish or chicken. Chutneys were first used in Indian cuisine as relishes or sauces. They rarely contain fat and are low in sodium. They can be, however, high in calories if prepared with large amounts of sugar.

4 servings

1 tablespoon vegetable oil
1/3 cup white wine vinegar
1 tablespoon fresh ginger, washed, peeled, grated
1 teaspoon ground turmeric or curry powder
1 pinch of saffron
1 teaspoon ground coriander
2 dashes ground red (cayenne) pepper
2 skinless, boneless whole chicken breasts, (20 ounces) cut in half, washed and patted dry
Mint or cilantro sprigs for garnish, optional
Peach Chutney (recipe follows)

■ In a small bowl, combine the vegetable oil, white wine vinegar, ginger, turmeric or curry powder, saffron, coriander and ground red pepper. Pour the mixture into a plastic sealable bag or a shallow nonreactive dish. Add the chicken and marinate, sealed in the bag or covered, in the refrigerator for 2 hours, turning the chicken 3 or 4 times.

Preheat the grill or broiler. Remove the chicken from the marinade and place the chicken over the grill or on the rack of the broiler pan. Baste with the marinade, turn, baste again. Cook the chicken for 8 minutes on each side, or until the chicken is well browned on both sides and is opaque throughout when cut with a knife.

Garnish the serving plate with mint or cilantro sprigs, and serve the chutney alongside the chicken.

Cook's note:

When using a marinade for basting, brush it on as you begin grilling to ensure that it is cooked.

Nutrition Information Per Serving

			% of daily value
Calories	251		
Calories from fat	18	%	
Fat	5	g	8%
Saturated fat	1.5	g	8%
Cholesterol	109	mg	36%
Sodium	111	mg	5%
Carbohydrate	7	g	2%
Fiber	0.5	g	
Sugar	4	g	
Protein	40	g	

Diabetic exchange

5 1/2 lean meat, 1/2 fruit

60

Fresh Peach Chutney

10 servings

2 ripe peaches, pitted, chopped; or 2 cups canned peaches in light juice, well drained
1 small red bell pepper, cored, seeded, chopped
1/2 medium white onion, peeled, ends removed, chopped
2 green onions, washed, ends removed, chopped
1/2 teaspoon ground ginger
1/8 teaspoon ground turmeric or curry powder
1/8 teaspoon ground cloves
1/4 cup white wine vinegar
2 tablespoons brown sugar

■ In a medium ceramic or glass bowl, combine the peaches, red bell pepper, onion, green onion, ginger, turmeric or curry powder, cloves, white wine vinegar and brown sugar. Stir the mixture until well combined.

Cover or seal and let sit at room temperature for 30 minutes to 1 hour to allow flavors to develop. Serve with Grilled Chicken Breasts.

Makes 2 1/2 cups.

Nutrition Information Per Serving 1/4 cup

			% of daily value
Calories	**30**		
Calories from fat	**0**	%	
Fat	**0**	g	0%
Saturated fat	**0**	g	0%
Cholesterol	**0**	mg	0%
Sodium	**2**	mg	1%
Carbohydrate	**8**	g	3%
Fiber	**0.5**	g	
Sugar	**6**	g	
Protein	**trace**	g	

1/2 fruit

Meat Lovers' Turkey Pizza

Like grown-ups trying to learn to live a healthier life, children must be taught the value of good nutrition and regular exercise. This pizza is a fun and tasty way to encourage your children to enjoy healthy foods.

8 servings

Vegetable oil cooking spray
1 tablespoon cornmeal
2 medium celery stalks, washed, ends removed, sliced
1 medium red onion, peeled, ends removed, cut into wedges
1 large sweet pepper, washed, cored, seeded, diced
1 teaspoon dried rosemary leaves, crushed
1/8 teaspoon freshly ground pepper
3 cups ground turkey breast
2 cups shredded fat-free mozzarella cheese, divided
1 1/2 ounces mushroom soup mix
1 pound hot roll mix (made according to pizza directions)

■ Preheat the oven to 425 degrees. Spray a baking sheet and large skillet with the cooking spray. Sprinkle the baking sheet with cornmeal. Set aside.

In a large skillet, saute the celery, red onion, sweet pepper, rosemary, ground pepper and ground turkey for about 10 minutes, breaking up the turkey.

Remove from heat and blot with a paper towel to remove excess moisture. Stir in 1 cup of the mozzarella cheese and the soup mix.

Spread the pizza dough on the prepared baking sheet. Bake for 10 minutes. Remove from the oven and sprinkle with the turkey-vegetable mixture, then sprinkle with the remaining 1 cup of cheese.

Bake for 15 to 20 minutes or until golden. Remove from the oven and serve.

Cook's note:

For a special garnish, reserve 1/2 cup of the dough. Cut into 3 sections. Roll each section into a 10-inch rope. After you add the turkey-vegetable mix and the last of the cheese, arrange the ropes like spokes on top of the cheese, pinching the ends of the ropes to attach to the crust on the sides; then bake.

Nutrition Information Per Serving

			% of daily value
Calories	**398**		
Calories from fat	**13**	%	
Fat	**6**	g	9%
Saturated fat	**trace**	g	1%
Cholesterol	**64**	mg	21%
Sodium	**900**	mg	38%
Carbohydrate	**54**	g	18%
Fiber	**1**	g	
Sugar	**1**	g	
Protein	**34**	g	

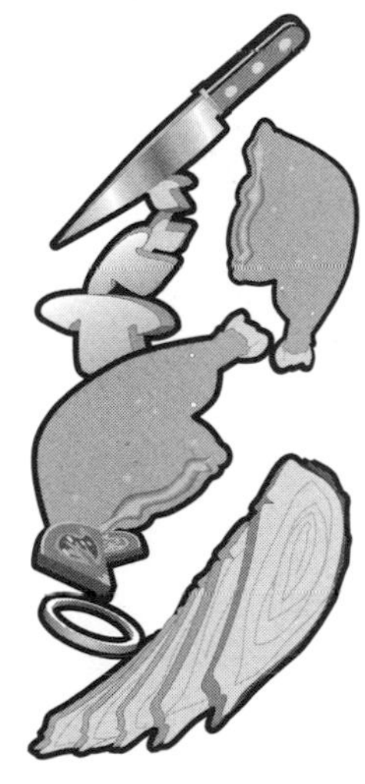

Diabetic exchange

3 lean meat, 3 bread, 1 vegetable

30

Microwave Stuffed Peppers

This recipe uses lean ground turkey in place of ground beef. By making this small change, you cut 100 calories and 8 grams of fat from each stuffed pepper without sacrificing taste. For those of you looking to make big changes in your diet, try leaving out the meat and have a vegetarian stuffed pepper.

Cook's note:

Microwave cooking time will vary depending on the wattage of the microwave.

4 servings

4 medium green, red or yellow peppers, washed
2 tablespoons water
3/4 pound lean ground turkey
1/2 cup finely chopped onion
1/2 cup finely chopped carrot
1 clove garlic, peeled, ends removed, minced
1 can (8 ounces) tomato sauce
1/2 cup cooked brown rice
1/4 cup raisins
1 teaspoon chili powder
1/8 teaspoon allspice
Few dashes hot pepper sauce, to taste

■ Cut the tops from the peppers; discard the cores, seeds and membranes. Chop enough of the tops to make 1/2 cup; set aside.

Place the peppers, cut side up, in an 8-by-8-by-2-inch baking dish. Add the water and cover with clear vented plastic wrap. Cook on 100 percent power in the microwave for 3 to 5 minutes, or until the peppers are barely tender; give the dish a half-turn once during cooking. Remove the peppers from the microwave, drain and set aside.

In a 2-quart casserole, crumble the ground turkey. Stir in the reserved 1/2 cup chopped green pepper, onion, carrot and garlic. Cover and microwave on 100 percent power for 5 to 6 minutes, or until the meat is no longer pink, stirring once.

Remove from the microwave and drain off the fat. Stir in the tomato sauce, rice, raisins, chili powder, allspice and hot pepper sauce. Evenly divide the mixture among the four pepper shells.

Cover with clear vented plastic wrap.

Cook on 100 percent power for 4 to 5 minutes or until the filling is hot and the peppers are crisp-tender, giving the dish a quarter-turn after 2 minutes. Remove from the microwave and serve.

Nutrition Information Per Serving

			% of daily value
Calories	195		
Calories from fat	28	%	
Fat	6	g	9%
Saturated fat	1.5	g	8%
Cholesterol	26	mg	9%
Sodium	411	mg	17%
Carbohydrate	25	g	8%
Fiber	3.5	g	
Sugar	9	g	
Protein	12	g	

Diabetic exchange

2 vegetable, 1/2 fruit, 1/2 starch, 2 meat

Parmesan Oven-Fried Chicken

Marinades are a simple way to tenderize foods. Some recipes — such as this one — use the marinade primarily for flavor. The benefits of tenderizing come through when cooking with lean cuts of meat such as round steak, flank steak or sirloin tip.

4 servings

1 1/4 pound boneless chicken breast, skinned, washed and patted dry
1/4 cup low-calorie Italian salad dressing
Vegetable oil cooking spray
1/2 cup fine, dry Italian bread crumbs
1/3 cup Parmesan cheese, grated
2 tablespoons fresh parsley, washed and chopped
1/4 teaspoon garlic powder
1/4 teaspoon pepper

■ Marinate the chicken in the salad dressing overnight.

Preheat the oven to 350 degrees. Spray a 9-by-13-inch baking dish with the cooking spray.

In a small bowl, combine the Italian bread crumbs, Parmesan cheese, parsley, garlic powder and pepper. Turn the chicken over in the salad dressing to moisten all sides. Dredge the chicken in the bread-crumb mixture.

Place in the prepared dish and bake uncovered for 35 to 45 minutes or until tender.

Nutrition Information Per Serving

			% of daily value
Calories	291		
Calories from fat	28	%	
Fat	9	g	14%
Saturated fat	3	g	15%
Cholesterol	104	mg	35%
Sodium	448	mg	19%
Carbohydrate	10	g	3%
Fiber	0.5	g	
Sugar	1	g	
Protein	41	g	

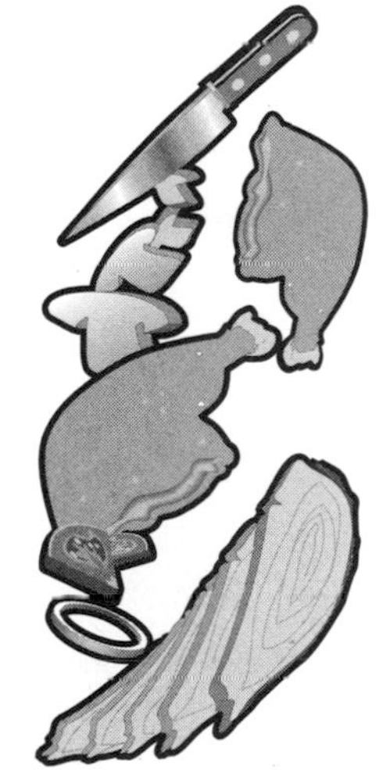

5 1/2 lean meat, 1/2 starch

150

Red Beans & Rice with Smoked Turkey

The smoked turkey used in this red beans and rice recipe adds a wonderful flavor. But all turkey products are not the same. It is important to read food labels carefully because many turkey products contain high amounts of fat from the use of fatty skin. You also need to check the amount of sodium in prepared turkey products. Some varieties of turkey bacon can have as much as 500 mg of sodium per ounce.

8 servings

10 cups water, divided
1 pound dry kidney beans, rinsed and sorted
1 pound smoked turkey (wings or breast), cut into 1/2-inch pieces (about 3 cups)
2 bay leaves
1 large green pepper, washed, cored, seeded, chopped
2 medium Spanish onions, peeled, ends removed, chopped
3 cloves garlic, peeled, ends removed, minced
1 cup coarsely chopped celery with leaves
1 tablespoon chili powder
1 teaspoon oregano
1 teaspoon basil
1/2 teaspoon Worcestershire sauce
1 1/2 cups uncooked long-grain brown rice
1/2 cup sliced green onion
1/2 red pepper, washed, cored, seeded, chopped
1/4 cup red wine vinegar

■ In a large saucepan, bring 6 cups of water to a boil. Add the beans and cook for 2 minutes. Remove from heat. Cover the saucepan and let stand for 1 hour.

Drain the beans. Return them to the saucepan. Add the remaining 4 cups of water, turkey, bay leaves, green pepper, Spanish onion, garlic, celery, chili powder, oregano, basil and Worcestershire sauce. Simmer uncovered, stirring occasionally, for 2 hours or until the beans are very tender.

Prepare the brown rice according to the package directions. Keep warm and set aside.

Remove and discard the bay leaves from the mixture. Add the green onion and red pepper to the saucepan. Simmer for 10 to 15 minutes. Stir in the red wine vinegar. Serve the bean mixture over brown rice.

Nutrition Information Per Serving

			% of daily value
Calories	303		
Calories from fat	14	%	
Fat	5	g	8%
Saturated fat	1	g	5%
Cholesterol	32	mg	11%
Sodium	506	mg	21%
Carbohydrate	46	g	15%
Fiber	3	g	
Sugar	1	g	
Protein	19	g	

1 1/2 lean meat, 3 starch

Rice-Stuffed Chicken

There's something wonderful about spooning hot stuffing onto the plates of your family. Steamy dressing is comfort food at its finest. This rice stuffing absorbs the juices of the roasted chicken, giving it a very satisfying flavor.

8 servings 

1 tablespoon oil
1/2 cup celery, washed, ends removed, chopped
1/2 cup onion, peeled, ends removed, chopped
1 1/2 cups cooked rice
1 can (16 ounces) tomatoes, crushed or cut up
1/2 teaspoon rubbed or ground sage
1/8 teaspoon pepper
1 roasting chicken (6 pounds), empty cavity, wash and pat dry

■ Preheat the oven to 375 degrees. In a large skillet, heat the oil over medium heat and cook the celery and onion for 3 minutes, until tender. Add the rice, tomatoes, sage and pepper to the celery mixture.

Loosely stuff the celery-rice mixture into the body and neck cavity of the chicken; truss.

Place the bird breast side up on a rack in a shallow roasting pan. Roast, uncovered, for 2 hours. Brush occasionally with pan drippings.

Nutrition Information Per Serving

			% of daily value
Calories	255		
Calories from fat	21	%	
Fat	6	g	9%
Saturated fat	1.5	g	8%
Cholesterol	97	mg	4%
Sodium	248	mg	10%
Carbohydrate	12	g	4%
Fiber	1	g	
Sugar	2	g	
Protein	37	g	

Cook's note:

Remove the leftover rice stuffing from the chicken cavity before storing.

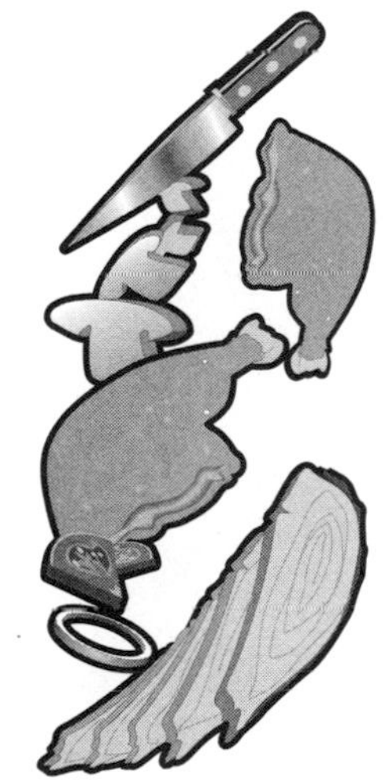

Diabetic exchange

4 1/2 lean meat, 1/2 starch, 1 vegetable

30

Stuffed Cabbage Rolls

Cabbage is the perfect summer vegetable, whether served in slaw, stuffed with meat and vegetables, or simply steamed. But who wants to steam vegetables in summer? Not us! This recipe calls for the cabbage to be prepared in the microwave, guaranteeing that it remains crisp, flavorful and packed with nutrients.

4 servings

1 can (8 ounces) tomato sauce
1 small carrot, peeled, ends removed, shredded (about 1/4 cup)
1/4 cup chopped zucchini
6 tablespoons water, divided
1/4 teaspoon dried basil
1/4 teaspoon dried oregano
8 large cabbage leaves, washed, tough center veins trimmed
2 egg whites
1/3 cup fine, dry, seasoned bread crumbs
2 stalks celery, washed, ends removed, finely chopped
1 small onion, peeled, ends removed, finely chopped
Dash of pepper
1 pound ground raw turkey

■ In a microwave-safe, medium-size bowl, combine the tomato sauce, carrot, zucchini, 2 tablespoons water, basil and oregano. Cover with plastic wrap or a natural cover, and microwave on high for 2 minutes. Remove from the microwave and set aside.

Place the cabbage in a microwave-safe dish. Cover with plastic wrap or a natural cover, and microwave on high for 3 to 5 minutes or until limp.

Meanwhile, in a medium-size mixing bowl, combine the egg whites, bread crumbs, celery, onion and pepper. Add the turkey and mix well.

Remove the cabbage leaves from the microwave and spread the leaves on a work surface.

Evenly divide the turkey mixture between the cabbage leaves. Fold in the sides; roll up. Place 8 rolls in an 8-by-8-inch or 9-by-9-inch microwave-safe baking pan. Sprinkle with the remaining 4 tablespoons of water. Cover with plastic wrap or a natural cover, and microwave on high for 6 minutes. Remove from the microwave.

Rearrange the cabbage rolls, moving those on the inside of the pan to the outside. Cover and microwave for 5 minutes. Drain.

Top with the sauce and serve.

Nutrition Information Per Serving

			% of daily value
Calories	**220**		
Calories from fat	**8**	%	
Fat	**2**	g	3%
Saturated fat	**trace**	g	1%
Cholesterol	**59**	mg	20%
Sodium	**578**	mg	24%
Carbohydrate	**18**	g	6%
Fiber	**3.5**	g	
Sugar	**3**	g	
Protein	**37**	g	

Diabetic exchange

4 1/2 lean meat, 1 starch, 1 vegetable

Teriyaki Chicken Kabobs

The combination of soy sauce, white wine and Russian salad dressing make this marinade especially potent. The concoction allows the chicken breast to soften and deeply absorb the flavors of the ginger and garlic.

6 servings

1/8 cup reduced-sodium soy sauce
1/2 cup dry white wine
1/4 cup reduced-calorie Russian salad dressing
1/4 teaspoon garlic powder; or clove of fresh garlic, peeled, ends removed, minced
1/2 teaspoon fresh ginger, grated; or 1 teaspoon powdered ginger
1 1/2 pounds chicken breast, boneless, skinless, washed, patted dry, cut into 1-inch cubes
2 medium red onions, peeled, ends removed, cut into 16 wedges
16 cherry tomatoes
1 large bell pepper, green or red, seeded, cored, cut into 16 pieces
2 small zucchini squash, diced into 16 cubes
Vegetable oil cooking spray
3 cups cooked rice

■ Combine the soy sauce, wine, Russian dressing, garlic and ginger in a container; mix well. Refrigerate one-third of the mixture to use when cooking the kabobs; pour the remaining two-thirds over the chicken and marinate in the refrigerator at least two hours.

Alternate the chicken and vegetables on four skewers.

Coat the grill with the cooking spray. Grill the kabobs 5 to 6 inches from medium-hot coals for 15 minutes, or until done. Coat often with the reserved marinade, turning frequently.

Serve over rice.

Nutrition Information Per Serving

		% of daily value
Calories	**286**	
Calories from fat	**13** %	
Fat	**4** g	6%
Saturated fat	**1** g	5%
Cholesterol	**73** mg	24%
Sodium	**342** mg	14%
Carbohydrate	**28** g	9%
Fiber	**2.5** g	
Sugar	**6** g	
Protein	**30** g	

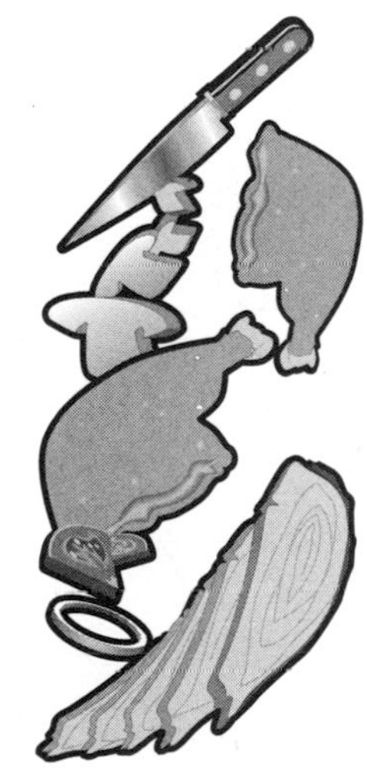

Diabetic exchange

3 lean meat, 1 1/2 starch, 1 vegetable

105

Tex-Mex Turkey Casserole

This turkey casserole is a spicy way to use turkey leftovers and, if you prepare extra, it can be frozen to be used as a quick meal later.

6 servings

1 tablespoon vegetable oil
1/4 cup onion, peeled, ends removed, chopped
1/4 cup green pepper, washed, seeded, cored, chopped
1 can (28 ounces) tomatoes, crushed (3 1/2 cups)
1 can (1 pint 2 ounces), tomato juice (2 1/4 cups)
1 teaspoon garlic powder
1/8 teaspoon black pepper
1/8 teaspoon ground red (cayenne) pepper
1 cup long-grain rice, uncooked
3 cups white meat turkey, cooked, bones removed, skinned, diced
Parsley, washed, dried (optional)

■ Preheat the oven to 350 degrees. In a large skillet, heat the vegetable oil and saute the onion and green pepper over medium heat, about 3 minutes.

Add the tomatoes, tomato juice, garlic powder, black pepper and ground red pepper. Mix well; stir in the rice.

Cover; bring to a boil.

Mix in the turkey and pour into a 3-quart ungreased casserole. Bake, covered, for 1 hour 25 minutes or until the rice is tender, stirring once. Garnish with parsley.

Serves 6.

Nutrition Information Per Serving

			% of daily value
Calories	**292**		
Calories from fat	**18**	%	
Fat	**6**	g	9%
Saturated fat	**1**	g	5%
Cholesterol	**49**	mg	16%
Sodium	**606**	mg	25%
Carbohydrate	**35**	g	12%
Fiber	**4**	g	
Sugar	**6**	g	
Protein	**26**	g	

2 1/2 lean meat, 2 starch, 1 vegetable

15

Turkey or Chicken Tetrazzini

There's no need to give up cream sauces in order to follow a low-fat diet. Tetrazzini, a traditional casserole combining turkey or chicken with pasta, usually is prepared with a thick cream sauce and grated cheese. But you can make a Heart Smart® version by substituting evaporated skim milk for cream and a small amount of vegetable oil for butter. Making these simple substitutions reduces the fat content per serving from 52 grams to 7 grams.

6 servings

1 tablespoon oil
1/4 cup all-purpose flour
1/4 teaspoon pepper
1 cup defatted chicken broth
8 ounces evaporated skim milk
2 tablespoons sherry
7 ounces spaghetti, cooked and drained
2 cups cooked cubed turkey breast or chicken breast
1 can (3 ounces) sliced mushrooms, drained
1/2 cup Parmesan cheese, grated

■ Preheat the oven to 350 degrees. In a large saucepan, heat the oil over low heat. Blend in the flour and pepper, stirring until the mixture is smooth and bubbly.

Slowly whisk in the broth and evaporated skim milk, stirring constantly. Bring to a boil; boil and stir for 1 minute. Stir in the sherry, spaghetti, turkey or chicken, and mushrooms.

Pour into an ungreased 2-quart casserole dish and sprinkle with Parmesan cheese. Bake, uncovered, for 30 minutes or until bubbly. To brown, preheat the broiler and place the casserole under the broiler. Watch so that it doesn't burn.

Nutrition Information Per Serving

			% of daily value
Calories	331		
Calories from fat	20	%	
Fat	7	g	11%
Saturated fat	2.5	g	13%
Cholesterol	41	mg	14%
Sodium	424	mg	18%
Carbohydrate	37	g	12%
Fiber	0.5	g	
Sugar	0	g	
Protein	27	g	

Diabetic exchange

3 lean meat, 2 1/2 starch

45 minutes

Turkey Cheddar Casserole with Noodles

Low-fat cheddar cheese keeps this satisfying entree Heart Smart® and provides flavor and color to the dish. Kids really go for this casserole, too.

6 servings

1 package (10 ounces) frozen broccoli, cooked according to package directions
2 tablespoons chicken broth
2 tablespoons flour
1/4 teaspoon white pepper
1/4 teaspoon prepared mustard
2 cups skim milk
1 cup low-fat cheddar cheese, grated
Vegetable oil cooking spray
2 cups turkey breast or chicken breast cooked, cubed
1/4 cup slivered almonds
4 ounces medium-wide noodles, cooked according to package directions, omitting salt and fat

■ Dice the broccoli stems, leaving the florets whole. Set aside.

In a medium saucepan over medium heat, heat the chicken broth. Blend in the flour. Add the pepper, mustard and skim milk. Cook, stirring constantly, until thickened. Remove from heat; stir in the cheese.

Preheat the oven to 400 degrees. Spray a 3-quart casserole with the cooking spray. Alternate layers of noodles, diced broccoli, turkey and cheese sauce in the casserole until all are used. Arrange the florets on top. Sprinkle with almonds. Cover.

Bake for 30 minutes or until bubbly throughout.

Nutrition Information Per Serving

			% of daily value
Calories	279		
Calories from fat	27	%	
Fat	9	g	14%
Saturated fat	3	g	15%
Cholesterol	64	mg	21%
Sodium	457	mg	19%
Carbohydrate	23	g	8%
Fiber	0.5	g	
Sugar	4	g	
Protein	27	g	

Diabetic exchange

3 lean meat, 1 starch, 1 vegetable

Desserts

Almond Biscotti

These delicious little cookies are low in saturated fat and high in flavor. Another bonus is this recipe makes enough batter for 4 dozen cookies.

48 servings

1/2 cup sugar
2 tablespoons oil
4 egg whites
1 teaspoon almond extract
1/4 teaspoon anise extract
1 3/4 cups all-purpose flour, divided
1/2 cup slivered almonds
1 teaspoon baking powder
Vegetable oil cooking spray

■ In a large bowl, combine the sugar, oil, egg whites, almond and anise extracts. Beat at medium speed with an electric mixer until well blended.

In a separate bowl combine 1 1/2 cups of the flour, almonds and baking powder. Add the flour mixture to the egg-white mixture, beating well. Stir in the remaining 1/4 cup flour to make a soft dough.

Cover and chill the dough in the refrigerator at least 2 hours. When the dough is chilled, remove from the refrigerator.

Preheat the oven to 350 degrees. Spray a baking sheet with the cooking spray.

Spray two sheets of heavy-plastic wrap with the cooking spray. Divide the dough in half. Place one half on one sheet of prepared plastic wrap. Using the plastic wrap as a guide, shape the dough into a 12-inch log. Repeat with the remaining half of dough. Transfer the dough logs to a prepared baking sheet. Flatten the logs to a 3/4-inch thickness. Bake for 20 minutes. Remove from the oven and transfer to a wire rack and let cool for 5 minutes. Reduce the oven temperature to 300 degrees.

Slice the logs diagonally into 1/4-inch slices. Place the slices on baking sheets, with the cut sides down. Bake for 15 minutes, turn the cookies over, and bake an additional 15 minutes or 30 minutes total. Remove from the oven and cool on wire racks.

Makes 4 dozen cookies.

Nutrition Information Per Serving

			% of daily value
Calories	**39**		
Calories from fat	**29**	%	
Fat	**1**	g	2%
Saturated fat	**trace**	g	1%
Cholesterol	**0**	mg	0%
Sodium	**12**	mg	1%
Carbohydrate	**6**	g	2%
Fiber	**trace**	g	
Sugar	**2**	g	
Protein	**1**	g	

Diabetic exchange

1/2 starch

Applesauce Carrot Cake

Applesauce is a wonderful Heart Smart® ingredient that adds body and texture to many cake and muffin recipes. Here, it's teamed with carrots to create a cake that is full-flavored and colorful.

16 servings

Vegetable oil cooking spray
2 cups flour, sifted
1/3 cup sugar
1/3 cup packed brown sugar
2 teaspoons baking powder
1 teaspoon cinnamon
1/4 teaspoon nutmeg
1/4 teaspoon ground ginger
1/4 teaspoon salt
3/4 cup unsweetened applesauce
1/4 cup vegetable oil
2 egg whites
3 cups coarsely grated carrots (about 12 carrots)
1/4 cup raisins

■ Preheat the oven to 350 degrees. Spray a 9-inch tube pan with the cooking spray. In a large mixing bowl, combine the flour, sugar, brown sugar, baking powder, cinnamon, nutmeg, ginger and salt. Set aside.

In a small bowl, combine the applesauce, oil and egg whites; blend well. Add to the flour mixture, stirring until well mixed. Add the carrots and raisins, and mix again.

Pour into the prepared pan.

Bake for 1 hour and 10 minutes, or until a wooden toothpick inserted into thickest part of the cake comes out clean. Set the cake pan on a wire rack to cool for 5 minutes. Run a knife around edges to loosen the cake, and turn onto the rack to cool completely.

Nutrition Information Per Serving

			% of daily value
Calories	**143**		
Calories from fat	**22**	%	
Fat	**4**	g	6%
Saturated fat	**0.5**	g	3%
Cholesterol	**0**	mg	0%
Sodium	**91**	mg	4%
Carbohydrate	**26**	g	9%
Fiber	**1.5**	g	
Sugar	**11**	g	
Protein	**2**	g	

Diabetic exchange

1 starch, 3/4 fruit, 1/2 fat

Bread Pudding with Lemon Raisin Sauce

Health professionals recommend that 50 to 60 percent of your calories come from carbohydrates. This Bread Pudding with Lemon Raisin Sauce is warm and filling, very low in fat and high in carbohydrates.

6 servings

Pudding:

Vegetable oil cooking spray
4 cups bread cubes (8 slices of bread)
4 egg whites, well beaten
2 3/4 cups of skim milk
1/2 cup firmly packed light brown sugar
1 1/2 teaspoons ground cinnamon
2 tablespoons lemon juice from concentrate

Sauce:

1/2 cup granulated sugar
1/4 cup firmly packed light brown sugar
2 tablespoons cornstarch
3/4 cup water
1/4 cup lemon juice
1/4 cup raisins

■ Preheat the oven to 350 degrees. Spray a 9-inch-square baking dish with the cooking spray. Arrange the bread cubes in the dish. In a medium bowl, add the egg whites, skim milk, brown sugar, cinnamon and lemon juice; mix well. Pour over the bread cubes.

Bake 40 to 45 minutes or until a knife inserted near the center comes out clean.

Meanwhile, to prepare the lemon raisin sauce, combine the granulated and brown sugars and cornstarch in a small saucepan. Gradually add the water and lemon juice; mix well. Over medium heat, cook and stir until the mixture comes to a boil. Reduce heat; cook and stir 3 to 4 minutes longer or until thickened and clear. Stir in the raisins and let stand 5 minutes.

Remove the bread pudding from the oven, and serve warm with 1/4 cup of the lemon raisin sauce over each slice.

Nutrition Information Per Serving

			% of daily value
Calories	**300**		
Calories from fat	**3**	%	
Fat	**1**	g	2%
Saturated fat	**0.5**	g	3%
Cholesterol	**2**	mg	1%
Sodium	**208**	mg	9%
Carbohydrate	**67**	g	22%
Fiber	**0.5**	g	
Sugar	**46**	g	
Protein	**8**	g	

Diabetic exchange

3 1/2 starch, 1/2 milk, 1/2 fruit

45

Carrot Raisin Snack Cake

If you're looking for new ways to include more fruits and vegetables in your diet, try using them in desserts. This Carrot Raisin Snack Cake provides a healthy dose of vitamins.

9 servings

Vegetable oil cooking spray
3 tablespoons vegetable oil
1/2 cup sugar
2 egg whites
1/4 cup skim milk
1/2 teaspoon vanilla
1/2 cup finely shredded carrots
1/2 cup raisins
1/4 cup crushed pineapple, well-drained
1 cup all-purpose flour
1 1/4 teaspoons baking powder
1/4 teaspoon ground cinnamon
Dash of ground nutmeg
2 teaspoons powdered sugar, sifted

■ Spray an 8-by-8-inch baking pan with the cooking spray. Preheat the oven to 350 degrees.

In a medium-size mixing bowl, beat the vegetable oil and sugar until blended. Beat in the egg whites, milk and vanilla. Stir in the carrots, raisins and pineapple. In a small bowl, combine the flour, baking powder, cinnamon and nutmeg. Add to the carrot mixture and stir until blended.

Pour the batter evenly into the prepared pan. Bake 20 to 25 minutes, or until a wooden pick inserted into the center comes out clean. Remove from the oven and cool on a wire rack. If desired, remove from the pan after cooling 10 minutes. Then cool completely.

When the cake is completely cooled, lightly dust with powdered sugar.

Cook's note:

A diet low in fat and high in vitamin C and beta carotene is beneficial to your immune system. If you take vitamins, they should be used to supplement a balanced diet that includes at least five servings of fruits and vegetables daily.

Nutrition Information Per Serving

			% of daily value
Calories	168		
Calories from fat	27	%	
Fat	5	g	8%
Saturated fat	0.5	g	3%
Cholesterol	trace	mg	1%
Sodium	65	mg	3%
Carbohydrate	30	g	10%
Fiber	1	g	
Sugar	17	g	
Protein	3	g	

Diabetic exchange

1 starch, 1 fruit, 1 fat

Chewy Oatmeal Bars

Many children participate in sports after school, so an afternoon snack low in fat and high in carbohydrates helps supply the fuel for practices and games. This recipe for Chewy Oatmeal Bars can be made ahead, wrapped in plastic, and sent in an equipment bag with a water bottle to give your young athlete the nutritional muscle he or she will need to perform well.

24 servings

Vegetable oil cooking spray
2 cups quick-cooking rolled oats
1 cup packed brown sugar
1/3 cup vegetable oil
3 tablespoons applesauce
2 egg whites
1/4 teaspoon salt
1/2 teaspoon almond extract
1/2 cup raisins

■ Preheat the oven to 325 degrees. Spray a 9-by-9-inch baking dish with the cooking spray. In a medium-size mixing bowl, stir together the oats, brown sugar, vegetable oil and applesauce.

Beat the egg whites until frothy and add to the oat mixture. Stir in the salt and almond extract. Stir in the raisins.

Spread the mixture into the prepared pan. Bake 30 to 35 minutes, or until the top is slightly golden and a wooden pick inserted into the center comes out clean. Remove from the oven and let cool 10 minutes. Cut into bars.

Cook's note:

Foods high in carbohydrates are a good source of energy. Such foods include fruits, fruit juices, milk, yogurt, vegetables, cereals, pastas and bagels.

Nutrition Information Per Serving

			% of daily value
Calories	103		
Calories from fat	29	%	
Fat	3	g	5%
Saturated fat	0.5	g	3%
Cholesterol	0	mg	0%
Sodium	30	mg	1%
Carbohydrate	17	g	6%
Fiber	0.5	g	
Sugar	11	g	
Protein	2	g	

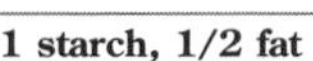

1 starch, 1/2 fat

40

Chocolate Brownies

Do you crave chocolate, but think it's a no-no on a Heart Smart® diet? Think again. Although chocolate candy is high in fat, foods made with cocoa powder and chocolate syrup can allow you to enjoy the taste of chocolate without consuming too much fat.

9 servings

Vegetable oil cooking spray or floured baking spray
3 tablespoons vegetable oil
3/4 cup sugar
2 egg whites, beaten
1/4 cup unsweetened cocoa
3/4 cup sifted flour
1 teaspoon baking powder
1 tablespoon water
1/2 teaspoon vanilla extract

Nutrition Information Per Serving

			% of daily value
Calories	**144**		
Calories from fat	**30**	%	
Fat	**5**	g	8%
Saturated fat	**0.5**	g	3%
Cholesterol	**0**	mg	0%
Sodium	**51**	mg	2%
Carbohydrate	**25**	g	8%
Fiber	**0.5**	g	
Sugar	**16**	g	
Protein	**2**	g	

■ Preheat the oven to 350 degrees.
Spray an 8-by-8-by-2-inch baking pan with vegetable oil cooking spray or floured baking spray; set aside.
In a medium bowl, blend together the oil and sugar. Stir in the beaten egg whites.
In a separate bowl, sift together the cocoa, flour and baking powder.
Add the flour mixture to the egg mixture and thoroughly combine.
Add the water and vanilla extract.
Pour the batter into the prepared pan and bake for 25 minutes. Remove from the oven and cool slightly.
Cut into squares.

Diabetic exchange

1 1/2 starch, 1 fat

Chocolate Chip Cereal Cookies

Cookies can be classified as bar, drop, rolled, pressed, molded, shaped and refrigerated. Bar and drop cookies are made with a soft dough, which is easier to adapt to a low-fat version. These Chocolate Chip Cereal Cookies are fun to make and contain a 1/2 gram of fiber and only 3 grams of fat per cookie.

24 servings

1 cup all-purpose flour
1/2 teaspoon baking powder
1/2 teaspoon baking soda
1/4 cup vegetable oil
1/2 cup sugar
1/2 cup firmly packed brown sugar
2 egg whites
1 teaspoon vanilla
1 cup fruit-nut-flake type cereal, such as Just Right or Basic 4
1/4 cup chocolate chips

■ Preheat the oven to 375 degrees.

In a medium-size bowl, mix together the flour, baking powder and baking soda; set aside.

In a large mixing bowl, blend the vegetable oil with the sugar and brown sugar. Beat in the egg whites and vanilla. Add the flour mixture, cereal and chocolate chips, mixing until just blended. Drop by teaspoonfuls on an ungreased baking sheet, about 2 inches apart.

Bake for 10 minutes; do not overbake. Cookies will puff up and then flatten. Remove from the oven and cool slightly on the baking sheet, then remove to a wire rack to cool completely.

How the Cookies Stack Up (1 ounce)

	Calories	Fat(g)	% fat calories	Fiber
Chocolate chip cookie	150	7.5	45	0.6
Fig bar (2)	106	2	16	1.2
Peanut butter cookie	150	7.5	48	0.6
Shortbread	140	7	43	0
Oatmeal cookie	132	5	38	0.3
Pecan shortbread	160	10	56	0
Heart Smart Chocolate Chip Cereal Cookie	93	3	29	0.5

Cook's note:

Americans' love affair with cookies began when the Dutch brought their "koekjes" to the New World. A cookie is basically a mixture of flour, sugar and fat. The taste and consistency are varied by tossing in everything from nuts to chocolate.

Nutrition Information Per Serving

		% of daily value
Calories	**93**	
Calories from fat	**28** %	
Fat	**3** g	5%
Saturated fat	**trace** g	1%
Cholesterol	**0** mg	0%
Sodium	**52** mg	2%
Carbohydrate	**16** g	5%
Fiber	**0.5** g	
Sugar	**10** g	
Protein	**1** g	

Diabetic exchange

1 starch, 1/2 fat

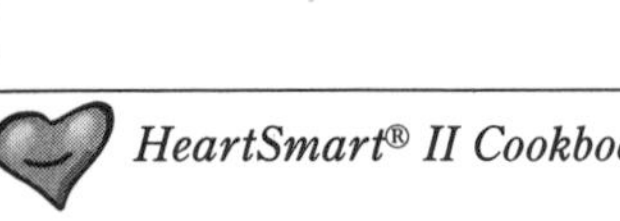

15

Crispy Marshmallow Bars

Sticky. Gooey. Delicious. Guaranteed to satisfy people who love to chew their after-meal treats. The hint of vanilla gives these marshmallow bars a special flavor not found in many rice cereal treats.

18 servings

Vegetable oil cooking spray
10 ounces miniature marshmallows
2 tablespoons vegetable oil
1 teaspoon vanilla
6 cups crisp rice cereal

■ Spray a 9-by-13-inch pan with the cooking spray. Place the marshmallows in a large microwave-safe bowl. Sprinkle with the vegetable oil and vanilla. Toss to coat so each of the marshmallows is coated with oil.

Microwave on high for 1 1/2 to 2 minutes or until the marshmallows are melted, stirring once. Stir until smooth.

Stir the cereal into the marshmallow mixture. Stir until equally combined. Press the mixture into the prepared pan as evenly as possible (if the mixture is sticking to hands, press with wax paper sprayed with cooking spray). Cool. Then cut into bars.

Nutrition Information Per Serving

			% of daily value
Calories	**101**		
Calories from fat	**18**	%	
Fat	**2**	g	3%
Saturated fat	**trace**	g	1%
Cholesterol	**0**	mg	0%
Sodium	**119**	mg	5%
Carbohydrate	**21**	g	7%
Fiber	**0**	g	
Sugar	**8**	g	
Protein	**2**	g	

Diabetic exchange

1 1/2 starch

Frozen Peach Yogurt Pie

Cold and crunchy, this freezer pie contrasts the smooth taste of frozen peaches and yogurt with the tang of gingersnap cookies. With only 5 grams of fat per serving, it's sure to become a family favorite.

8 servings

3/4 cup plus 2 tablespoons finely ground gingersnap cookies, about 16 cookies, divided
2 teaspoons diet margarine, melted
1 1/2 pounds ripe peaches, washed, dried, unpeeled, cut in half, pits removed
2 tablespoons fresh lemon juice
1 teaspoon grated lemon zest (see note)
1 tablespoon grated orange zest (see note)
1 1/2 cups plain nonfat yogurt
1/4 cup egg substitute
1/3 cup honey

■ To prepare the crust: Preheat the oven to 350 degrees. Reserve 2 tablespoons of the gingersnap crumbs. Combine the remaining 3/4 cup gingersnap crumbs and diet margarine in the bottom of a 9-inch pie plate. Press the mixture up sides. Bake for 5 minutes. Remove from the oven. Cool and set aside.

To prepare the filling: In a blender or food processor fitted with a metal blade, place the peach halves, lemon juice, lemon zest and orange zest. Puree. Add the yogurt, egg substitute and honey. Blend the mixture for 5 seconds.

Pour the mixture into the prepared crust. Freeze the pie for 2 to 3 hours or until set. Just before serving, sprinkle the remaining 2 tablespoons gingersnap crumbs on top of the pie.

Cook's note:

Plan to serve this pie the day you make it because ice crystals will form after one day. For lemon or orange zest, use only the colored part of the citrus, leaving the white part, which is bitter.

Nutrition Information Per Serving

			% of daily value
Calories	**192**		
Calories from fat	**23**	%	
Fat	**5**	g	8%
Saturated fat	**0.5**	g	3%
Cholesterol	**trace**	mg	1%
Sodium	**119**	mg	5%
Carbohydrate	**34**	g	11%
Fiber	**2**	g	
Sugar	**25**	g	
Protein	**5**	g	

Diabetic exchange

1 starch, 1 fruit, 1 fat

45

Gingerbread with Pear Sauce

This recipe for Gingerbread with Pear Sauce uses oil in place of solid fat and egg whites instead of whole eggs. It tastes just as good as traditional gingerbread but has less than half the fat.

9 servings

Vegetable oil cooking spray
3 tablespoons vegetable oil
2 tablespoons maple syrup
1/4 cup brown sugar
2 egg whites
1 1/2 cups all-purpose flour
1 teaspoon baking powder
1/2 teaspoon baking soda
1 teaspoon cinnamon
1 1/2 teaspoons ginger
1/2 teaspoon allspice
1/4 teaspoon grated nutmeg
1 cup low-fat buttermilk
2 cups water
5 tablespoons sugar, divided
3 ripe pears, peeled, cored, seeded

Nutrition Information Per Serving

			% of daily value
Calories	211		
Calories from fat	21	%	
Fat	5	g	8%
Saturated fat	1	g	5%
Cholesterol	1	mg	1%
Sodium	130	mg	5%
Carbohydrate	38	g	13%
Fiber	2	g	
Sugar	16	g	
Protein	4	g	

■ Preheat the oven to 350 degrees. Spray an 8-inch-by-8-inch baking pan with the cooking spray. In a medium bowl, mix the oil, maple syrup and brown sugar. Beat in the egg whites. Set aside.

In a large bowl combine the flour, baking powder, baking soda, cinnamon, ginger, allspice and nutmeg. Add the flour mixture to the oil-sugar mixture, mixing alternately with the buttermilk. Mix until smooth.

Pour the batter into the prepared pan and bake for 30 minutes, or until a wooden pick inserted into the center comes out clean. Remove from the oven and cool. Let stand 10 minutes, then invert onto a wire rack.

As the cake is baking, prepare the sauce. In a large saucepan, combine the water and 4 tablespoons sugar and bring to a simmer. Poach the pears in the simmering sugar water for about 10 minutes or until soft. Drain and cool the pears. When the pears are cool, puree them with remaining 1 tablespoon sugar in a blender or food processor until smooth.

Spread the sauce over the cooled cake and cut into 9 squares.

Cook's note:

Eggs are an important ingredient in many cookie and cake recipes. But considering the amount of cholesterol — 214 mg — and fat — 5 g — in one egg yolk, it is important to limit the number in baked goods.

2 starch, 1/2 fruit, 1 fat

Lemon Poppy Seed Cake

Seeds such as poppy, pumpkin, sesame and sunflower can serve as garnishes or flavor accents. A teaspoon of seeds gives a crunchy, nutty taste to foods such as low-fat yogurt, applesauce, hot cereals or muffin batters. Seeds should be used in small amounts because they contain fat. One teaspoon of poppy seeds, for example, contains 1.5 grams of fat. Store seeds at room temperature, tightly closed, in a dry place for up to three to four months, or freeze them, tightly wrapped, for up to one year.

9 servings

Floured baking spray
1 2/3 cups all-purpose flour
3/4 cup sugar
1 tablespoon poppy seeds
1 teaspoon baking soda
3/4 cup skim milk
3 tablespoons fresh lemon juice
3 tablespoons vegetable oil
1 teaspoon grated lemon rind
2 egg whites, beaten

Nutrition Information Per Serving

			% of daily value
Calories	**202**		
Calories from fat	**23**	%	
Fat	**5**	g	8%
Saturated fat	**0.5**	g	3%
Cholesterol	**trace**	mg	1%
Sodium	**116**	mg	5%
Carbohydrate	**35**	g	12%
Fiber	**0.5**	g	
Sugar	**17**	g	
Protein	**4**	g	

■ Preheat the oven to 375 degrees.

Spray an 8-by-8-inch square baking dish with floured baking spray.

In a large bowl, combine the flour, sugar, poppy seeds and baking soda. Stir well, and make a well in the center.

In a medium-size bowl, combine the skim milk, lemon juice, oil, lemon rind and egg whites. Add this mixture to the well in the flour mixture. Stir just until the dry ingredients are moistened.

Spoon the batter into the prepared baking dish. Bake for 28 minutes, or until a wooden pick inserted into the center comes out clean. Remove from the oven and cool 10 minutes in the pan on a wire rack.

Diabetic exchange

2 starch, 1 fat

45

Microwave Chocolate Pudding Cake

The walnuts in this Microwave Chocolate Pudding Cake provide a welcome crunch that contrasts with the smooth pudding texture of the cake. Remember when microwaving to rotate the dish at regular intervals to ensure even cooking.

10 servings

Vegetable oil cooking spray
6 tablespoons unsweetened cocoa powder, divided, plus 1 teaspoon for pan
1/2 cup plus 1/3 cup sugar
1 cup cake flour
2 teaspoons baking powder
1/2 cup skim milk
2 teaspoons safflower oil
1 1/2 teaspoons pure vanilla extract, divided
1/4 cup chopped walnuts (about 1 ounce)
1/3 cup light brown sugar
1 cup water
1 tablespoon confectioners' sugar

Nutrition Information Per Serving

			% of daily value
Calories	**172**		
Calories from fat	**16**	%	
Fat	**3**	g	5%
Saturated fat	**trace**	g	1%
Cholesterol	**trace**	mg	1%
Sodium	**208**	mg	9%
Carbohydrate	**36**	g	12%
Fiber	**0.5**	g	
Sugar	**23**	g	
Protein	**3**	g	

■ Lightly spray a deep 9-inch pie pan with the cooking spray and dust it with 1 teaspoon unsweetened cocoa powder.

In a bowl, sift together 3 tablespoons of the cocoa powder, 1/2 cup of sugar, the cake flour and the baking powder. Add the milk, oil and 1 teaspoon of vanilla, then stir to combine. Stir in the walnuts and spread the cake batter evenly in the pie pan.

Mix together the remaining 3 tablespoons cocoa powder, the remaining 1/3 cup sugar and the brown sugar. Stir in the remaining 1/2 teaspoon of vanilla and 1 cup of water. Pour this liquid over the batter in the pie pan.

Microwave the cake on medium (50 percent power) for 18 to 25 minutes, checking for doneness after 18 minutes. The cake is done if the batter is evenly moist but not wet. Rotate the dish a quarter-turn every 3 minutes during cooking.

Let the cake stand 5 minutes. Serve warm. Just before serving, sift the confectioners' sugar onto the cake.

Diabetic exchange

2 1/2 starch

Nutty Apple Cake

60

This delicious, crunchy apple cake is low in fat but high in soluble fiber and taste. Although apples are not high in any one nutrient, they contain moderate amounts of many vitamins and minerals.

8 servings

Floured baking spray
4 cups tart apples, washed and unpared, cored, diced
1 cup sugar
1/2 cup flour
2 teaspoons baking powder
2 egg whites
1 tablespoon vegetable oil
1 teaspoon vanilla
1/4 cup chopped walnuts
1/2 cup raisins
2 cups low-fat vanilla frozen yogurt

Cook's note:

When selecting apples, consider how they will be used. For example, Red Delicious is a crisp eating apple, while Northern Spy and McIntosh provide the best results in baked goods. Store fresh apples in a plastic bag in your refrigerator. They should keep for up to six weeks.

■ Preheat the oven to 400 degrees. Spray an 8-by-8-inch baking dish with floured baking spray.

In a large bowl, combine the apples and sugar; set aside.

In a medium bowl sift together the flour and baking powder; set aside.

In a small bowl mix the egg whites, oil and vanilla. Combine the flour mixture and the egg mixture with the apple mixture. Stir, do not beat, until thoroughly mixed. Fold in the walnuts and raisins. Pour the mixture into the prepared pan.

Bake for 30 to 40 minutes, piercing the apples with a wooden pick to check for doneness.

Remove from the oven and cut into 8 rectangles. Serve hot or cold. Top each serving with 1/4 cup of frozen yogurt.

Nutrition Information Per Serving

			% of daily value
Calories	**287**		
Calories from fat	**15**	%	
Fat	**5**	g	8%
Saturated fat	**0.5**	g	3%
Cholesterol	**1**	mg	1%
Sodium	**98**	mg	4%
Carbohydrate	**59**	g	20%
Fiber	**2.5**	g	
Sugar	**38**	g	
Protein	**5**	g	

Diabetic exchange

2 starch, 2 fruit, 1/2 fat

60

Pears Baked in Brandy

The ground cinnamon and ginger brandy pay a rich compliment to this simple but elegant dessert. The natural sugars blend with the brown sugar and lemon juice to make this an after-dinner treat everyone will enjoy.

4 servings

4 small pears, such as Bosc or Bartlett, peeled, cored, halved lengthwise
1 tablespoon lemon juice
1/2 cup ginger brandy
1 1/2 tablespoons light brown sugar
1/8 teaspoon ground cinnamon
1 tablespoon chopped walnuts

■ Preheat the oven to 375 degrees. Rub the pear halves with the lemon juice. Place cut side down in an 8-by-8-inch or larger baking dish. Pour the brandy over and around the pears.

In a small bowl, combine the brown sugar and cinnamon. Sprinkle over the pears. Bake uncovered for 40 to 50 minutes, basting occasionally with the pan juices, or until the pears are tender and the juices are slightly thickened.

To serve, place the pears onto dessert plates, spoon the juices on top and sprinkle with walnuts.

Nutrition Information Per Serving

			% of daily value
Calories	**221**		
Calories from fat	**7**	%	
Fat	**2**	g	3%
Saturated fat	**trace**	g	1%
Cholesterol	**0**	mg	0%
Sodium	**2**	mg	1%
Carbohydrate	**39**	g	13%
Fiber	**4.5**	g	
Sugar	**31**	g	
Protein	**1**	g	

Diabetic exchange

2 fruit, 1/2 starch, 1 fat

Springtime English Trifle

Specialty desserts, such as the elegant English Trifle, can contain a whopping 600 calories per serving. Rather than avoid these treats altogether, it's more sensible to eat them in moderation in lower-calorie forms. The Springtime English Trifle trims the calories by substituting low-fat ingredients and using less sugar than the traditional recipe.

10 servings

1 quart strawberries, washed, hulled and sliced (reserve some whole for garnish)
2 tablespoons sugar
15 ounces angel food cake, crust trimmed, cut into 1-inch cubes
3 tablespoons Triple Sec or liqueur of your choice (amaretto, Frangelico), divided
2 tablespoons slivered almonds, divided
1 package (3.4 ounces) vanilla pudding mix, made according to package directions, using 2 cups of skim milk

Cook's note:

Making small changes in your diet can make a big difference. If you cut 100 calories per day, in one year you would lose 10 pounds.

■ In a large bowl, place the sliced strawberries and sprinkle with the sugar. Gently toss to coat.

Line the bottom of a glass serving bowl with half of the cake cubes. Sprinkle the cake with 1 1/2 tablespoons of Triple Sec or other liqueur.

Layer half the strawberry mixture and 1 tablespoon of the almonds on the cake cubes. Layer half of the prepared pudding over the strawberries and almonds. Repeat the layers using the remaining cake, liqueur, strawberries, almonds and pudding. Cover and chill for 3 to 4 hours. Garnish with the remaining whole strawberries.

Nutrition Information Per Serving

			% of daily value
Calories	**242**		
Calories from fat	**4**	%	
Fat	**1**	g	2%
Saturated fat	**trace**	g	1%
Cholesterol	**1**	mg	1%
Sodium	**223**	mg	9%
Carbohydrate	**51**	g	17%
Fiber	**1.5**	g	
Sugar	**14**	g	
Protein	**7**	g	

2 1/2 starch, 1 fruit

Strawberry Shortcake

This version of Strawberry Shortcake contains some sugar, but with only 181 calories per serving, it fits into most diets including those of many diabetics.

8 servings

1 quart fresh strawberries, washed, hulled, sliced
1 tablespoon plus 2 teaspoons sugar, divided
1 1/4 cups all-purpose flour, divided
1 teaspoon baking powder
1/8 teaspoon baking soda
1/3 cup buttermilk
2 tablespoons vegetable oil
1 cup nonfat vanilla yogurt
1 tablespoon brown sugar
2 tablespoons Grand Marnier, optional

Nutrition Information Per Serving

		% of daily value
Calories	**181**	
Calories from fat	**19** %	
Fat	**4** g	6%
Saturated fat	**0.5** g	3%
Cholesterol	**1** mg	1%
Sodium	**84** mg	4%
Carbohydrate	**31** g	10%
Fiber	**2.5** g	
Sugar	**8** g	
Protein	**4** g	

■ Preheat the oven to 450 degrees. Place the strawberries in a large bowl and sprinkle with 1 tablespoon of the sugar. Toss to coat and set aside.

In a medium bowl, sift together 1 cup of flour, baking powder, baking soda and the remaining 2 teaspoons of sugar. Set aside.

In a small bowl, stir together the buttermilk and oil. Pour over the flour mixture; stir well.

Sprinkle the work surface with the remaining 1/4 cup flour. Knead the dough gently on the floured surface for 10 to 12 strokes. Roll or pat the dough to 1/2-inch thickness. Using a 2-inch biscuit cutter, dipping the cutter in flour between cuts, cut eight biscuits. Transfer the biscuits to an ungreased baking sheet.

Bake for 10 to 12 minutes or until golden.

In a small bowl, mix the yogurt and brown sugar. Add Grand Marnier if desired.

Remove the biscuits from the oven. Cut the biscuits in two. Use half the strawberries between the layers. Replace the top halves of biscuits. Spoon the remaining strawberries on the biscuits. Top with the yogurt sauce.

Diabetic exchange

1starch, 1 fruit, 1/2 fat

Strawberry Cheesecake

By using fat-free cream cheese and cottage cheese, 200 calories and 14 grams of fat have been sliced from each serving of this Strawberry Cheesecake.

12 servings

Vegetable oil cooking spray
1/2 cup graham cracker crumbs
2 packages (8 ounces each) fat-free cream cheese
1 cup fat-free cottage cheese
1/2 cup sugar
2 teaspoons vanilla extract
2 whole eggs
2 egg whites
10 ounces frozen strawberries in light syrup, thawed, drained, syrup reserved; or 2 pints fresh strawberries, washed, hulled, divided
3/4 cup sugar, optional
1 1/2 to 2 tablespoons cornstarch
3 tablespoons lemon juice
5 drops red food coloring
Mint leaves, optional

■ Preheat the oven to 350 degrees.

Spray a 9-by-9-inch baking dish with the cooking spray.

Spread the graham cracker crumbs in the bottom of the baking dish. Set aside.

In a food processor fitted with a metal blade, place the cream cheese, cottage cheese, sugar and vanilla. Process until smooth.

Add the eggs and egg whites one at a time; process well after each addition. Carefully pour the batter into the prepared dish.

Bake for 18 to 20 minutes or until almost set. Remove from the oven and let cool 30 minutes.

Meanwhile, prepare the glaze:

If you are using frozen strawberries, place them in a food processor fitted with a metal blade. Process until smooth. In a small saucepan over medium heat, mix together the reserved syrup and the cornstarch. Add the strawberry puree. Add the lemon juice and red food coloring. Cook until the mixture is thick enough to coat the back of a spoon. When the cheesecake is cooled, spread the glaze over it and serve. Or serve the sauce on the side.

If you are using fresh strawberries, place 1 cup of strawberries in a food processor fitted with a metal blade. Process until smooth. Place the sugar and cornstarch in a shallow pan; slowly add the strawberry puree. Add the lemon juice and red food coloring. Cook until thick. Remove from the heat and cool. Arrange the remaining strawberries on top of the cheesecake and pour the glaze over it.

Garnish with more whole strawberries or mint leaves if desired.

Nutrition Information Per Serving

			% of daily value
Calories	185		
Calories from fat	7	%	
Fat	1	g	2%
Saturated fat	0.5	g	3%
Cholesterol	43	mg	14%
Sodium	315	mg	13%
Carbohydrate	32	g	11%
Fiber	1.5	g	
Sugar	22	g	
Protein	11	g	

Cook's note:

Before substituting an ingredient, make sure it's appropriate for your recipe. If the product label does not provide adequate information, call the consumer information number on the label before trying a new product. It will be worth the extra effort.

1 lean meat, 1 starch, 1 fruit

45

Sugar Cookies

Traditional holiday cookies use dough that is high in fat, with each cookie containing 4 or 5 grams of fat. By substituting egg whites for whole eggs and including nonfat yogurt, this dough yields cookies with only 1 gram of fat each.

48 servings

3/4 cup sugar
1/3 cup tub margarine
2 egg whites
1 teaspoon vanilla
1/3 cup vanilla nonfat yogurt
3 cups all-purpose flour, divided
1 teaspoon baking powder
1/2 teaspoon baking soda
1/4 teaspoon ground nutmeg
Vegetable oil cooking spray

Nutrition Information Per Serving

			% of daily value
Calories	**51**		
Calories from fat	**24**	%	
Fat	**1**	g	2%
Saturated fat	**trace**	g	1%
Cholesterol	**trace**	mg	1%
Sodium	**36**	mg	2%
Carbohydrate	**9**	g	3%
Fiber	**trace**	g	
Sugar	**3**	g	
Protein	**1**	g	

■ In a medium bowl, cream the sugar and margarine until fluffy, about 2 to 3 minutes. Add the egg whites one at a time, beating after each addition. Add the vanilla and yogurt; mix well.

In a separate medium bowl, sift together 2 2/3 cup flour, baking powder, baking soda and nutmeg. Add gradually to the yogurt mixture. Mix well. Divide the dough into 3 equal parts and press into disc shapes. Cover and chill for at least 3 hours.

At baking time preheat the oven to 425 degrees. Spray two baking sheets with the cooking spray.

Sprinkle the remaining 1/3 cup of flour on the work surface. Roll each part of the dough to 1/4-inch thick on the floured surface. Cut with 2-inch cookie cutter. Place cookies on the prepared baking sheets.

Bake until no indentation remains when touched, about 6 to 8 minutes. Remove from the oven and place on a cooling rack.

Makes 4 dozen cookies.

Diabetic exchange

3/4 starch

Valentine Meringues

Valentine Meringues are a delicious way to say "I love you" to your sweetheart. Assembling the dish is not difficult if you follow instructions. Baking, too, is simple. Just don't open the oven door. Meringues need an even, consistent baking temperature and cooldown to turn out right.

8 servings

3 eggs whites, at room temperature
1/4 teaspoon cream of tartar
3/4 cup superfine or regular sugar
2 drops red food coloring
10 ounces frozen raspberries, sweetened, defrosted
1 tablespoon cornstarch
4 cups nonfat frozen yogurt

Nutrition Information Per Serving

		% of daily value
Calories	204	
Calories from fat	0 %	
Fat	0 g	0%
Saturated fat	0 g	0%
Cholesterol	0 mg	0%
Sodium	91 mg	4%
Carbohydrate	48 g	16%
Fiber	1.5 g	
Sugar	42 g	
Protein	5 g	

■ Preheat the oven to 275 degrees. Cover a cookie sheet with parchment or heavy brown paper. Using a pencil, draw 8 heart shapes on the paper, leaving space between them.

In a medium mixing bowl, beat the egg whites until foamy. Add the cream of tartar. Beat in the sugar 1 tablespoon at a time until the mixture is stiff and shiny. Add 2 drops of red food coloring and mix.

Spoon the meringues into heart shapes on the paper, or place the meringue in a pastry bag fitted with a coupler and large star. Fill in the hearts, leaving a higher ridge along outside edge. Bake 1 hour (do not open the door), then turn the oven off. Leave the meringues in oven with the door closed for 1 1/2 to 2 hours, or until the oven is totally cool.

Prepare the sauce while the meringues are cooling. Place the raspberries with juice in a small saucepan, and sprinkle with cornstarch. Gently stir until the cornstarch dissolves and is lump-free. Heat over low heat until boiling and the mixture has thickened. Remove from heat and cool.

After the meringues have completely cooled, top with 1/2 cup nonfat frozen yogurt and drizzle with the raspberry sauce.

Diabetic exchange

1 1/2 starch, 1 1/2 fruit

60

Noel Cake

Using a low-fat cake mix for this beautiful cake saves approximately 4 grams of fat per serving. It's a great dessert to make ahead and bring to your next holiday party.

24 servings

2 layers white cake, prepared from a low-fat cake mix
1 cup bourbon, divided
1/2 cup chopped walnuts
2 cups assorted candied fruits
1 cup quartered candied cherries
1/2 cup light brown sugar
1 cup frozen cran-raspberry juice concentrate, defrosted
1 cup candied cherries, halved

■ Slice each cake layer horizontally into 2 layers. Using 1/2 cup of the bourbon, drizzle each layer with about 2 tablespoons of the bourbon; set aside and allow the bourbon to soak in.

In a medium saucepan, combine the walnuts, assorted candied fruits, quartered candied cherries, remaining 1/2 cup bourbon, brown sugar and cran-raspberry juice. Stir over medium heat for about 10 minutes, until the mixture is syrupy and almost caramelized.

Using 2 spatulas, carefully place one bourbon-soaked cake layer on a serving plate. Divide 1 cup of the fruit mixture over the layer. Repeat with the remaining layers, using the last 1 cup of the fruit mixture on top of the cake. Decorate with the halved cherries, placing them around the top rim of the cake.

Cover tightly with plastic wrap and let sit in a cool place for at least 3 to 4 days. Serve in thin slices. This cake will keep for up to 3 weeks.

Nutrition Information Per Serving

			% of daily value
Calories	**255**		
Calories from fat	**11**	%	
Fat	**3**	g	5%
Saturated fat	**0**	g	0%
Cholesterol	**0**	mg	0%
Sodium	**255**	mg	11%
Carbohydrate	**51**	g	17%
Fiber	**1**	g	
Sugar	**34**	g	
Protein	**28**	g	

Diabetic exchange

1 starch, 2 1/2 fruit, 1/2 fat

Volume One Favorites

We hope you have been using new products and cooking techniques to make healthier versions of your favorite recipes.

Heart Smart® staff members have also been busy in the kitchen. They have modified a dozen of readers' favorite dishes from the first Heart Smart® Cookbook. Try these revised recipes to discover how new food products and different ways of preparing them can add to your Heart Smart® selections.

Apple Cinnamon Oat Bran Muffins

Traditional muffin recipes call for as much as 1 cup of fat. You can use only a fraction of that by including nonfat yogurt or pureed fruit. You don't need to sacrifice taste to enjoy these great Heart Smart® muffins.

16 servings

Vegetable oil cooking spray
2 1/4 cups oat bran
1/4 cup brown sugar
1 1/4 teaspoons cinnamon
1 tablespoon baking powder
1/2 cup raisins
1/2 cup evaporated skim milk
3/4 cup frozen apple juice concentrate, defrosted
2 egg whites
3 tablespoons applesauce
1 medium apple, peeled, cored, seeded, chopped

■ Preheat the oven to 425 degrees. Spray muffin pans with the cooking spray.

In a large bowl, mix together the oat bran, brown sugar, cinnamon, baking powder and raisins.

In a medium-size bowl, mix together the evaporated skim milk, apple juice concentrate, egg whites and applesauce. Add the milk mixture to the oat bran mixture and stir to mix. Fold in the chopped apple.

Fill the prepared muffin pans with the batter. Bake for 17 minutes, or until a wooden pick inserted into the center comes out clean. Remove from the oven and cool. After cooling, store the muffins in a large plastic bag to retain moisture.

Nutrition Information Per Serving

		% of daily value
Calories	98	
Calories from fat	8 %	
Fat	1 g	2%
Saturated fat	0 g	0%
Cholesterol	0 mg	0%
Sodium	83 mg	3%
Carbohydrate	24 g	8%
Fiber	2 g	
Sugar	8 g	
Protein	4 g	

Diabetic exchange

1 starch, 1/2 fruit

Heart Smart® Vegetable Dip

Cottage cheese made from whole milk is high in fat even though the label reads 4 percent fat. Don't be fooled. Read the entire label, and choose a fat-free cottage cheese whenever possible.

32 servings

1 cup fat-free cottage cheese
1/3 cup buttermilk
1 tablespoon lemon juice
3 tablespoons fat-free mayonnaise
1 package (10 ounces) frozen spinach, thawed, drained and chopped
1/3 cup finely shredded carrots
1/2 cup finely chopped onion
2 teaspoons dill weed
1 tablespoon parsley
1 1/2 teaspoons celery seed

■ In a medium-size bowl, blend together the cottage cheese, buttermilk, lemon juice and mayonnaise until smooth. Add the spinach, carrots, onion, dill weed, parsley and celery seed. Blend well. Chill the mixture at least 1 hour and serve with fresh vegetables.

Nutrition Information Per Serving

			% of daily value
Calories	**11**		
Calories from fat	**7**	%	
Fat	**trace**	g	1%
Saturated fat	**0**	g	0%
Cholesterol	**trace**	mg	1%
Sodium	**30**	mg	1%
Carbohydrate	**1**	g	1%
Fiber	**trace**	g	
Sugar	**0**	g	
Protein	**1**	g	

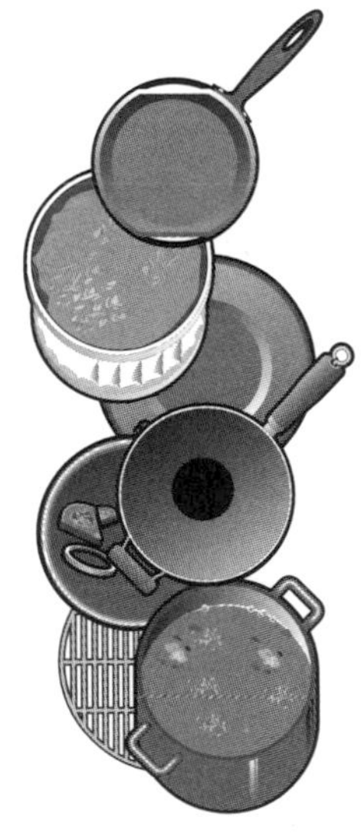

Diabetic exchange

free food (up to 2 tablespoons)

45

Potato Salad

All those summer salads made with mayonnaise that you have been avoiding can be trimmed down. If you have been using low-fat mayonnaise, go that extra step and use the fat-free variety. You may notice that the fat-free kind adds more sweetness to your potato salad, so we used a little lemon to cut the sweetness.

6 servings

1 pound medium round white potatoes, scrubbed, eyes removed
3 cups water
1/4 cup finely chopped green onions (include green tops)
1/4 cup finely chopped red bell pepper
1/2 cup chopped celery
1/3 cup fat-free mayonnaise
2 tablespoons plain nonfat yogurt
1 teaspoon prepared mustard
1 teaspoon horseradish
1/8 teaspoon white pepper
Dash of paprika
1/4 cup shredded carrots

■ In a large saucepan, combine the whole unpeeled potatoes and water. Bring to a boil. Reduce heat and simmer until tender, about 35 minutes. Drain the potatoes and allow to cool to the touch. Peel the potatoes. Cut into cubes and set aside.

In a large bowl combine the green onion, red bell pepper, celery and cubed potatoes. Chill for at least 2 hours.

In a small bowl, mix together the mayonnaise, yogurt, mustard, horseradish and white pepper. Pour the mixture over the chilled vegetables and toss gently to evenly coat. Sprinkle with paprika on top and garnish with shredded carrots.

Nutrition Information Per Serving

			% of daily value
Calories	**86**		
Calories from fat	**1**	%	
Fat	**trace**	g	1%
Saturated fat	**0**	g	0%
Cholesterol	**0**	mg	0%
Sodium	**206**	mg	9%
Carbohydrate	**20**	g	7%
Fiber	**1.5**	g	
Sugar	**2**	g	
Protein	**2**	g	

Diabetic exchange

1 starch

45

Pasta Primavera

A traditional white sauce is prepared with butter. But butter is high in fat, and we were all warned not to use it. Then we switched to margarine, which also has been shown to raise cholesterol. The answer is to find ways to replace the solid fats in recipes with vegetable oils or fat-free products as we have with the white sauce used in our Pasta Primavera.

4 servings

1 tablespoon olive oil
3 medium cloves garlic, peeled, ends removed, minced
1 1/2 cups cauliflower florets
1/2 cup julienned carrot strips
1 cup broccoli florets
1/2 cup diced yellow squash
1/2 of a red bell pepper, washed, cored, seeded, julienned
2 green onions, washed, ends removed, diced (including green tops)
1 1/2 cups sliced mushrooms
1/2 cup water
1 tablespoon fat-free tub margarine
2 teaspoons cornstarch
1 cup skim milk
1/4 cup fat-free Parmesan cheese
1/4 cup fat-free Romano cheese
1/4 teaspoon white pepper
1/2 pound linguine or other pasta, cooked al dente according to package directions, omitting salt and fat, drained
1/2 cup chopped fresh parsley

■ In a large skillet or wok, heat the oil over medium-high heat until hot but not smoking. Add the vegetables one at a time and saute each a few seconds, starting with the garlic, then cauliflower, carrots, broccoli, yellow squash, red pepper, green onion and mushrooms. Saute until the vegetables soften a little and turn golden, about 3 minutes total.

Add the water and cover.

Steam the vegetables until just tender, approximately 2 to 3 minutes, depending on how crisp you like vegetables. Drain the vegetables and set aside. Keep them warm. Meanwhile, in a small saucepan, melt the margarine over medium heat. Using a wire whisk, whip in the cornstarch and skim milk until smooth.

Sprinkle in the Parmesan and Romano cheeses and white pepper; stir to combine. Bring the mixture to a gentle boil over medium-low heat, stirring constantly. Reduce the heat and simmer until the mixture lightly thickens, about 2 to 3 minutes.

Place the cooked hot linguine in a large serving bowl. Immediately add the cooked vegetables, sauce and parsley. Gently toss until thoroughly mixed.

Nutrition Information Per Serving

			% of daily value
Calories	374		
Calories from fat	14	%	
Fat	5	g	8%
Saturated fat	1	g	5%
Cholesterol	1	mg	1%
Sodium	295	mg	12%
Carbohydrate	61	g	20%
Fiber	3	g	
Sugar	6	g	
Protein	18	g	

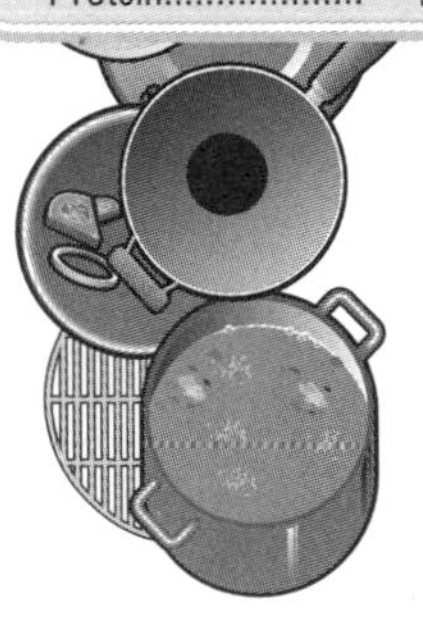

3 starch, 3 vegetable, 1/2 meat

Heart Smart® Spinach Lasagna

This Spinach Lasagna was a real hit in the first Heart Smart® cookbook. With new products, we have trimmed the fat per serving from 10 grams to 1 gram without sacrificing any of the taste.

8 servings

1 package (10 ounces) frozen spinach
Vegetable oil cooking spray
1 large onion, peeled, ends removed, finely chopped
2 to 3 cloves garlic, peeled, ends removed, minced
1 teaspoon dried oregano
1 teaspoon dried basil
1/2 teaspoon dried rosemary
1 can (15 ounces) low-sodium tomato puree
1/4 cup tomato paste, low-sodium if available
1/2 cup dry red wine
12 no-yolk lasagna noodles, such as white, green or whole-wheat
1 egg white
2 cups (1 pound) fat-free ricotta cheese
Freshly ground pepper to taste
1/4 teaspoon ground nutmeg
1 cup shredded fat-free mozzarella cheese
1/2 cup grated fat-free Parmesan cheese

■ Cook the spinach according to the package directions. Drain well and let cool. Press to remove as much water as possible. Set aside.

Spray a large nonstick skillet with the cooking spray. Place over medium heat. Add the onion, garlic, oregano, basil and rosemary. Cook, stirring often, until the onion is soft, about 10 minutes. Add the tomato puree, tomato paste and wine. Cover and simmer for about 10 minutes. Uncover and cook until the sauce thickens and is reduced to about 2 1/2 cups, about 10 minutes.

Preheat the oven to 350 degrees.

Meanwhile, cook the lasagna noodles according to the package directions, omitting salt and fat. Drain and set aside. When cool enough to handle, carefully separate the noodles.

Spoon about 1/4 of the sauce into a 9-by-13-inch baking dish. Arrange four noodles lengthwise on the bottom and sides of the dish, overlapping as needed and bringing noodles up the side of the dish. Spread half of the spinach over the noodles.

In a medium-size bowl, lightly beat the egg white. Blend in the ricotta cheese, pepper and nutmeg. Spread half the cheese mixture over the spinach. Sprinkle with about 1/3 cup of the mozzarella cheese and 2 1/2 tablespoons of the Parmesan cheese.

Repeat with 2 more layers in the same order using the remaining noodles, tomato sauce and cheese.

Cover with foil and bake for 50 minutes. Remove foil and bake for 10 minutes more.

Nutrition Information Per Serving

			% of daily value
Calories	306		
Calories from fat	4	%	
Fat	1	g	2%
Saturated fat	trace	g	1%
Cholesterol	5	mg	2%
Sodium	380	mg	16%
Carbohydrate	49	g	16%
Fiber	3	g	
Sugar	2	g	
Protein	21	g	

2 vegetable, 2 1/2 starch, 1 1/2 lean meat

30

Chicken in a Pocket Sandwich

When fat-free cream cheese came on the market, it had a warning on the label that it was not to be used in cooking or baking. Now there is a fat-free cream cheese that can be used in all recipes and melts well in the microwave. For best results, be sure to choose the cream cheese in a block, not the tub.

6 servings

2 ounces fat-free cream cheese (block), cut into chunks
1 green pepper, washed, cored, seeded, diced
4 to 5 green onions, washed, ends removed, diced
2 stalks celery, washed, ends removed, diced
1/8 to 1/4 teaspoon garlic powder, optional
12 ounces cooked boneless, skinless chicken breast, diced
2 tablespoons fat-free ranch dressing
3 pita rounds (6-inch), cut in half crosswise to make 6 pockets
1 cup shredded lettuce or spinach leaves
1/2 cup alfalfa sprouts
1 to 2 carrots, peeled, ends removed, shredded
2 ounces shredded fat-free cheddar cheese

■ In a 1-quart microwave-safe dish, combine the cream cheese, green pepper, green onion, celery and, if desired, garlic powder. Microwave on low just until the cheese softens, about 1 minute. If you don't have a microwave, heat gently in the top of a double boiler over simmering water until the cheese softens.

Remove from the microwave and stir in the cooked chicken and ranch dressing. Microwave on low for 1 minute. If using a double boiler, stir and cook until heated through, about 3 to 4 minutes. Remove from the microwave or heat and keep warm.

Evenly divide the shredded lettuce or spinach and sprouts among the 6 pita pockets. Divide the chicken mixture among each sandwich. Evenly divide the carrots and cheddar cheese among each sandwich, sprinkling on top.

Place the sandwich on a microwave-safe platter and microwave on low about 20 to 30 seconds, just until the cheese melts. Or place on a broiler pan and broil about 30 seconds. Serve.

Nutrition Information Per Serving

			% of daily value
Calories	**195**		
Calories from fat	**11**	%	
Fat	**2**	g	3%
Saturated fat	**0.5**	g	3%
Cholesterol	**52**	mg	17%
Sodium	**430**	mg	18%
Carbohydrate	**18**	g	6%
Fiber	**2**	g	
Sugar	**2**	g	
Protein	**24**	g	

Diabetic exchange

2 1/2 lean meat, 1 starch, 1 vegetable

Spicy-Hot Tofu

Tofu is not a miracle food. But it is a good source of protein to be used in place of meat. Although tofu contains a good type of fat, a 1/2 cup of firm tofu can pack in as much as 11 grams of fat. There is now a low-fat tofu with at least half the fat removed.

6 servings

Vegetable oil cooking spray
8 ounces low-fat, firm tofu, drained and cut into 1/2-inch cubes
1 medium onion, peeled, ends removed, quartered, separated into pieces
2 cloves garlic, peeled, ends removed, minced
1 teaspoon minced ginger root
1 teaspoon ground cumin
1 teaspoon ground coriander
1/8 teaspoon ground red (cayenne) pepper
1/4 teaspoon sugar
1 sweet red pepper, washed, cored, seeded, thinly sliced
3/4 cup green pea pods, washed, stems trimmed
1/4 head green cabbage (about 8 ounces), shredded
1 1/2 cups mushrooms, cleaned, quartered
1 teaspoon cornstarch
1/2 cup chicken bouillon broth
1 tablespoon white vinegar
3 cups cooked, brown rice

■ Spray a wok or large skillet with the cooking spray. Add the tofu and stir-fry until lightly browned over medium heat. Remove with a slotted spoon and set aside.

Add the onion, garlic, ginger root, cumin, coriander, sugar and ground red pepper to the wok or skillet. Cook, stirring constantly, for 30 seconds. Do not brown the garlic. Add the sweet red pepper and pea pods. Stir-fry for 2 minutes. Add the cabbage and mushrooms. Cook, stirring for 2 minutes or until the cabbage wilts.

In a small bowl, combine the cornstarch and chicken bouillon. Gradually stir the cornstarch mixture into the wok or skillet. Cook, stirring until the mixture slightly thickens. Stir in the reserved tofu and vinegar. Heat through. Serve over brown rice.

Nutrition Information Per Serving

			% of daily value
Calories	161		
Calories from fat	11	%	
Fat	2	g	3%
Saturated fat	0.5	g	3%
Cholesterol	0	mg	0%
Sodium	102	mg	4%
Carbohydrate	30	g	10%
Fiber	2.5	g	
Sugar	2	g	
Protein	7	g	

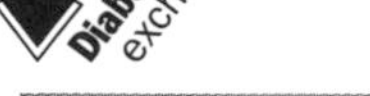

1 1/2 starch, 2 vegetable

15

Hawaiian Tossed Chicken Salad

With all of the fat-free salad dressings available, if you have not found one you like, you haven't been trying hard enough. This recipe is great with a fat-free ranch dressing, but if you have another favorite, don't hesitate to use it.

4 servings

1/2 pound grilled boneless and skinless chicken breast, chopped
1 small head iceberg lettuce, washed, dried, shredded (about 6 cups)
1 medium tomato, washed, cored, chopped
1/2 cucumber, peeled, ends removed, sliced
1 can (8 ounces) pineapple chunks canned in juice, drained
1/4 cup dry roasted cashews
4 tablespoons favorite fat-free salad dressing

■ In a large bowl toss together the grilled chicken, lettuce, tomato, cucumber and pineapple. Sprinkle with cashews.

Serve with your favorite fat-free salad dressing (1 tablespoon per serving).

Nutrition Information Per Serving

			% of daily value
Calories	**197**		
Calories from fat	**28**	%	
Fat	**6**	g	9%
Saturated fat	**1.5**	g	8%
Cholesterol	**49**	mg	16%
Sodium	**245**	mg	10%
Carbohydrate	**15**	g	5%
Fiber	**2.5**	g	
Sugar	**7**	g	
Protein	**21**	g	

Diabetic exchange

3 lean meat, 1/2 fruit, 1 vegetable

Sole Fillets with Curry Sauce

Choosing a margarine to meet your needs is not easy because there are so many available. Whipped margarine has air added to improve the way it spreads, and it will melt differently than regular margarine. Diet margarine adds water to the ingredients to reduce the calorie content. The fat-free margarines will not work with every recipe, but this delicious curry sauce made with the fat-free margarine proves that, in small amounts, they will work in many of them.

4 servings

Fillets:

1 1/2 pounds sole fillets, rinsed, patted dry, cut into 6-ounce servings
2 tablespoons lemon juice
1/4 teaspoon paprika
Parsley to taste

Curry sauce:

1 tablespoon fat-free margarine
1 tablespoon all-purpose flour
1/8 teaspoon curry powder
Dash of pepper
1/2 cup skim milk

Nutrition Information Per Serving

			% of daily value
Calories	**152**		
Calories from fat	**11**	%	
Fat	**2**	g	3%
Saturated fat	**0.5**	g	3%
Cholesterol	**77**	mg	26%
Sodium	**136**	mg	6%
Carbohydrate	**4**	g	1%
Fiber	**trace**	g	
Sugar	**2**	g	
Protein	**29**	g	

■ To prepare the fish: Arrange the fish in a 9-by-13-inch microwave-safe dish. Drizzle with lemon juice and sprinkle with paprika.

Cover tightly and microwave on high (100 percent power) for 5 minutes, rotating the dish 1/2 turn halfway through the cooking. Microwave until the fish flakes easily with a fork, about 2 to 4 minutes longer. Remove from the microwave and let stand for 3 minutes. Remove and place on a platter; keep warm.

To make the curry sauce: Place the margarine in a microwave-safe bowl. Microwave uncovered on high until the margarine is melted, about 15 to 30 seconds. Stir in the flour, curry powder and pepper. Gradually stir in the skim milk.

Microwave uncovered on high, 2 to 3 minutes, stirring every minute until thickened.

Remove from the microwave and pour the sauce over the fish. Sprinkle with parsley.

4 lean meat

Macaroni and Cheese

One cup of macaroni and cheese prepared with regular cheese contains 430 calories and 22 grams of fat. When the recipe was adjusted five years ago using low-fat cheeses, we cut it to 281 calories and 7 grams of fat per serving. Now, with all the fat-free cheeses available, we were able to trim the recipe to 225 calories and 3 grams of fat.

8 servings

Vegetable oil cooking spray
2 cups uncooked macaroni
2 egg whites, slightly beaten
1 cup skim milk
2 cups fat-free cottage cheese, pureed in a blender or food processor
1 cup (4 ounces) fat-free cheddar cheese
1 cup (4 ounces) low-fat cheddar cheese
1/8 teaspoon salt
1/2 teaspoon white pepper
1 tablespoon chopped fresh parsley
2 tablespoons bread crumbs
2 teaspoons grated fat-free Parmesan cheese
1/2 teaspoon paprika

■ Preheat the oven to 350 degrees. Spray a 2 1/2-quart baking dish with the cooking spray; set aside.

Cook the macaroni according to the package directions, omitting salt and leaving slightly undercooked; drain.

In a medium-size bowl, combine the egg whites, skim milk, cottage cheese, fat-free and low-fat cheddar cheese, salt, pepper and parsley; blend well. Mix the sauce with the slightly undercooked macaroni. Spoon into the prepared baking dish.

In a small bowl combine the bread crumbs, Parmesan cheese and paprika. Sprinkle the top of the macaroni mixture with the bread-crumb mixture. Cover the pan with aluminum foil. Bake for 50 minutes, uncover, bake for 5 to 10 minutes.

Nutrition Information Per Serving

			% of daily value
Calories	225		
Calories from fat	13	%	
Fat	3	g	5%
Saturated fat	1	g	5%
Cholesterol	18	mg	6%
Sodium	565	mg	24%
Carbohydrate	28	g	9%
Fiber	0	g	
Sugar	1	g	
Protein	20	g	

Diabetic exchange

2 lean meat, 2 starch

Submarine Sandwich

The introduction of low-fat lunch meats was a real treat for people watching the fat in their diet. Today you will find a variety of fat-free luncheon meats. But watch the serving size. Remember that fat-free means less than half a gram of fat per serving. If you put 6 servings on your sandwich, you may be adding more fat to your diet than you realize.

6 servings

1 loaf (16 ounces) unsliced French bread (about 16 inches long)
2 tablespoons prepared mustard
4 ounces fat-free mozzarella cheese, thinly sliced
4 ounces fat-free sliced turkey
2 ounces fat-free ham
2 cups shredded lettuce leaves
2 medium tomatoes, washed, cored, thinly sliced
1 medium onion, peeled, ends removed, thinly sliced
1 medium green pepper, washed, cored, seeded, thinly sliced
1/4 cup fat-free Italian dressing

■ Cut the loaf of bread horizontally in half. Spread the bottom half with the mustard. Layer the mozzarella cheese, turkey and ham on the bottom half. Top with shredded lettuce, tomatoes, onion and green pepper.

Drizzle the dressing over the loaf. Top with the remaining bread half. If necessary, secure the loaf with wooden picks or skewers and cut into 6 servings.

Nutrition Information Per Serving

			% of daily value
Calories	305		
Calories from fat	12	%	
Fat	4	g	6%
Saturated fat	0.5	g	3%
Cholesterol	23	mg	8%
Sodium	732	mg	31%
Carbohydrate	47	g	16%
Fiber	3	g	
Sugar	6	g	
Protein	20	g	

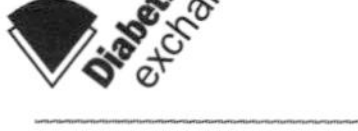

Diabetic exchange

3 starch, 1 1/2 lean meat, 1 vegetable

Beef Stroganoff

Traditionally, beef stroganoff is prepared with sour cream, making it a very high-fat meal. Regular sour cream contains 208 calories and 20 grams of fat per 1/2 cup. By using fat-free sour cream, the fat content in one serving of this dish is limited to 7 grams.

4 servings

Vegetable oil cooking spray
1 clove garlic, peeled, ends removed, finely chopped
1 small onion, peeled, ends removed, finely chopped
1 pound lean sirloin or lean beef tenderloin, cut into strips
8 ounces fresh wild mushrooms, cleaned, sliced (such as shiitake, crimini, oyster)
1 1/2 cups beef broth, divided
1 tablespoon Worcestershire sauce
1 teaspoon paprika
3 tablespoons all-purpose flour
1 cup fat-free sour cream

■ Spray a large skillet with the cooking spray. Add the garlic and onion. Saute over medium heat until onion is lightly brown. Add the beef strips and brown quickly over medium-high heat. Add the sliced mushrooms and heat until the mushrooms are lightly brown.

In a small bowl, stir together 1 cup plus 3 tablespoons of the beef broth, the Worcestershire sauce and paprika. Stir the beef broth mixture into the skillet. Bring to a boil, then reduce the heat to simmer and cover. Simmer until the beef is tender, about 10 minutes.

Meanwhile in a small bowl or container with a tight-fitting lid, stir together or shake the flour and the remaining beef broth. Gradually stir the flour mixture into the beef mixture. Return to a boil, stirring constantly. Boil and stir for 1 minute, then reduce the heat. Stir in the sour cream and heat through. Serve over hot cooked noodles.

Nutrition Information Per Serving

			% of daily value
Calories	**269**		
Calories from fat	**23**	%	
Fat	**7**	g	11%
Saturated fat	**2**	g	10%
Cholesterol	**68**	mg	23%
Sodium	**433**	mg	18%
Carbohydrate	**22**	g	7%
Fiber	**1**	g	
Sugar	**1**	g	
Protein	**29**	g	

1/2 starch, 2 vegetable, 3 1/2 lean meat

Appendix

Food Pyramid

Fats (naturally occurring and added)
Sugars (naturally occurring and added)

Use sparingly

Dairy
One serving equals: 1 cup milk or yogurt or about 1 1/2 ounces of cheese.

2–3 servings

Meat, Poultry, Fish, Dry Beans
Daily total equals 4 - 6 ounces.

2–3 servings

peanut butter

Vegetables
One serving equals: 1 cup raw leafy greens, 1/2 cup of other kinds.

3–5 servings

Fruits
One serving equals: 1 medium apple, orange or banana; 1/2 cup of fruit, 3/4 cup of juice.

2–4 servings

Source: U.S. Department of Agriculture

Martha Thierry / Detroit Free Press

Grain products
One serving equals: 1 slice bread; 1/2 bun; bagel or English muffin; 1 ounce of dry ready-to-eat cereal; 1/2 cup of cooked cereal, rice or pasta.

6–11 servings

Glossary

Amino acids:
Compounds that can be linked together to form protein. Many of these amino acids can be manufactured in the body. Some, however, must be supplied by food. Good sources are meats, milk and milk products, vegetables and grains.

Atherosclerosis:
A disease that involves thickening and hardening of the major blood vessels. Deposits of fat, cholesterol and other minerals in the walls of the blood vessels interfere with the normal blood flow.

Blood pressure:
The force of the blood against blood vessel walls as it is pumped by the heart to all parts of the body.

Calorie:
A unit of heat that measures the energy in food. Calories come from carbohydrates, proteins, fats and alcohol.

Carbohydrate:
A nutrient that is the body's main source of energy. Complex carbohydrates are found mainly in fruits, vegetables, breads and cereals. Simple carbohydrates (sugars) are found naturally in foods such as fruits and in sweeteners such as sugar and honey.

Cholesterol:
A fat-like substance made in the liver and also found in foods of animal origin. It is a major part of the fatty deposits found in the arteries of people with atherosclerosis.

Coronary arteries:
Blood vessels that supply blood to the heart.

Diabetes:
A disease in which the body does not use carbohydrates for energy because of inadequate production or use of insulin.

Digestion:
The breakdown of foods in the digestive tract into simple substances the body can use for energy and nourishment.

Fat:
A nutrient whose main function is to provide energy. It also aids in the transportation of fat-soluble vitamins and insulates and cushions the organs. It is found mainly in meats, eggs, milk and milk products, oils, margarines, salad dressings and nuts.

Fiber:
That part of food that is not digested and adds bulk but no calories to the diet.

Gram:
A unit of weight in the metric system; one ounce equals 28.5 grams.

Heart attack: Damage to an area of the heart muscle, caused by the blockage of an artery supplying blood to the heart.

High density lipoprotein (HDL):
A lipoprotein thought to remove cholesterol from the blood. A high level of HDLs decreases the risk of heart disease.

Hydrogenation:
The process of adding hydrogen to an unsaturated fat to make it more solid.

Legumes:
Plants that have edible seeds within a pod. These include peas, beans and lentils.

Lipid:
A fat or fat-like substance such as cholesterol and triglycerides.

Lipoprotein:
A compound containing a lipid and a protein.

Low density lipoprotein (LDL):
A lipoprotein that transports most of the cholesterol in your body. An elevated LDL cholesterol level increases the risk of heart disease.

Minerals:
Nutrients necessary for life that are found in small amounts in many different foods. They are important because they are needed to form and maintain the skeleton (calcium), are needed to help nerves and muscles function (potassium and calcium), and are oxygen-carriers (iron).

Monounsaturated fat:
An unsaturated fat that tends to lower blood cholesterol levels. Oils high in monounsaturated fats are canola oil, olive oil and peanut oil.

Nutrient:
A substance found in food that is needed by a living thing to maintain life, health and reproduction.

Plaque:
The abnormal build up of fatty deposits on the inner layer of an artery. Plaques reduce the internal diameter of the artery and may lead to total blockage.

Polyunsaturated fat:
A fat that is mainly found in foods of plant origin and that is usually in liquid form at room temperature. Examples of polyunsaturated fats are corn oil, sunflower oil, safflower oil and soybean oil. These fats tend to lower blood cholesterol levels.

Protein:
A major nutrient needed for building and repairing cells. It is found in meats, eggs, milk, and milk products.

Saturated fat:
A fat that cannot absorb additional hydrogen. It is found mainly in foods of animal origin, such as meat and milk. It is usually solid at room temperature. This type of fat tends to raise blood cholesterol levels.

Sodium:
An essential mineral that is necessary, in small amounts, to keep fluids distributed in the body. It is found in most foods, but the main source of sodium is table salt (sodium chloride). A diet high in sodium may increase the risk of high blood pressure in salt-sensitive people.

Stroke:
An interruption of the blood flow to the brain, causing damage to the brain.

Triglyceride:
A fat normally present in the blood. Elevated levels of triglycerides may be caused by obesity or alcohol and sugar in the diet.

Vitamins:
Organic compounds that are necessary for growth, development and maintenance of health. Although many foods contain small amounts of vitamins, fruits and vegetables are the best sources.

Index

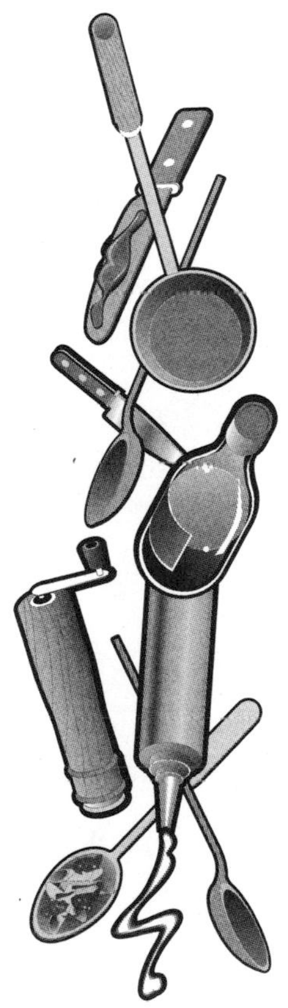

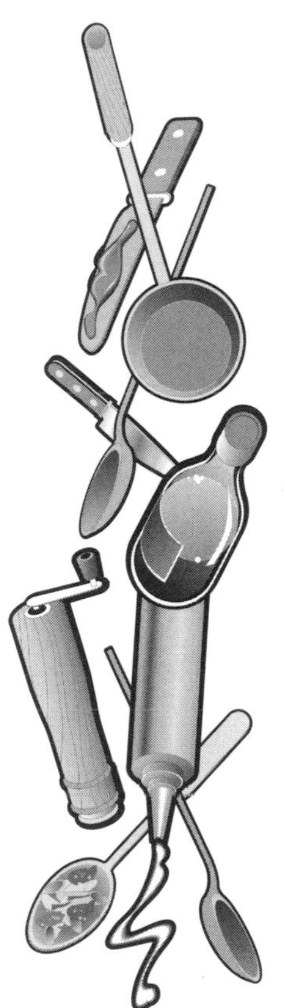

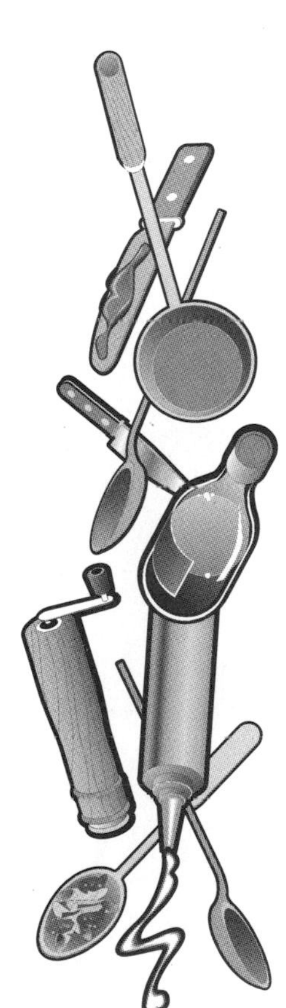

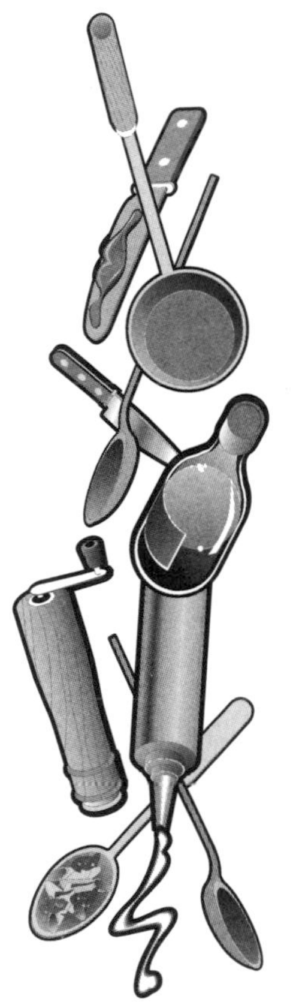

■ Seafood 159

■ Poultry 177

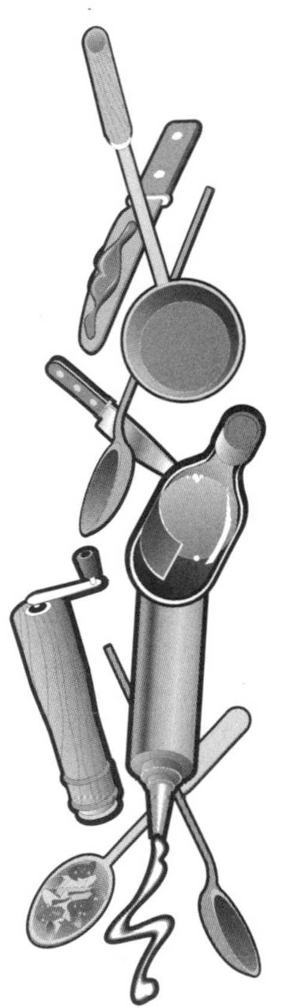

■ Desserts 201

■ Volume One Favorites 223

■ Appendix 237

Notes

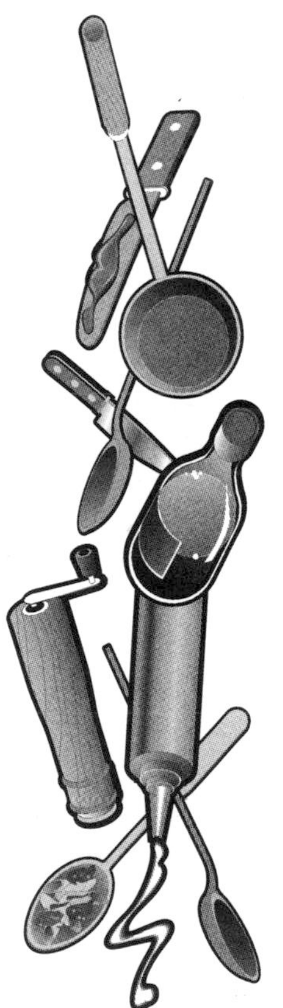

Notes

Notes

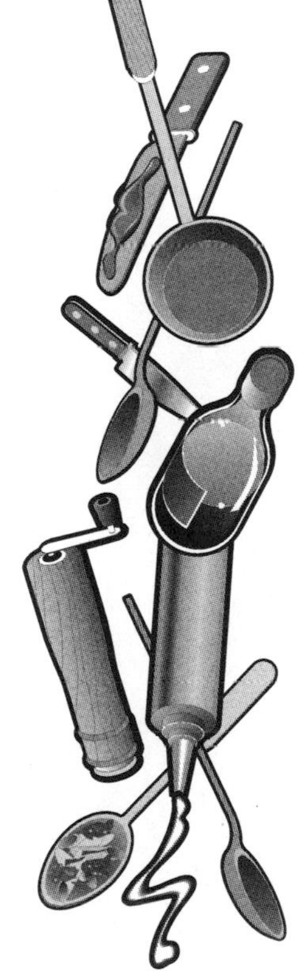

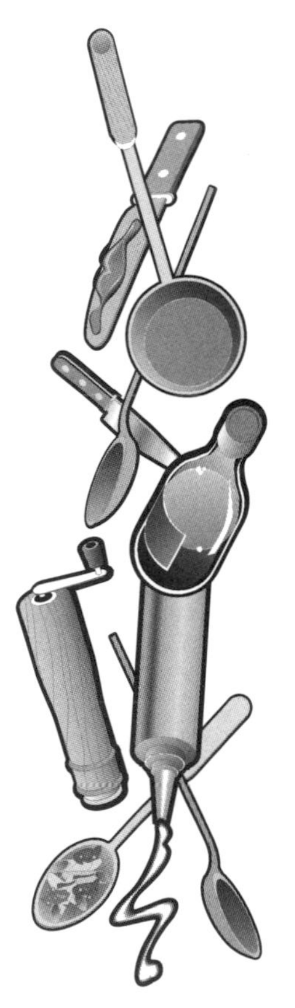

Notes

Notes

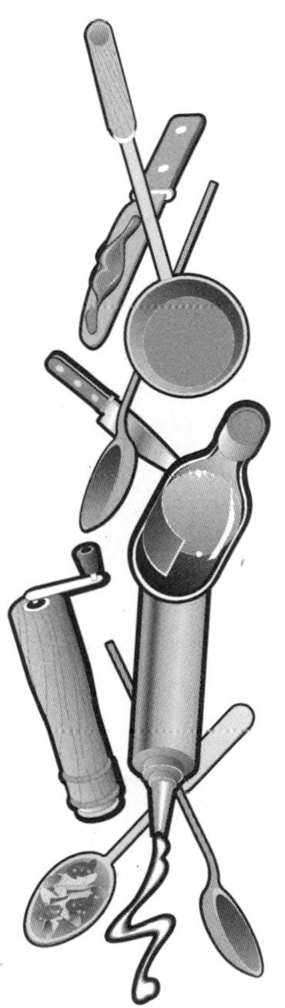